School of Divinity

Gardner-Webb University
School of Divinity

This book donated
by

Dr. Rick Prassel

Early Christianity
and Society

Early Christianity and Society

SEVEN STUDIES

Robert M. Grant

COLLINS
St James's Place, London
1978

William Collins Sons & Co Ltd
London · Glasgow · Sydney · Auckland
Toronto · Johannesburg

First published in the United States of America 1977
by Harper & Row, Publishers, Inc , 10 East 53rd Street,
New York, N.Y. 10022
First published in Great Britain 1978
© 1977 by Robert M. Grant
ISBN 0 00 211375 9
Made and printed in Great Britain by
William Collins Sons & Co Ltd, Glasgow

Contents

Preface

THIS BOOK is intended for people whose interest in the life and thought of early Christianity is not strictly academic. In having to deal with the modern world, such readers have necessarily become interested in facts and figures, population trends, attitudes toward the government, taxes and deductions, pros and cons of different occupations, property and charitable gifts, and buildings and capital funds. They are likely to be concerned about such matters not only for themselves and their families, but quite possibly for religious groups with which they are involved.

Early Christianity and Society was written in Chicago and Rome, cities where one is not likely to forget practical Christianity. The chapter on private property is a slightly revised version of an Andrew W. Mellon Lecture delivered at Dumbarton Oaks for the program in Early Christian Humanism of the Catholic University of America. Much of the chapter on work and the work ethic was delivered as a lecture for the Institut for Kirkehistorie of Copenhagen University.

Far too often in modern religious thought one jumps from the Bible to the world today without paying attention to any of the practical problems religionists had to face in antiquity. Too often we are content with a mythical or even fabulous picture of the religious past and thus are unable to relate ourselves to it or it to ourselves. According to Acts 14, crowds at Lystra in Asia Minor thought that the apostles Barnabas and Paul were Zeus and Hermes. The two vigorously denied this, claiming to be men just like the others. Unfortunately the writers of church history have not always taken advantage of this insight.

Modern historians are usually fascinated with figures and speak of quantification. Ancient Christians undoubtedly had more figures than they passed on to us, but the rhetorically-minded preachers and theologians whose writings tended to be preserved usually talked about "myriads" rather than precise numbers of people or monetary units. In Chapter I I have tried to overcome this situation and examine what evidence there is. After we consider the possible number of Christians in the Roman empire, we go on to observe their attitudes toward the empire and the emperor. We shall also investigate how Christians interpreted one of their earliest dogmas concerning the kingdom or reign of God. What could this concept of kingdom have meant in the Palestine of Jesus' time? What later on? As throughout the book, I emphasize the practical effect of the church's gradually becoming a well-organized state within a state—the main subject of Chapter II.

In Chapter III we turn to even more mundane concerns, viewed in one context when Jesus discussed the payment of tribute to Caesar. These are also explored in other contexts which relate his thinking to various Roman taxes and the exemptions provided some pagan priests and all orthodox clergy, as well as Jewish leaders under Constantine. In the same vein, Chapter IV examines, in some detail, work and occupations in early church society. Was there a special Christian or Jewish view of work or "work ethic"? Were certain occupations off limits for Christians and Jews alone? This chapter will show that Jews and Christians shared the ideas of the dominant groups in their society and did not innovate. The same is true of their ideas regarding private property (Chapter V).

There is a considerable measure of agreement between my own views and those of G. E. M. de Ste. Croix, whose essay on "Early Christian attitudes to property and slavery" appeared in 1975. Perhaps as a Marxist, he is unenthusiastic about almsgiving and charity, but I view this expression of human concern more favorably and have devoted Chapter VI to it. The last chapter treats the "triumph of Christianity" in the fourth century as an economic matter involving the closing of pagan temples, the building or at least remodeling of churches, and the concomitant attacks on pagan endowments and the obtaining of Christian ones.

What I am discussing here is not the whole story about early Christianity. There is not much about the history of doctrine as such or of exegesis or even about the wrangles among churchmen that constitute so much of church history. To write a scenario based on such themes is both legitimate and necessary, but not my goal. If taken by itself, this book could rightly be viewed as an extreme answer to the extreme "churchiness" of Eusebius of Caesarea, who mentioned events in the life and history of the Roman world only when Christians were being persecuted by the state. An adequate history of the church needs to take all these aspects into account. But this is not a history of the early church. It is a venture into the reconstruction of early Christian practicality.

Years ago, when some friends of mine were discussing the menace of secularism, I suggested that we could most readily examine it by considering the way we ourselves think and act. I still think that to differentiate the sacred and the secular too

sharply is a mistake. In this book I attempt to show that many
early Christians had concerns remarkably like some of our
own. In spite of this, or perhaps because of it, the church did
survive.

My thanks are due to many colleagues, including students,
who have labored with me in these areas, and especially to
Professor R. Krautheimer for guidance at Rome. My book is
obviously related to my father's study of *The Economic
Background of the Gospels,* published fifty years ago. Many of the
New Testament quotations are taken from the Revised Standard Version. Others are my own translations.

ROBERT M. GRANT

Chicago
October 1976

Abbreviations

AJP	*American Journal of Philology*
BGU	Griechische Urkunden . . . Berlin
Chrest.	L. Mitteis and U. Wilcken, eds., *Grundzüge und Chrestomathie der Papyruskunde* (cited by editor's name)
CIL	Corpus Inscriptionum Latinarum
CSEL	Corpus Scriptorum Ecclesiasticorum Latinorum
ESAR	T. Frank, ed., *Economic Survey of Ancient Rome*
FIRA	S. Riccobono et al., eds., *Fontes Iuris Romani Antejustiniani*
H.E.	*Historia Ecclesiastica*
HTR	*Harvard Theological Review*
IG	Inscriptiones Graecae
IGRR	Inscriptiones Graecae ad Res Romanas Pertinentes
ILS	Inscriptiones Latinae Selectae
JBL	*Journal of Biblical Literature*
JRS	*Journal of Roman Studies*
JTS	*Journal of Theological Studies*
MAMA	Monumenta Asiae Minoris Antiqua
OGIS	Orientis Graeci Inscriptiones Selectae

P.	Papyrus: collections Aberdeen, Cairo Isidore, London, Lund, Oxyrhynchus, Tebtunis, Yale
PG	Migne, Patrologia Graeca
PL	Migne, Patrologia Latina
RAC	*Reallexikon für Antike und Christentum*
RE	*Realencyclopädie der classischen Altertumswissenschaft*
SB	Sammelbuch griechischer Urkunden aus Ägypten
SHA	*Scriptores Historiae Augustae*
SIG	Sylloge Inscriptionum Graecarum
SVF	Stoicorum Veterum Fragmenta
TAPS	*Transactions* of the American Philosophical Society
TU	*Texte und Untersuchungen*
VC	*Vigiliae Christianae*
ZKG	*Zeitschrift für Kirchengeschichte*
ZKTh	*Zeitschrift für Katholische Theologie*
ZNW	*Zeitschrift für die neutestamentliche Wissenschaft*
ZPE	*Zeitschrift für Papyrologie und Epigraphik*
ZThK	*Zeitschrift für Theologie und Kirche*

I

The Christian Population
of the Roman Empire

It took a long time for Christianity to emerge as a dominant force in its social world. The "existing powers," according to Paul the apostle ordained by God, were not eager to acknowledge that they were "passing away." They were primarily concerned with propping up and maintaining the existing order. One of the basic points is expressed in remarks ascribed to representatives of the Jews in the Gospel of John: "If you release this man [Jesus], you are not Caesar's friend; everyone who makes himself a king sets himself against Caesar. . . . We have no king but Caesar."[1] We do not know whether or not Pilate was really entitled to the honorific name "friend of Caesar," valued by oriental kings and Roman administrators alike. Pilate's patron Sejanus, however, was certainly a counselor of the emperor Tiberius until the year 31, when he was executed for treason. And it is remarkable how often the early Christians came in contact with such "friends." The Agrippa who put James, son of Zebedee, to death was a friend and

adviser of Caligula. His son, Agrippa II, was a friend of both
Claudius and Vespasian. The apostle Paul, who appeared before him, had already been dismissed at Corinth by Junius
Gallio, whom Claudius called "friend" on a Delphic inscription.[2] In the earlier years of the first century, then, the Christian movement was known, and not always unfavorably, to the
advisers of various Roman emperors. It is hard to tell what
Nero's advisers made of Christianity. Many of them were ac-
tively plotting against him at the time when he blamed Christians for the great fire at Rome.

During the reign of Trajan, early in the second century, three
prominent Roman administrators and authors paid attention
to the Christians. The oldest of them, Cornelius Tacitus, belonged to the senatorial aristocracy and was a friend of few emperors, though the senatorial emperor Nerva made him suffect
consul in 97 and Trajan approved his proconsulship in Asia for
112–113. In his *Annals,* apparently published only a few years
later, Tacitus described the Christians as Nero's scapegoats for
the fire at Rome. He had no enthusiasm for them, any more
than for the Jews already described in his *Histories.* He could
not decide whether the "pernicious superstition" was detest-
able more because it originated in Judaea or because it succeeded at Rome, a sink of iniquity. He stated that a "great multitude" was put to death, justly hated for its crime and for its
"hatred of the human race." But he could not escape from the
suspicion that Nero had unjustly blamed the Christians for his
own misdeeds.[3]

Plinius Secundus, another senator but a member of Trajan's
council,[4] was suffect consul in 100 and about a decade later
went out to Bithynia and Pontus, on the southern shore of the
Black Sea, as the emperor's agent to reform the government
and the finances of these provinces. While he was there, many
persons were accused of being Christians. Uncertain as to how

to deal with the situation—he had not been present at earlier investigations—he asked the emperor how to proceed and reported on the results of his interrogations. The kinds of questions he asked may have been derived from his memories of Livy's account of the Bacchanalia or else, as Sherwin-White suggested, from annalistic accounts of "measures taken to repress Druids, Magians, or Jews."[5] Pliny, like his friend Trajan, regarded Christianity as a "depraved and immoderate superstition." He thought the contagion could be checked.

Our third witness from this period is Suetonius, an equestrian government official with full access to the archives; he used his opportunities to round out his *Lives of the Twelve Caesars,* published early in Hadrian's reign, just before the emperor removed him from office. He was one of Pliny's protégés. He shared the distaste of the senatorial group for Judaism, and perhaps thought that Christ was at Rome urging the Jews toward rioting during the reign of Claudius.[6] Certainly he justified Nero's punishment of the Christians, on the ground that they were adherents of a novel and harmful superstition.[7]

We thus see that toward the beginning of the second century influential government officials shared hostility toward the Christian movement. This attitude inevitably led toward trouble for the Christians, no matter how many defenses and explanations the apologists might provide. The basic view was that Christianity was simply an unnecessary, possibly a harmful, religion. It was neither protected by past treaties, as Judaism was, nor assimilable to other religions, as pagan cults were.

It is not my intention to write a history of Christianity, and I therefore refrain from discussing the gradual extension of the Christian churches during the second century. I note only that the "prophet" Alexander of Abonuteichus, an active oraclemongerer about the year 160, was able to claim that he was opposed because "Pontus was full of atheists and Christians," while even earlier the charlatan (as Lucian describes him) Peregrinus lived handsomely off what the Christians of Palestine and Asia sent him in prison.[8] By the end of the century the Carthaginian apologist Tertullian could say that "though we are but of yesterday, we have filled all that is yours, cities, islands, fortified towns, country towns, centers of meeting, even camps, tribes, classes of public attendants, the palace, the senate, the forum." He obviously exaggerates when he states that "nearly all the citizens you have in nearly all the cities are Christian."[9] Almost a century earlier, Pliny had reported to Trajan that Christianity was attracting adherents from every class. Now Tertullian claimed that there were Christians everywhere. In his tract addressed in 212 to Scapula, proconsul of Africa, he gave more details. Good governors had favored Christians; bad ones had persecuted. A Christian in the palace had cured the emperor Septimius Severus by using oil, and the emperor protected senatorial Christians, women and men alike, against the mob. When Scapula persecuted Christians, he was "decimating" Carthage.[10]

It may be that the numerical expansion of Christianity around this time was helped by an increase in the population of the Roman empire, not yet affected by the series of plagues that began in the last third of the second century. Writing after 180, Theophilus of Antioch stated that "the whole world is now filled with inhabitants," while Tertullian himself held that the population was steadily increasing, since new regions were being opened up for food production. (In spite of this, food shortages were constant.)[11] It is in this period that we find evidence for many who were Christians by upbringing rather than conversion, and for attempts to keep church offices in particular families.

Christians themselves were given to fantasy when discussing such subjects. The later population decline explains Eunomius' idea, late in the fourth century, that the world was only half-full; it cannot account for his view that there were fifty thousand births a day.[12] To be sure, this would have been reduced by the thirty thousand daily deaths revealed by Jesus according to the *Gospel of Bartholomew*.[13] Even so, more than seven million added to the population annually would be an incredible figure.

What was the Christian population? This question has received a good deal of attention over the years and it cannot be regarded as close to a solution. If we take two figures and try to make inferences, we shall see some of the kinds of difficulties that arise. First, some early martyrs. In general, Origen, writing about 248, tells us that the total number to his time was small. Martyrdoms had been only occasional and were easily enumerated.[14] So we turn to two numbers. Eusebius gives us the whole number of martyrs in Palestine during the ten years of the Diocletianic–Maximinian persecution, and G. E. M. de Ste Croix has examined the accounts. The total number was ninety-one, of whom forty-four suffered at the copper mines of southern Palestine toward the end. Of the other forty-seven, thirteen were volunteers, while eighteen managed to draw attention to themselves. This leaves sixteen who were actually sought out by the authorities, or fewer than two a year during the whole period.[15] The other number is given by the martyrologies for the persecution in Gaul under Marcus Aurelius. At first glance, one would suppose that forty-eight martyrs were listed. But "in some instances two names (nomen and cognomen) belong to one person."[16] It is therefore obvious that the number of martyrs was considerably less than forty-eight. This is not to deny that whatever the number it seemed large.[17]

The second group of figures leads us into deeper complexities. It comes from a letter which Cornelius of Rome addressed to Fabius of Antioch in the year 251, informing him that in the church of Rome there were "forty-six presbyters, seven deacons, seven subdeacons, forty-two acolytes, fifty-two exorcists, readers, and doorkeepers, and more than fifteen hundred widows and poor people, all supported by the favor and humanity of the Master." Cornelius referred to this group as a "multitude, in God's providence rich [i.e., large] and growing." Outside it there was a very large, indeed innumerable, group of laity.[18] Obviously Cornelius has listed the numbers on the payroll of the Roman church, nearly seventeen hundred in all. In order to make a guess about the total number of Christians we must find a model for the relation between the supporters and the supported.

At first glance it might seem rather easy to find an analogy. We could look for the population of the city of Rome and for the number of persons there supported by the government's grain distributions. Then we should find that the most reliable modern studies, those of von Gerkan, suggest a population of approximately seven hundred thousand.[19] Now we are fortunate enough to have Dio Cassius tell us that to celebrate his tenth anniversary the emperor Septimius Severus gave the equivalent of a thousand sesterces to each person entitled to the grain ration and to the praetorian guards, and that the total was two hundred million sesterces.[20] We see, then, that the gift was made to two hundred thousand persons, and that, since the praetorian guard numbered between twelve and twenty-four thousand, the number of those on the ration was about a hundred and seventy-five thousand.[21] The proportion of those on the ration to the total population would be one to four, and one could perhaps conclude that there were seven thousand Christians.

Before we can make this jump, however, we must try to determine whether the Roman grain distribution was made as a matter of right or on the basis of charity. Or does it make any difference, since the widows in the Roman church, and presumably other beneficiaries as well, were enrolled on official lists?[22] (We shall go into this in Chapter VI.)

We tentatively conclude that it is possible to apply this model to the situation of the Roman church and find at least seven thousand Christians at Rome. But the Roman church was different from the Roman state in that it sent money out rather than chiefly taking it in. Dionysius of Corinth testifies to this practice in the second century. The Roman church is accustomed "to send contributions to many churches in every city; now relieving the poverty of the needy, now making provision . . . for brethren in the mines." Dionysius actually speaks of the funds as distributed "for the saints," thus recalling the provision made by Paul for the church of Jerusalem.[23] Even when another Dionysius, bishop of Alexandria in the third century, was forced to appear before the deputy prefect of Egypt in 258, he was attended by "one of the brothers who had come from Rome."[24] We should therefore assume that the number of Christians in the Roman church was greater than the figure already given, though it is hard to tell how much greater. In part it depends on the economic class of the church members, to which we shall later return. Here it may be enough to suggest that there need not have been more than fifteen or twenty thousand Christians. After all, Josephus seems to imply that at the beginning of the first century there were no more than eight thousand Jews at Rome.[25]

The triumph of the church in the fourth century meant that the situation was greatly changed, though one must always remember that figures in antiquity (and not only then) were part of rhetorical exercises. The figure-giver is always trying to

prove something. Most of the populace of Antioch was Christian, according to the emperor Julian; he was explaining why
they were so unenthusiastic about him.[26] There are fully a
hundred thousand Christians in Constantinople, says Chrysostom, soon after arriving there as bishop. He believes that they
could pay much more than they do for the support of the
poor.[27] Oddly enough, he gives the same number for the
Christians at Antioch, where he had preached before moving
to Constantinople. There, too, he gives the figure in an effort
to get more money from his flock.[28] Did he actually know just
how many Christians there were, or how many inhabitants,
in either city? No, it looks as if his figures are just as impres-
sionistic as his statement that there are more Christians than
pagans.[29]

Because of problems like these, and because of our need to
use Christian propaganda literature, we cannot accept the
figures worked out by L. von Hertling in his study of "the
number of Christians at the beginning of the fourth century."
The higher figure he proposes, fifteen million, is much too
high, and even the lower figure, half that, seems excessive.[30]
One of the main problems has to do with the question of what
year exactly is being discussed, or who is discussing the population then or what place is being considered. Consider only two
examples, both related to Alexandria. First, Origen like other
Christian apologists says much about the miracle of Christian
expansion. At just one point, however, when he is arguing that
the Roman empire could be defended by prayer alone, he
takes a different line and states that now there are just a few
(Christians) who agree in prayer, compared with the population of the whole Roman world.[31] This seems a more honest
statement than the claim to be everywhere. Second, the population varied, especially under the adverse circumstances of
plague and famine. Zosimus gives a somber account of the

disastrous plague of the mid-third century.[32] Dionysius, bishop of Alexandria, well acquainted with city officials, is more precise. Writing in 260, he states that the total population of the city is now less than the "elderly" in a former time, while the figure for the elderly, those between forty and seventy, was larger than the present number of those from fourteen to eighty enrolled for the public grain distribution.[33] J. C. Russell rejects this statement because of the tables he has constructed to show what the population ought to have been, and he rightly points out that "Eusebius was no demographer."[34] But Eusebius was quoting Dionysius, who was in a position to know the facts. The effect of the plague on the population, Christian and non-Christian alike, must have been very severe.

Now we take a lead from Russell and turn to another aspect of the growth of the Christian population. He states that "only when the masses became the ruling class did the subject of demography become important."[35] It seems that the Romans actually were interested in statistics about the empire, but the literary-minded persons who wrote history or even handed down chronicles were not interested. Quantification was often regarded as mere counting and looked down upon. Perhaps we could put it thus: to whose interest would it have been to publish accurate figures?

The point here is that in one instance, presumably unusual, we actually possess figures for the progress of Christianity. These have to do with life at Gaza in Palestine between 395 and 402, and they come from Mark the Deacon's *Life of Porphyry Bishop of Gaza.*[36] Before giving the statistics, however, we need to say something about the size of Gaza altogether. Rates of increase on very small beginnings can be startling but they are not usually significant. Grégoire's guess of fifty or sixty thousand citizens may not seem far wrong, especially since he quotes the emperor Arcadius on the large revenues derived from the taxes of Gaza.[37] On the other hand, Ammianus Marcellinus lists Gaza as the fifth of five Palestinian cities, while fifth- and sixth-century information in Hierocles and Georgius make it the seventeenth or the eleventh city of Palestina I.[38] It might be safer to guess at a size half what Grégoire supposed.

Gaza had long been insignificant among Christian churches. When a synod met early in 325 to lay the groundwork for Nicaea, the bishop of Gaza was the fiftieth out of fifty-six signatories. At Nicaea itself he was the seventeenth out of nineteen from Palestine. It is no wonder that he could be deposed a year later and that his successor could suffer deposition too—though we have to admit that the second bishop was replaced by the first! The city of Gaza was a stronghold of the old paganism. It had eight temples, including the very famous temple of Marnas ("the Lord"), apparently dating from the time of Hadrian and perhaps built by that emperor. In the year 395, eighty years after the toleration of Christians in the eastern empire, there were two hundred and eighty Christians in Gaza. During the year the new bishop was able to offer a timely prayer for rain, and new converts numbered seventy-eight men, thirty-five women, nine boys, and five girls. During the same year thirty-five more converts were added and the total thus reached four hundred and forty-two. Apparently no further conversions took place until 398, when an imperial letter closed seven of the eight temples. That year the bishop was able to save a prominent pagan woman from death in childbirth. In consequence of the miracle he could baptize mother and child, and sixty-four further conversions took place. Even so, the rate of conversion was low, and the bishop headed for Constantinople in order to persuade the empress Eudoxia to destroy the temples instead of merely closing them. After a long struggle, he won the promise of a church at Gaza. On his return, a statue of Aphrodite spontaneously crashed and broke; the conversion of thirty-two men and seven women immediately followed. Recognizing their impending defeat, the rich pagans of Gaza took refuge elsewhere. After the temple of Marnas was destroyed, "many came over to the holy faith, some out of fear, others rejecting their former way of life." By "many" the author meant about three hundred, although "each year after that the number of Christians increased."

All this information comes from the *Life of Porphyry,* which clearly reveals the extent to which imperial power and money was needed in order to make Gaza Christian. Such was not necessarily the case everywhere. Conversions in such urban centers as Rome, Antioch, Alexandria, and Carthage must have been more numerous and more spontaneous. But we should not forget that according to John Chrysostom's figures, at the end of the fourth century in Antioch, where Christian missions had been active for three and a half centuries, Christians numbered no more than half the total population.

Our conclusions in regard to population are important for our further investigations, since they determine the way in which we shall view the Christian movement as a whole. We regard it not as a proletarian mass movement but as a relatively small cluster of more or less intense groups, largely middle class in origin. At the time when the emperor Constantine turned toward Christianity, the aristocracy was definitely pagan. Its Christianization took place only during the fourth century and even into the fifth.[39] What made the Roman world Christian is what Eusebius and others said made it Christian: the conversion of Constantine. The triumph of Christianity in a hierarchically organized society necessarily took place from the top down.

From such considerations we now turn to two closely related

topics: first, Christian devotion to the monarchical ideal both in the state and in the church (Chapter II), and second, Christian insistence upon paying taxes to the state and, at the same time, obtaining exemptions and immunities for clerical officers (Chapter III).

II

Christian Devotion to the Monarchy

CHURCH AND STATE

The social world into which Christianity spread was governed monarchically. To be sure, many Romans followed the lead of their Greek admirer Polybius and claimed that their form of government had all the best features of monarchy, aristocracy, and democracy.[1] Others were more candid and admitted that though the early Roman emperors did not care for the title of king, they eagerly seized the powers associated with the name.

When Jesus preached his gospel in Palestine the Roman empire was not much more than half a century old. What he preached about could easily have been understood as seditious, for he proclaimed the coming of the reign of God. Exactly what he meant by this has been the subject of controversy for centuries. Perhaps we can best approach it in its Palestinian, first-century setting. What was meant by the expression "the king of the Jews"?

When Jesus was growing up in Galilee, there were no kings in Palestine. To the east lay the kingdom of the Arabian Aretas, who had made himself king in 9 B.C. and had been reluctantly confirmed by the Roman emperor.[2] To the north, when the king of Commagene died in A.D. 17 there was local conflict over the government. Many advocated traditional kingship. The Romans sided with those who wanted Commagene to become a Roman province.[3] Similarly in Cappadocia, the next year saw kingship replaced by provincial administration, though the Romans were willing to appoint a king in Armenia.[4] In Palestine (not to mention Egypt and Syria) there were no kings at all. A Roman procurator governed Judaea; two sons of Herod the Great, Herod Antipas and Philip, bore the title "tetrach" and ruled in Galilee and to the north.

Somewhat earlier there had been a king or, in the view of most of his subjects, a tyrant in Palestine. During the first half of the first century B.C. there had been Hasmonean kings and queens in Jerusalem, but many Jews had welcomed the arrival of Roman governors after Pompey took the city in 63 B.C.[5] As the Roman republic was gradually transformed into the Roman empire, the Roman senate confirmed the seizure of power in Palestine by the Idumaean adventurer Herod, and after a decade of civil war in the Mediterranean world Augustus reconfirmed his position as king.[6] Herod's last years were poisoned by plots among his wives and sons. According to his will, his son Antipas was to succeed him as king; according to a codicil, Antipas was merely to become a tetrarch, while Archelaus would be king.[7]

Herod's death in 4 B.C. was followed by revolutionary turmoil. The sons vied with one another. They were opposed by new pretenders such as a runaway slave of the Herodian household, a shepherd, and a Galilean named Judas. All three claimed the title of king. Indeed, as Josephus puts it, "anyone might make himself king as the chief of a band of rebels whom he fell in with."[8] Under these circumstances the case was referred to Rome, where in any event the succession had to be confirmed.

At Rome the emperor and his council met with a delegation of fifty Jews from Palestine, supported by more than eight thousand of the Jews in Rome. What the Jews demanded, in opposition to the Herodian princes and their allies, was what they called "autonomy," that is, deliverance from kingship and union with the Roman province of Syria, to be governed by the Roman officials sent there. Augustus did not grant their petition, but he took it seriously enough so that he partitioned Herod's old kingdom. Half went to Archelaus, with the offer of the title of king if he could earn it. The other half was divided between Antipas and Philip.[9]

Less than a decade later Archelaus was so unpopular in Judaea that another delegation brought about his summons to Rome and exile to Gaul. At this point Judaea became a Roman province somehow appended to Syria. The taking of a Roman census for tax purposes led to revolt again. In Galilee, Judas insisted that no tribute could be paid the Romans and that Jews could have no mortal masters. God alone was their lord.[10]

It is evident, then, that in Jesus' time there were at least three ideas about the nature of kingly power in Palestine. The view we have just mentioned was that there was to be no king but God. What this meant, if we may accept Josephus' analysis of it in political terms, was not monarchy, nor oligarchy, nor democracy, but "theocracy," or "entrusting all sovereignty and authority to God."[11] But what does this mean? Perhaps it is not surprising that Judas had as his ally a certain Pharisee named Sadok, that is, Zadok, a priestly name. For later Josephus tells us that in this polity God was "governor of the universe," while the most important administrations were assigned to the whole body of priests, with the high priest supreme over the others.[12] In other words, theocracy means government by priests.[13]

The second idea about kingly power was government by members of the Herodian family. When the evangelist Mark wrongly called Antipas a king, he was actually reflecting the ambitious plans of Antipas' wife Herodias, whose efforts to make him king led to the downfall of both.[14] Herod's grandson Agrippa became king of Judaea under Caligula after encouraging the young emperor against Tiberius. Four years later Agrippa survived Caligula's murder and helped Claudius gain the Roman throne. His skill in surviving was much like his grandfather's. At Rome there were those who thought he taught tyranny to Caligula,[15] but his reign, like his son's, was marked by considerable administrative ability.

The third idea about kingly power involved direct rule by the Romans. The Romans themselves firmly rejected the title of king for their emperors, since they wanted to maintain the form of republican government.[16] But popularly, as in some New Testament documents, emperors were called kings.[17] In Jesus' time, as we have already seen, there was considerable enthusiasm for Roman rule among Jewish leaders. Thus according to Luke 23:2, the high priests and others accused Jesus of leading the nation astray, of hindering the payment of tribute to Caesar, and of calling himself "an anointed king." The point is made even more forcefully in John 19:12–15. There "the Jews" say to Pilate, "If you release this man, you are no friend of Caesar's; everyone who makes himself king is opposed to Caesar." And then "the high priests" make their political affirmation: "We have no king but Caesar."

This, then, is the background of the ministry of Jesus of Nazareth, during which he proclaimed the arrival or even the dawning stages of what he called "the reign of God." Did he mean a priestly theocracy by this? It appears that he did not, for according to the Gospels he was regularly in trouble with the priestly authorities. Jesus himself "was—or was to be—God's Agent in the final establishment (or re-establishment) of the divine reign in this world."[18] And in what the four canonical Gospels describe as taking place shortly before Jesus' arrest, that is, the "triumphal entry" into Jerusalem, we see an action apparently intended to provoke some sort of political response. To be sure, Mark, the earliest Gospel, does not describe the event as explicitly related to the prophecy in Zechariah of the coming of a "peaceable king" (Zech. 9:9). And John states that it was only when Jesus was "glorified" that his disciples "remembered that these things were written of him and that they did these things to him" (John 12:16). In other words, the definite associations with the prophecy may be due to later reflection. This is especially the case in Matthew 21:4–7, where, since Zechariah mentions, in Hebraic style, an ass and a colt the foal of an ass, we find both animals and Jesus seated on both. With or without detailed reference to Zechariah, however, it appears that some disturbance took place. It involved blessings upon the one who was coming (or was to come?) in the name of the Lord. It must have occasioned anxiety on the part of priestly and military authorities, ever mindful of the likelihood of trouble at the great festivals like Passover.[19]

More than that, if one can accept the sequence of events as described by the synoptic evangelists, the entry into Jerusalem was followed by the cleansing of the outer court of the temple. Obviously the evangelist John views matters differently. While the synoptists mention only one Passover in the ministry of Jesus, John refers to the approach of three such festivals, and he tells about the cleansing of the temple in relation to the first, not the last (2:13). But he was almost certainly exercising his theological creativity, for at the end of this story we find the same kind of statement he appended to the story of the entry into Jerusalem. Here we read that "when he was raised from the dead, his disciples remembered that he said this and they believed the scripture and the word which Jesus said" (2:22). This looks like an explanation for splitting up an earlier sequence into two parts. The Gospels agree that Jesus drove sellers of "religious articles" out of the temple; most add that he overturned the tables of money-changers. Only Mark 11:16 says that he did not permit anyone to carry a vessel through the temple. This point, neglected by the other evangelists, shows that Jesus, at least in the tradition Mark knew, was concerned with the ritual purity of the temple.[20] "In that day every vessel in Jerusalem and in Judah will be holy for the Lord almighty" (Zech. 14:21).[21] The political implications of this action could not escape anyone. After Antiochus Epiphanes defiled the temple and interrupted the sacrifices for three and a half years, Judas Maccabaeus gained control of the temple, cleansed the whole area, and replaced the old and polluted vessels with new ones.[22] The Roman general Pompey ordered the temple servants to cleanse it after his own brief visit.[23] Now Jesus was obviously claiming that it had been defiled again. One could put it this way: there was need for a new Dedication, even a new Feast of Lights.

What was wrong with the temple? According to the synoptists, Jesus alluded to Jeremiah 7:11 and called it "a den of thieves." According to John, he called it a business office. Too much commercial business was going on. But would this justify the tradition that he predicted the destruction of the temple? Or even that he said he himself would destroy it? It may be that John gives us a clue when he transforms the prediction and the charge into symbolic language. Jesus says, "Destroy this temple, and I will raise it up in three days." "The Jews," for John always literalists, reply, "This temple has been built for forty-six years, and will you raise it up in three days?" (2:19–20). The

temple that had been under construction for about forty-six
years was the grandiosely rebuilt edifice provided by Herod
the Great, and begun in the eighteenth year of his reign (i.e.,
roughly 20/19 B.C.).[24] This work itself had aroused the ap-
prehension of Herod's contemporaries. As Josephus says,
"they were dismayed by the thought that he might tear down
[destroy] the whole edifice [i.e., the old temple] and not have
sufficient means to bring his project to completion."[25] Such
fears would inevitably revive when Jesus spoke of destruction
and rebuilding. But why destroy? Is not the simplest answer
that the temple was indeed Herodian, that it was the creation of
the royal family with whom Jesus, like many other Jews, had no
sympathy?[26] Antipas had killed Jesus' great forerunner, John
the Baptist, a murder that many Jews thought deserving of
punishment by God.[27] A temple built by such a family was not
one in which God wanted worship (cf. John 4:19–24).

It was appropriate, then, that Jesus should have been asked
by Pilate, "Are you the king of the Jews?" and that the title on
the cross should contain these words.[28] No one had been called
"king of the Jews" since the death of Herod. An Essene named
Menahem had called Herod "king of the Jews," and Josephus
fairly often uses this title of him.[29] Symbolically, the conflict
between two kings is expressed in the Matthaean story of the
Magi who actually came to Jerusalem in Herod's time and
asked, "Where is he who has been born as king of the Jews?"
(Matt. 2:2). Presumably to Herod this would have meant, if
he heard it, an inquiry about the future fortunes of his sons
Antipas or Archelaus or even Philip. It was just at that time,
actually, that conflicts over the Herodian temple began. Over
the great gate of the temple in Jerusalem the king had set up
a golden eagle as a votive offering, possibly in honor of Jupi-
ter or Rome as well as Yahweh. Two Jewish legal experts encouraged their hearers to chop down this illegal image and,

though many were later executed, the deed was done. Violence
arising out of this episode ultimately led to the downfall of
Archelaus, beginning with his failure to become king.[30]

We do not know whether or not Jesus considered becoming
"king of Israel." He refused to answer Pilate's questions and,
according to John 6:15, he avoided an attempt by others to
make him king. It may be that he had no definite political
program. But it is virtually certain that he would not have
commended Herod the Great for his vast expenditures "in
God's honor"—as the king described them in a speech in the
amphitheater at Jericho.[31] The story of the widow's mite (Mark
12:41–44) proves the point.

While the kingdom of God is prominent in the Gospels,
other New Testament writings place much less emphasis on it.
Paul says that it is not related to dietary regulations; it is "righteousness and peace and joy in the Holy Spirit." It is not a
matter of words but of divinely given power. The unrighteous
will not "inherit" it, and God himself calls men to be in it.[32] In
these passages whatever political overtones the kingdom once
had have been transformed into morality with an individual
emphasis. In addition, its coming or men's reception of it is
placed in the indefinite future. According to Paul, Christ will
return and wage war upon hostile spiritual powers, all of which
he will make subject to himself. Then he will hand over his
kingdom to God the Father.[33] In the writings of the Apostolic
Fathers the kingdom of God is occasionally mentioned as
something lying in the future, but with the passage of time its
importance tends to decline.[34] Within the Montanist sect, in
the third quarter of the second century, there was a great deal
of concern for the imminent descent of the "heavenly
Jerusalem" in Phrygia, but this expectation, too, gradually
faded away.

To a remarkable extent what took the place of the primitive

Christian concern for the kingdom of God was a double concern for the Christian church and for the state as the sphere of the church's life. We shall deal with the attitudes toward the state first and then turn back to the ways in which the church took on the shape of the state.

Some of the most prominent early Christian leaders expressed their loyalty to the state under highly inauspicious circumstances. When the apostle Paul spoke about "the powers that be," the principal power at the time was the emperor Nero, though he may have been enjoying an auspicious first five years on the throne.[35] Again, Clement of Rome almost certainly wrote his letter to the Corinthians late in the reign of Domitian, and his attitude toward existing political structures was much like Paul's. But Domitian was murdered because of his "tyranny."

Philo of Alexandria was luckier in his choices, perhaps because he stood closer to political life. He had actually participated in an embassy sent by Alexandrian Jews to Gaius Caligula. He was, therefore, able to provide a remarkably full account of Caligula's wickedness, safe enough to describe under Claudius, but balanced by a panegyric on the virtues of Augustus and, more briefly, some praise of Tiberius.[36] To Philo, who largely followed the pro-Roman historian Polybius, we owe an analysis of ideal forms of government. In his view the state founded by Moses combined the best aspects of monarchy, aristocracy, and democracy.[37] Other authors of his time held that this combination was exemplified in the Roman state. What is especially remarkable about Philo is his fondness for what he calls "democracy," though he was certainly opposed to "ochlocracy," mob rule; his idea of equality was the traditional Platonic-Aristotelian one involving proportion, not nose counting.[38]

In Philo's time, enthusiasm for democracy was limited by the

transition at Rome from republic to empire, or what Ronald
Syme called "the Roman revolution." Two authors whom Syme
cited reflect the general attitude. Appian summarized it toward the beginning of his history of the civil wars: "out of
multifarious civil commotions *(staseis)* the Roman state passed
into harmony and monarchy." Or, much more ambiguously,
Lucan's words: *Cum domino pax ista venit;* this must mean "when
peace comes, a tyrant will come with it."[39]

From Appian we pick up the word *stasis,* which means not
only "civil commotion" but also "faction," "revolt," even "party
spirit." It is never a virtue. In the gospels of Mark and Luke it is
what led the political criminal Barabbas to commit murder. In
Acts it is occasioned by disputes related to the apostle Paul, but
only among Jews. Josephus uses the words *stasis* and *apostasis* to
denote the situation at Jerusalem in the year 66 as revolt developed into war. And significantly it is one of the key words of
the letter to the Corinthians sent by Clement in the name of the
Roman church.[40]

According to Clement's letter, Christians serve as soldiers in
what must be God's army. They observe order, discipline, and
obedience as they do what they are commanded. Not all of
them are officers, but each in his own rank obeys the emperor
and his generals or governors. From the military metaphor,
Clement turns to the benefits derived from the mixture *(syn-
krasis)* of great and small, necessary for the existence of both.
Finally he revises Paul's picture of the church as a body,
explicitly referring to its members as "breathing together" and
joining in a "common subjection" for the preservation of the
whole (chap. 37).

A prayer at the end of the letter clearly expresses the ideas he
wants to remain in his reader's minds. Clement asks God to
"grant that we may be obedient to thy almighty and glorious
name, and to our rulers and governors upon earth" (60, 4).

This surprising juxtaposition clearly shows that the Roman political authorities are to be honored with the honor expressed toward God. It turns out that God has given them their authority and that Christians are to be subject to them, in no respect resisting God's will (61, 1–2). No wonder "humility" is frequently recommended as a prime Christian virtue! In 1951 Eggenberger argued that Clement's ideas were derived from Dio Chrysostom, a Stoic friend of the emperor Trajan.[41] The parallels are striking. But whereas Eggenberger thought that one had to wait for Trajan's reign to find loyalist philosophers, MacMullen has drawn attention to a few "turncoats" who supported Domitian.[42] There were such people, and Clement may well have known one or more of them. Or does what he says really go far beyond Paul's words in Romans 13?

Also during the reign of Domitian we find some of the most important writing by the Jewish general Josephus. His work is interesting not only in itself but also because of its influence upon the many Christian authors who used it. As we should expect, he uses the traditional analysis of societies as governed by monarchs, by oligarchs, or by the masses. He also tries to classify the various systems of government found in Old Testament history. Moses himself held that aristocracy was the best form of life, though it was permissible to have a limited monarchy.[43] In the time of the judges the aristocracy became corrupt. That is why the judges governed them.[44] They restored aristocracy—which Josephus sometimes calls monarchy, presumably because the judges ruled one at a time.[45] He differentiates monarchy from kingdom, the state of government under the kings from Saul onward.[46]

History repeated itself after the Babylonian exile. First came a period of what could be called either aristocracy or even democracy.[47] Then there were kings of the Hasmonean line, followed by aristocracy for a brief period.[48] The kings Herod and Archelaus were followed by the final aristocracy.[49] Josephus uses similar language in discussing Roman history. Before Julius Caesar there was either aristocracy or democracy; either was better than tyranny.[50]

We expect to find Josephus rather loyal to his superiors at Rome. When he was taken prisoner during the Jewish revolt he predicted that both Vespasian and his son Titus would become emperors.[51] In turn, Vespasian took Josephus back to Rome with him, lodged him in his own private house, gave him Roman citizenship, and provided him with a pension. Later he gave him land in Judaea.[52] Titus also honored him, while Domitian exempted his Judaean property from taxation. The empress Domitia was his benefactor as well.[53] It is, therefore, rather odd to find him speaking favorably, though not often, of democracy. (The references are only in *Antiquities* XIX and XX). A date helps explain this feature. Josephus finished the *Antiquities* in the thirteenth year of Domitian, that is, in 93/94. This was just the time when Domitian was executing senators and exiling philosophers. Indeed, one of the senators, Junius Rusticus, had published panegyrics on enemies of Nero and Vespasian.[54] Perhaps Josephus was tacitly indicating some sympathy with the opposition. Tacitus did not feel free to publish his life of Agricola, dead in 93, until the reign of Trajan.[55] In any case, both Josephus and Tacitus could recognize tyranny when they saw it.

The attitude of Josephus, then, is to be contrasted with that of Clement. Of course we have no clear idea as to who Clement was, but it is at least possible that he was a freedman of the Flavian family. In 95 Domitian executed his own cousin, Titus Flavius Clemens, and banished Clemens' wife, Domitilla. She may have been a Christian, for there is a catacomb of Domitilla at Rome. Perhaps it could be argued that the intense loyalism of I Clement is partly owing to the author's personal need to express loyalty to the state and all its officers. Peter, Paul, and other Roman Christians, says the author, suffered as martyrs simply because of jealousy and envy, not because of any basic conflict between church and empire.[56]

Around the same time, "toward the end of the reign of Domitian," as Irenaeus states, we find a Christian book with a very different attitude toward the state.[57] This is the Revelation of John. Bitterly hostile toward Rome and all its works, the author begins his book by writing letters to seven churches in Asia Minor. He himself has been banished to the Aegean island of Patmos. Now he praises the church at Pergamum for keeping faith even though a certain Antipas has been put to death in the city "where Satan's throne is." By "Satan's throne" he seems to refer to the famous altar of Zeus at Pergamum. The author has complaints to make about all the churches but two, those at Smyrna and Philadelphia; the complaints suggest that there are many who do not share his apocalyptic enthusiasm. Insofar as one can discover contacts with social reality in the book, the author seems perturbed by the threat of compulsory emperor-worship (13:8, 15) and by famine prices which appeared "all over the eastern provinces in ca. 93"[58] (6:6). The book ends with an awesome prediction of the destruction of Babylon (Rome) and with the descent of the new Jerusalem from heaven to earth. There is no loyalty to Rome here.

But Revelation presented a problem, not an affirmation of faith, for most Christians in the second century and after. The words of Paul and of Clement were much more influential than those of John. Indeed, as we move toward the ideas of the Christian apologists we find a remarkable affinity with those of the upper-class literary personages of Trajanic–Hadrianic times. Dio Chrysostom and Plutarch are the real forerunners of second-century Christian monarchism.

Dio devotes no fewer than four discourses to kingship.

Apparently he delivered them at Rome before Trajan, who like
Nerva had allowed and encouraged him to return from exile.
In the third discourse we find a treatment of the forms of
government. The best is rule in accordance with "one good
man's judgment and virtue"—as Homer indicated in *Iliad* II
204f.: "The rule of many is not good; let there be one lord, one
king. . . ." Next comes "so-called aristocracy," an impracticable
form. Even more impracticable is "democracy," harmless but
impossible.[59]

The quotation from Homer is interesting. Philo liked it and
referred it to the reign of Augustus, the emperor who "dis-
placed the rule of many" *(polyarchia)*; he also referred it to the
reign of God.[60] The reference to Augustus is significant, for it
occurs in Philo's account of the badness of Gaius Caligula; and
according to Suetonius, Caligula himself was fond of the quotation.[61] Judgments on monarchy seem to depend on who is
monarch. Domitian, too, liked the verse.[62] Later on, we find
both the anti-Christian writer Celsus and the Christian Origen
quoting it.[63]

Like Dio, Plutarch discussed kingship and thought highly of
it. He referred to kingship, indeed, as "the most perfect and
the greatest of all political offices."[64] Epictetus apparently has
nothing to say about monarchical theory, but he is aware that
Roman rule has brought peace and the absence of battles,
brigandage, piracy. Travel is safe even though Caesar cannot
give peace from troubles.[65]

Finally one should mention the *Roman Oration (Or.* 26) by the
famous rhetorician Aelius Aristides. Delivered in the year 143,
it lavishes praise upon the city of Rome and the empire, especially because of the way administration is actually carried on
and because of the nature of its constitution. In Rome, Aristides found the perfect combination of kingship, aristocracy,
and democracy. As J. H. Oliver put it, "Aristides agrees with

Polybius that Rome has a mixed constitution, but the mixture is now concentrated in one institution which is monarchical in the best sense but through which both the Many and the Few realize their aims. . . . Aristides seems to have accepted the official interpretation of the role of the emperor at its face value, but so did Antoninus Pius and Marcus Aurelius."[66] The whole oration, it should be noted, ends with a prayer. "Let all the gods and the children of the gods be invoked to grant that this empire and this city flourish forever and never cease until stones (float) upon the sea and trees cease to put forth shoots in spring, and that the great governor and his sons be preserved and obtain blessings for all."[67]

We now turn directly to the major Christian apologists of the second century. Our first witness is Justin, who wrote at Rome about the year 150. He addressed his apology to Antoninus Pius and to his sons Marcus Aurelius and Lucius Verus, both called philosophers. He argues that they owe him a hearing because they bear such titles as pious, philosophers, guardians of justice, and lovers of culture. What he has in mind is that they should investigate the Christians rather than rely on rumors about them. "Subjects should give a straightforward account of their life and thought, and rulers should give their decision as followers of piety and philosophy, not with tyrannical violence. From this both rulers and subjects would gain. As one of the ancients said somewhere, 'Unless both rulers and those they rule become lovers of wisdom cities cannot prosper.'"[68] "One of the ancients" is Plato; "somewhere" is in the *Republic* (473d–e); Justin himself has added the words about the subjects as philosophers. The philosophers he has in mind are the Christians. If any member of the imperial household read his words, did they evoke a response? As a whole, the *Augustan History* dates from the late fourth century, and it is hard to separate the wheat from the chaff. But it is generally agreed that the life of Marcus Aurelius in this collection contains some good materials; and among them is the story that he was always quoting Plato's notion that cities flourished if philosophers were kings or kings philosophers.[69]

The Christians, Justin claims, exercise the virtues of philosophers, and the "kingdom" they look for is not merely human. It is a kingdom with God. If Christians were revolutionists they would remain in hiding in order to reach their goal. Actually, however, death does not trouble them, for their hopes are not set on the present age. And they are the emperors' best allies in the cause of peace and good order.[70]

Justin is by no means uncritically loyal. He hopes that the emperors will have a sound mind to match their power, and reminds them that eternal fire awaits those who disobey God. "Look at the end of each of the former emperors, how they died the common death of all."[71] More than that, one of them (Hadrian) deified his favorite, Antinous.[72] Justin's criticism, though implicit, is obvious.

From the period toward the end of Marcus Aurelius' reign we probably have four works, or parts of them, which can be roughly classified as apologies. The first is not really an apology but a vitriolic attack on Graeco-Roman culture by a self-styled barbarian from Syria, Tatian. For our purposes he deserves mention only because he accuses the Greeks of favoring the "rule of many," rather than monarchy, because they follow demons.[73] Since he applies a monarchical political tag to theology and we know he was a militant monotheist, it seems likely that he was a monarchist on earth too. Theophilus of Antioch criticizes the payment of divine honors to emperors while insisting that the emperor is appointed by God, and that no one else can be given his title—just as only God can be called God.[74] Like Tatian, Theophilus moves from the political to the theological without difficulty.

Two other apologists have more to say about the empire. The first, Melito of Sardis, provides a brief sketch of the history of church and empire, both arising under Augustus and flourishing together.[75] In his view the empire's success is due to its protection of the church, which only the bad emperors persecuted. These were Nero and Domitian. According to Herodian, Marcus Aurelius held the same opinion of them.[76] Marcus is the successor of the good emperors, and Melito hopes that he will continue to reign along with his son. Just so, as we have seen, Aelius Aristides believed that there was divine protection for Rome and for the emperor and his heirs.

The second apologist, Athenagoras, seems even closer to the traditions of rhetoric. Presumably it was Justin whom he followed when he addressed the emperor and his son as philosophers. His other remarks go far beyond the ideas of the earliest apologist. He begins by referring to the "gentle and mild" nature of the emperors, their "peaceableness and humanity toward all," as resulting in equality before the law for individuals, equality in honor for cities, and "profound peace" for the empire.[77] Such emperors should provide benefits for Christians like those they provide for individuals and cities. The Christians ask for nothing but justice.[78] Athenagoras' attitude of reverence toward the emperors becomes even clearer when he compares the imperial palace with the world, the emperors with God.[79] A page or so further on, we find this analogy: "As all things have been subjected to you, a father and a son, who have received your kingdom from above, . . . so all things are subordinated to the one God and the Word that issues from him whom we consider his inseparable Son."[80] The work ends with something close to adulation. Athenagoras praises the emperors again and insists that Christians "pray for your reign that the succession to the kingdom may proceed from father to son, as is most just, and that your reign may grow and increase as all men become subject to you." The prayer is also advantageous to Christians themselves: "that we may lead a quiet and peaceable life [I Tim. 2:2] and at the same time may willingly do all that is commanded"—presumably by the emperors.[81] The prayer is the prayer of I Timothy, I Clement, and Aelius Aristides.

Irenaeus of Lyons wrote his five books against heresies only a few years after Athenagoras' *Embassy.* Times had changed. Quite a few Christians had been put to death at Lyons by order of the philosopher-emperor Marcus Aurelius. There is no adulation in Irenaeus' work, which in any case was concerned primarily with struggles for power inside the church, not outside. Words for "faction" and similar ideas are used, as in I Clement, in regard to internal dissension.[82] Irenaeus' opposition to the Gnostics leads him to discuss the interpretation of "the powers that be" in Romans 13. The apostle Paul was speaking not of angelic powers or invisible principalities, but of human authorities. Power on earth was established by God for men's benefit, not by the devil. Some apparently claim that the whole world is governed by the devil.[83] The real situation is this: various kinds of subjects deserve, and get, various kinds of rulers. Sometimes the people need a king who reforms and helps his subjects and preserves justice. At other times, they need fear, punishment, and reprimand; or again, mockery, insolence, and pride.[84] Irenaeus gives no examples, and so we do not know which rulers had had in mind. It is clear that he has touched upon, and drawn away from, the problem of tyrannical rulers. He has already said that good magistrates will not be punished, while those given to injustice and tyranny will perish.[85]

In his view (as in that of Aelius Aristides and others) it is because of the Romans that the world is at peace, and thus one can freely travel both by land and by sea.[86]

On the other hand, several Christian writers at the end of the second century and the beginning of the third are less enthusiastic about Rome, and it is worth noting that two of them became sectarians: Hippolytus and Tertullian. In Hippolytus' view the empire was created by the power of Satan.[87] He expected it to perish, for he believed that this was indicated by Nebuchadnezzar's dream in the book of Daniel. Nebuchadnezzar had dreamed of an image with parts made of gold, silver, bronze, iron, and clay. Gold indicated the Babylonians, silver the Persians, and bronze the Greeks from Alexander onward. The iron empire of the Romans was mixed with clay, which cannot be bound with iron, and therefore the Roman empire would perish. The feet were of clay and since there must have been ten clay toes, sooner or later the empire would be divided into ten states and indeed into ten democracies.[88] This prediction reflects an attitude both anti-Roman and anti-democratic.

The apologist Tertullian discussed governments in dealing with the question of the origin of Roman power. Did Roman reverence for the gods bring the empire into existence? In Tertullian's view, Roman religion began to flourish only after the empire came into existence; therefore it did not cause the empire. Moreover, "every kingdom or empire is gained by wars and extended by victories." Wars and victories are produced by the capture and destruction of cities, including temples. Therefore the Roman empire was created by sacrilege, not piety. In any case, God regulates kingdoms and kings, fixing the alternations of power and raising and crushing states. It is this God to whom Christians pray for the safety of the emperors, as their Scriptures command them. They have a special reason for so praying, for they are asking for the continuation of the Roman empire in order to keep back "the great force which threatens the whole world and the end of world-history." But they are simply loyal, too, to the ruler whom God has chosen.[89]

In his treatise *Against Praxeas,* Tertullian shows that he is well aware of the nature of monarchy and its theological implications. To a theological "monarchian" he replies that monarchy cannot be so restricted as to exclude rule through a son, either natural or adopted, or through other administrators. Political experience teaches that a monarchy can be held by a father and a son together.[90] Doubtless he has Septimius Severus and Caracalla in mind.

The great third-century theologian, Origen, also discussed the nature of the Roman state in late writings such as his commentary on Romans and his treatise *Against Celsus.* Commenting on Romans 13:1–2, he followed Melito's lead by pointing out the fact that Christianity and the empire arose at the same time; in his view the connection was providential. He also held that emperors ruled by divine right and that monarchy was the best form of government.[91] Questions, he said, arose when there were savage and tyrannical emperors or rulers who drifted into debauchery.[92] He answered the questions when he wrote that "it would be right for people to form associations secretly to kill a tyrant who had seized control of their city."[93] Origen's monarchism was not absolute.

During the decade after the persecution under Decius, the Christian churches first experienced the perils of barbarian raids, later to become barbarian invasions. Dionysius of Alexandria tells how an aged Egyptian bishop fled with his wife to the mountainous desert east of the Nile and then disappeared. Many others in the area were enslaved by barbarian Saracens, and only some of them could be ransomed.[94] Within a year or so we find Cyprian of Carthage sending 100,000 sesterces to the churches of Numidia for the ransoming of Christians kidnaped in a Berber uprising.[95] Around 255 the Goths from the Danube, along with the Borani, a tribe apparently from southern Russia, broke into Pontus.[96] After "the barbarian invasion" was over, Gregory Thaumaturgus, once the pupil of Origen and now bishop in Neocaesarea, wrote to another bishop on the subject of discipline. He had to deal with such problems as those of women raped by the invaders, of receivers of looted goods, of refugees enslaved by fellow Romans, of collaborators who "forgot that they were natives of Pontus and Christians" and assisted in killings undertaken by the barbarians or acted as their guides, of men who seized the houses of others or kept what the barbarians left. Finally, there were those who informed for the Romans or returned runaway slaves or lost property but requested rewards. Gregory created an elaborate system of penance to take care of the various cases. The church in Pontus was disastrously divided, at least for the time.[97]

A dozen years later, Dionysius of Alexandria reached the conclusion that pestilence was about to produce the total disappearance of the human race. Civil wars added to his eschatological gloom. After Gallienus recovered control of the situation, however, he could write that "the empire has, as it were, cast off its old skin and cleansed itself from its former wickedness and now blossoms forth in fuller bloom, is seen and heard more widely, and spreads abroad everywhere." Dionysius urged Christians to participate in the celebration of the emperor's decennial year.[98] It is not surprising that in an undated treatise against Epicurean philosophy, Dionysius complained against a system that involved "the marvelous democracy of the atoms."[99] He did not care for democracy either among human beings or among atoms. The loss of dignities, glory, and influence that he suffered during the persecutions was real and what he lost was valuable to him.[100]

It is clear that Eusebius of Caesarea, writing during the first third of the fourth century, shared the admiration of the Roman empire expressed by his predecessors. He went beyond

them, however, when he interpreted the history of the empire
as proving the superiority of monarchy to any kind of state
with more than one ruler. Local rule, whether democratic or
tyrannical, produces wars, while monarchy produces peace.
This lesson he derives from the reign of Augustus—as understood in the reign of Constantine. In his view monarchy and
monotheism go together, while multiple authority, based on
equality, is actually anarchy or revolt.

He makes this point toward the beginning of his work on the
"preparation for the gospel." Before Christ came into the
world, the human situation, or at any rate that of the Roman
world, was intolerable. "In each nation innumerable kings and
local governors held power, and in the various cities some were
governed by a democracy and some by tyrants and some by a
multitude of rulers; hence wars of all kinds naturally arose."
When Christ came, however, by a "divine and secret power"
the human race was immediately liberated from "the multitude of rulers among the nations." This analysis is of course
based on Eusebius' idea of Roman history, derived from his
apologetic predecessors like Melito, Origen, and Dionysius.
"The whole multitude of rulers among the Romans began to be
abolished when Augustus became sole ruler at the time of our
Savior's appearing. And from that time to the present you
cannot see, as before, cities at war with cities nor nation fighting
with nation, nor life being worn away in the old confusion."[101]
This fantastic picture has no relation whatsoever to the actual
situation of the Roman world. It is based on the theory that
monarchy is the earthly counterpart of the sole rule of God. It
is therefore superior to either tyranny or democracy (forms of
polyarchy).[102]

Apparently his view was shared by other Christians. At any
rate, he describes the first martyr of Palestine as called upon to
pour out a libation in honor of the four tetrarchs. The martyr

refused, citing the traditional tag from the *Iliad:* "The lordship of many is not good; let there be one lord, one king." In consequence, he was immediately beheaded.[103]

In Eusebius' opinion, after Diocletian and Maximian abdicated they "let public affairs fall into disorder." Civil war broke out and peace did not return until it was provided for the Christians "throughout the whole of the world that was under the Roman principate." The empire then "recovered its traditional concord and once again became stable, harmonious, and peaceful."[104]

This means that under Constantine the empire enjoyed a transition from polyarchy to monarchy like the original experience under Augustus. The tetrarchs persecuted Christianity, but the "tyrants" at Rome and in the Orient, Maxentius and Maximin, neither a ruler in lawful succession, perished miserably in conflict with the allies of God.[105] At the end, Constantine defeated Licinius and put him to death. The monarchy was finally restored.

We should not suppose that these Christian writers were unusual when they gave their seal of approval to the monarchy and to the hierarchical social structure. In fact, they did not go as far as did the second-century dream expert Artemidorus, who classified the pagan gods in relation to their helpfulness to the three classes of society. The Olympians provided benefits for the very powerful. The "heavenly" gods like the sun helped the middle class. The gods on earth, including Asclepius, Heracles, and Dionysius, gave assistance to the poor.[106]

In addition, Eusebians and other courtiers did not express the only attitude toward the emperor to be found in the fourth-century church. The state-churchman Ossius of Cordova changed his mind about submissiveness toward the end of his life. The years Athanasius spent in exile prove clearly enough what his attitude was. In his *Apology for His Flight* he refers to Constantius as a heretic, while in his *Apology to Constantius* references to the emperor as "beloved of God" and as having received the kingdom from God are either ambiguous or ironical.[107] We sometimes forget the other bishops who violently criticized the emperor.[108] Before the fourth century such men would have been put to death. The triumph of Christianity made it possible for an opposition to exist. For the moment, anyway, absolutism was checked, not least by a great official-bishop like Ambrose.

THE CHURCH AS A STATE

The most obvious place for beginning our discussion of the church as a state within the state is in I Corinthians 12, with Paul's extended use of the metaphor of the body. Like a physical body, the political body of the church has many members and is constituted by the union of these diverse parts. The various members cannot deny their membership on the ground that they are inferior to others, and in return the superior members must pay honor and concerns to the inferior ones. All are joined together in suffering and in acceptance of praise. This metaphor is primarily and essentially political. It becomes Christian only because Paul mentions Christ, explains that membership in the body comes through baptism, states that position in the body is due to God's choice, and calls Christians the "body of Christ." Otherwise it is the metaphor found in various areas of ancient literature.[109]

Something like it is ascribed to Socrates in Xenophon's *Memorabilia,* where two brothers are urged to work together as do hands and feet and eyes, since God made them for this.[110] In Livy's account of the early fifth century there is a more fully political fable. The belly, analogous to the patricians, seemed to do nothing but enjoy what the other members, such as hands, mouth, and teeth, transmitted to it. When they tried to dominate the belly by starving it, they themselves lost all their strength.[111] With or without the fable, the figure of speech was extremely common. Cicero speaks of the need for members of the body to work together, and (in another connection) insists that nature has covered up the less seemly parts.[112] Epictetus says that if foot or hand could reason they would work for the good of the whole.[113]

Seneca naturally makes the same comparison. "What if the hands should desire to harm the feet, or the eyes the hands? As all the members of the body are in harmony one with another because it is to the advantage of the whole that the individual members be unharmed, so mankind should spare the individual man. . . ."[114] With remarkable lack of political foresight, he can say that Nero is the mind of the state, while the state is his body, or that his mind is like a head, the state like a body.[115]

We find the idea without Seneca's excesses in Hellenistic Jewish writers. Philo, for example, says that the high priest prays "that every age and all the members of the nation, as of a single body, may be united in one and the same fellowship, aiming at peace and good order."[116] Even proselytes have common concerns and "seem to be the separate parts of a single living being which is compacted and unified by their fellowship in it."[117] Josephus compares kingdoms with the bodies of individuals and discusses sedition as like disease. "As in the body when inflammation attacks the principal member all the members catch the infection. . . ."[118]

The point of our parallels (taken from the commentaries) is that the political picture intended by the metaphor of the body is that of a society combining diversity with unity and allowing for a stratified unity. John Hurd reasonably suggests that Paul is encouraging diversity as he uses it.[119] If this is so, Paul has returned to something like the fable of the belly and the other parts of the body. Harmony is essential. So is hierarchical order.

Proof that Paul thought this metaphor was important is given by his return to it in Romans 12:4–5 and, as in I Corinthians, the ensuing list of functions within the community. In Romans he speaks of "gifts that differ according to the grace given to us," and names prophecy, service, teaching, exhorting, contributing, giving aid, and doing acts of mercy. In dealing with the Corinthians he seems more specifically concerned with administrative and other offices, and he insists that "God has appointed in the church first apostles, second prophets, third teachers." Then come various other spiritual gifts or aptitudes. He has artfully placed the Corinthians' specialty, speaking in tongues, at the end.

In I Clement, where good order is vehemently stressed, the metaphor of the body recurs, along with comparisons between church life and army discipline and, indeed, explicit comments on "the great" and "the small."[120] The author also offers comparisons with Jewish priests and Levites as described in the Old Testament, and he is the first Christian writer to set forth a picture of apostolic succession as coming down from God through Christ to apostles and then to bishops.[121] But this is theoretical. Ignatius of Antioch had a high idea of episcopal authority but said nothing about succession. In the Didache readers are encouraged to appoint their own bishops and deacons. Let us look at some of the practical features of church organization.

One aspect of church life which must have been based on Jewish models was the court, in which church legislation was enforced. From Josephus and the book of Acts we learn that Jews dealt with cases involving their own laws.[122] The "forty lashes less one" was a regular, though severe, penalty imposed by such courts.[123] It is not clear that they could impose the death penalty. The execution of Jesus seems to have been carried out by the Roman governor.[124] Stephen was stoned in a kind of judicial lynching, and this is presumably what the evangelist John has in mind as he writes about the Jews and Jesus.[125] According to the story of the woman taken in adultery, a late addition to the Gospel of John, "the scribes and the Pharisees" believed themselves competent to stone women in such cases, and Philo of Alexandria certainly writes as if there were many crimes, not regarded as capital offenses by the Romans, for which the Jews could execute criminals either officially or informally.[126] Doubtless executions or lynchings sometimes took place. Both Origen and the author of the *Didascalia apostolorum*, however, state that under Roman rule the Jews were not able to inflict the death penalty.[127] Admittedly they may have been influenced by John 18:31: "It is not lawful for us to put any man to death." But Origen goes out of his way to state that only by personal observation in Palestine was he able to learn that Jews enforced the death penalty "neither fully in the open nor without the emperor's notice."[128]

Comparable church courts are described in Matthew 18:15–20 and in Paul's first letter to the Corinthians. In the letter we find two discussions, first on how to deal with the particular case of a man who is living with his stepmother, second on the necessity for setting up courts to deal with lawsuits between Christians. The case was a serious one according to Leviticus 20:11. "The man who lies with his father's wife has uncovered his father's nakedness; both of them shall be put to death, their blood is upon them." The Mishnaic tractate *Sanhedrin* specified stoning. Even if the father had died, the son of a first marriage could not marry the stepmother.[129] Paul certainly did not try to impose the death penalty, at least overtly. Like the rabbis he tried to enforce "punishment at the hand of Heaven for transgressions about which it is written, 'The souls that do them shall be cut off from among their people.'"[130] More than that, however, Paul has decided, with the congregation assembled, to "deliver such a man to Satan for the destruction of the flesh, that his spirit may be saved in the day of the Lord." This was a curse, intended to be just as effective as the self-imposed judgments that resulted in sickness and death at Corinth.[131] But it was a limited curse, not unlike the divine action depicted in the book of Job. "The Lord said to the devil, 'Behold, I deliver him to you, only preserve his soul'" (Job 2:6, LXX).

More generally, Paul notes that Christians are having recourse to pagan courts. He argues that Christian judges are perfectly capable of handling such cases, and he denounces the Corinthians for laying them "before those who are least esteemed by the church"—or "in the church."[132] The model Paul seems to have in mind is to be found in Deuteronomy 16:18. "Appoint judges and officers for yourself in all your towns. . . . and they shall judge the people with righteous judgment." The ones who are least esteemed seem to be pagans, outside the church. At Corinth there are no church courts. Here Paul demands that one be set up.

The church at Corinth is a state within a state in another regard. Christians had been expected to recognize those who labored among them and were above them in the Lord and admonished them. At Corinth the household of Stephanas "devoted themselves to the service of the saints," and Paul urged others "to be subject to such persons and to every fellow worker and laborer."[133] The line of argument is the same as the one developed in regard to the state in Romans 13. There Paul tells Christians to be subject to the state authorities and speaks of the individual authority as a "servant of God" (Rom. 13:1–4).

By the time we reach the Pastoral Epistles the situation has come to be regularized. There are requirements for the chief officers, now defined as bishops, presbyters, and deacons. There is a clearly defined list on which widows sixty years old can be enrolled. Presbyters who rule well (presumably as bishops) are to receive double pay. Charges brought against presbyters are not to be accepted unless there are two or three witnesses (I Tim. 5:9–11, 17–19). Here again we find echoes of the Deuteronomic courts.[134] So too in the Didache, when the author is going beyond the ministry of prophets and teachers, he gives this instruction: "Appoint for yourselves bishops and deacons worthy of the Lord, men who are humble and no lovers of money and genuine and approved" (15:1). The sentence echoes the words of Deuteronomy on the appointment of judges, including even the requirement that the judges must not take bribes.

Courts also provided a setting for the pronouncements of "holy law."[135] Indeed, one could follow Käsemann's classification of I Corinthians 3:19 ("if anyone destroys God's temple, God will destroy him") as holy law, and go on to find echoes of this kind of pronouncement even in Ignatius of Antioch, notably in his letter to Polycarp: "Pay attention to the bishop so that God will pay attention to you."[136] For the context of the message we may compare his letter to the Philadelphians: "When I was with you I cried out, I spoke with a loud voice, God's own voice, 'Pay attention to the bishop and the presbytery and the deacons.'"[137]

The courts are clearly under the control of the bishops according to the *Didascalia apostolorum*, and from the very earliest times there is thus a development to the episcopal courts of Constantine's time and the attendant right to appeal from civil to episcopal authority.[138]

Naturally the court was not the only institution to develop within the early Christian communities. Christians did not

spend all their time suing one another. They were concerned
with carrying on liturgical worship, with baptisms, weddings,
and funerals, and above all with the maintenance of the work
of charity. The offices of bishops and deacons seem to be related to both liturgy and the administration of alms.[139] Not
every bishop was enough of a theologian to spend his time
fighting heresy.

In addition, the church came to be more a state within a state
as the episcopal network was bound together (and sometimes
separated) by the meetings of provincial synods. The obvious
model for the synods themselves was the provincial assembly
within the empire, and the procedures followed in the synods
were based on local adaptations of Roman senate meetings.[140]
It should not be supposed that there was anything democratic
about these proceedings. The idea of "consensus" excluded
open disagreement or the use of voting.

It is also obvious that the development of the episcopate, not
to mention the papacy, meant that hierarchical and even imperial ideas were reinforced. When the Didachist counseled his
readers to "appoint bishops and deacons" for themselves, his
view of the episcopate was a much less exalted one than what
we find, for example, in Ignatius. For Ignatius, the bishop is
virtually God on earth. The later imperial notion that the emperor is emperor by divine grace is anticipated in what Ignatius
says of the bishop and, therefore, of himself.

Can we find traces of democratic elements in the Christian
societies? If the bishops had been elected by the whole community, this could be viewed as a democratic procedure, but it
is evident that various modes of selection were in use. Origen
mentions at least three methods: selection by the previous
bishop (or even mention in his testament), acclamation by all,
or election by the presbyters of the church.[141] Fabian of Rome
was "in the mind of nobody" before a dove settled on his head

"in clear imitation of the descent of the Holy Spirit in the form of a dove upon the Savior." The voters could respond only by crying out with one soul, "Worthy is he."[142] This is consensus, not an election. Where real disagreements existed they were accompanied by riots and murders, as in the fourth-century Roman scenes on which Ammianus Marcellinus comments unfavorably.[143]

We therefore conclude that the pattern of government within the church was close to that of the larger state around it. The precise relationship between the two states was not worked out during the fourth century, though we see some guidelines in existence by the time of Ambrose. To gain a clearer picture of the interrelations we now turn to the question of taxation. Do Christians pay taxes to the Roman state? To what extent are any of them to be granted exemption, and on what grounds?

III

Taxation and Exemption

TAXATION

Taxation plays a larger part in the New Testament and early Christian literature than one might expect, and the question of exemption was one that agitated pagan priests and Christian clerics over a period of centuries. C. J. Cadoux argued that "injunctions to obey the magistrates and pay the government-taxes are meaningless, unless there was a considerable number of Christians who were more or less strongly disinclined to do so."[1] Apart from the obvious fact that taxpayers are always "more or less strongly disinclined" to pay taxes, Christians were not especially opposed to them. More probably there was a persistent suspicion that Christians were in fact not paying properly. According to the Gospel of Luke, Jesus himself had been accused of forbidding the payment of some taxes, and the question had been important in Palestine before his time.

A. H. M. Jones refers to "the great native temples of Syria and central Asia Minor, whose high priests had often under the Hellenistic kings been territorial dynasts," and notes that "in several cases Strabo asserts that their power was broken when Rome took over the government, and it is probable that in general they were brought under municipal control."[2] At Jerusalem there had been priest-kings under the Hasmoneans; Herod the Great took over from them in 38 B.C., as a client-king under the Romans. Herod's revenues, amounting to at least a thousand talents annually, were derived largely from taxation, and at his death in 4 B.C. his subjects bitterly protested the amounts they had to pay.[3] In addition, they were subject to "tribute" exacted by the Romans.

The tribute to the Romans caused trouble in the first century. A decree of Julius Caesar, probably from the year 47 B.C., mentions a tax on produce amounting to 25 percent but payable only every other year. All years but the sabbatical year were taxed, however. (In addition, tithes were to be paid to the high priest and his sons.)[4] There were also land taxes, perhaps at the rate of 1 percent of the valuation.[5] When Judaea was taken away from Herod's son, Archelaus, in A.D. 6 and placed under direct Roman administration, a census was taken for the purpose of instituting further taxation. At this point a certain Judas rebelled in Galilee, denouncing the measure and urging Jews not to pay tribute to the Romans or acknowledge any mortal masters.[6] Presumably he agreed with Philo that the land belonged to God, not to men.[7] Though Judas failed to prevent the census, his memory lingered on; Josephus mentions his son as a rebel killed by the Romans; another relative was Eleazer, the "despot of Mesada."[8] Unaffected by this kind of struggle was the matter of customs duties, collected by the men described in the synoptic Gospels. A chief customs inspector is mentioned in Luke 19:1–2.

According to Suetonius, the emperor Tiberius told provincial governors to shear their sheep, not skin them, and in the year 17 the provinces of Syria and Judaea petitioned for a reduction in their tribute.[9] Interestingly enough, this was the third year of a prefect of Judaea who stayed for eleven years in all and was followed by Pontius Pilate. The prefect, Valerius Gratus, had the power to remove and appoint high priests, and he exercised it vigorously during his first three years, until in 18 he found Joseph Caiaphas, who remained in office until 36. One is tempted to suppose that the high priests were somehow involved in the dispute over payment of tribute.

The synoptic evangelists make it clear that Jesus took a stand on the tribute money. According to Mark 12:13–17 Pharisees and supporters of Herod Antipas, tetrarch of Galilee, asked Jesus if it was right to pay "census" (poll tax plus property taxes) to Caesar or not. Jesus asked to see a denarius, that is, a typical Roman coin. "Whose image and superscription is this?" Obviously they were the Roman emperor's. He then concluded thus: "Pay what is Caesar's to Caesar and what is God's to God." The conclusion does not make clear what Jesus' stand was. In the light of the original question, the answer must mean that it is right to pay taxes to Caesar if you are using Caesar's money. But the addition of the comment on paying what is God's to God introduces an element of ambiguity. Is Jesus pointing to the fact that his questioners were carrying unclean Roman money?[10] Or is there a different point, based on the idea that what bears someone's image, at least in the case of coinage, belongs to that person? If so, according to the creation story it is man who bears God's image and therefore he belongs to God.[11] Or is it that God is the ultimate one to whom man owes allegiance? All these explanations seem a little forced.

Luke is the only evangelist who takes such responsibilities toward Rome with full seriousness. He tells of Joseph as registering for the census taken by Quirinius, governor of Syria. He claims that among the charges brought against Jesus was that of forbidding the payment of tribute to Caesar; the Roman governor Pilate found him innocent. When Judas the Galilean led a rebellion in "the days of the census," he perished—and apparently deserved to perish.[12] So when Luke writes about the tribute money he changes the word from "census" to "tribute" because he wants to make the political reference clear. Like the Roman citizen Paul, who in Acts appeals to Caesar, Jesus was no enemy of the Roman state and its tax system. Christians are not rebels against Rome.

The synoptic evangelists also agree that Jesus favored the collectors of customs and other taxes as contrasted with conventional religionists. Matthew goes so far as to have him say that tax collectors and prostitutes who accepted the message of John the Baptist had precedence over the chief priests and the elders of the people. Luke tells a parable in which a penitent tax collector is favored over a proud Pharisee. There was sometimes room for repentence. Also in Luke we find the story of the chief customs collector of Jericho who, upon conversion, offered half his property to the poor and quadruple damages to those he had defrauded.[13]

Josephus tells us of two occasions, at the beginning and the end of the reign of Caligula (37–41), when rulers reduced various taxes paid at Jerusalem. On the first occasion, the legate of Syria, after removing Pilate from office, visited Jerusalem and canceled all the taxes on the sale of agricultural produce. On the second, the new Jewish king, Agrippa, appointed by Claudius, remitted the tax paid on every house by the inhabitants of Jerusalem.[14] The first of these taxes was presumably Roman, but the second was natively royal, producing part of Agrippa's twelve-million drachma revenues.[15] We doubt that the precise nature of the taxes made much difference. Both kinds were paid to those who ruled Judaea directly.

Roman taxation was a cause of provocation just before the revolt. Albinus, procurator from 62 to 64, "burdened the whole nation with extraordinary taxes."[16] Riots followed

Florus' confiscation of seventeen talents from the temple in 66, and Agrippa II had to denounce the nonpayment of tribute to the Romans. His counsel to pay up was accepted, and in the spring of that year "the magistrates and the members of the council dispersed to the various villages and levied the tribute; the arrears, amounting to forty talents, were rapidly collected."[17] It proved harder and, indeed, impossible to collect the taxes in the countryside. Resistance became war.

The question of civil obedience and taxation arises toward the end of Paul's letter to the Romans, written in the year 56. Paul's primary concern is with obedience to governmental authorities as appointed by God. As his discussion becomes more general, he explains that Christians pay "tribute" because the state endeavors to enforce justice. "Pay all their dues, tribute where tribute is due, tax where tax is due, fear where fear is due, honor where honor is due." Then the discussion moves to another subject. "Owe no one anything, except to love one another." But "Owe no one anything" sums up the discussion on taxes.[18]

Irenaeus refers to some who "audaciously interpret" this passage as referring to angelic powers and invisible rulers. Evidently he has Gnostic exegetes in mind. In his view the reference to taxes was enough to refute their view.[19] He could not foresee or did not know that Gnostic exegetes—specifically, the Naassenes—took "taxes" to mean the seeds scattered in the world from the uncharacterized Being above. "We," they said, "are the tax collectors to whom the taxes of the aeons have come."[20] "To whom the taxes of the aeons have come" is a meaningless but literal rendering of I Corinthians 10:11, "on whom the ends of the ages have come." These Gnostics viewed themselves as the "tax collectors," if not the prostitutes, who were to be the first to enter the kingdom of the heavens.[21] Presumably none of this is what Jesus or Paul had in mind.

Beyond Roman taxes, Jews in Palestine and outside paid taxes for the support of the temple. A good deal of information about the temple revenues is given us by Philo. They come "not only from landed estates but also from other and far greater sources which time will never destroy." What he means is that as long as the population remains constant or increases, the regular contributions of "first-fruits" by everyone aged twenty and up will provide for the temple. The contributions are also called "ransom money"; they are expected to supply "release from slavery or healing of diseases or the enjoyment of liberty fully secured and also complete preservation from danger." (Philo's treatise *Every Good Man Is Free* shows that the slavery in question was not literal.)

The contributions of Jews outside Palestine were especially important. "In practically every city," Philo continues, "there are local treasuries for the holy money, where people regularly come and give their offerings. And at stated times sacred envoys chosen on their merits are appointed to carry the money, from every city those of the highest repute, who will forward in safety the hopes of each and all. For the hopes of the pious rest on these legitimate firstfruits."[22]

Other sources, notably Josephus and the Mishnaic tractate *Shekalim,* give more precise information. How much was the tax? Half a shekel, or two drachmas. When paid? During the month before Passover, Pentecost, and Tabernacles. How paid? In local currency, shipped to Jerusalem and exchanged for "holy shekels" there. The money shipments were protected not only by agents and guards but also by the Roman government.[23]

The funds were used for providing whatever was regularly sacrificed in the temple, as well as for the expenses of guards and maintenance. Normally there was a surplus from these operations, used for civic purposes or simply kept in reserve. Rabbi Ishmael suggested that speculation in produce would be beneficial to the temple, but others refused to permit the operation.

Important Romans also made contributions. According to Philo, the emperor Augustus not only adorned the temple but provided funds from his private account for the daily offering of two lambs and a bull in perpetuity. His wife Livia donated golden vials and libation bowls.[24] It is not clear that the revenues outlasted his lifetime. Josephus indicates that the sacrifices on behalf of the Roman emperor were provided "from the common account of all the Jews," that is, from the temple funds.[25] When the revolt began in A.D. 66 the sacrifices were halted, and during the war the rebel chief John of Gischala melted down the imperial gifts.[26]

Because of its reputation for wealth and sanctity, the temple served as a bank for the valuables of the rich, as Josephus indicates. "In the treasury-chambers lay vast sums of money, vast piles of raiment, and other valuables."[27] This was the case in spite of occasional difficulties with Roman generals or governors. Pompey had been generous enough to leave untouched the two thousand talents he found there, but Crassus took it and, in addition, eight thousand talents' worth of gold.[28] After the death of Herod, Roman soldiers got at least four hundred talents.[29] Pilate took enough to build an aqueduct almost a mile long.[30] Just before the revolt, money was being spent in large sums in order not to leave it for Roman confiscation. Even toward the end of the war some of the treasure was still left, and it was privately surrendered to the Romans.[31] Presumably loot from the temple was among the glut of gold which, according to Josephus, forced its price throughout Syria down to half the prewar level.[32]

At the end of August 70, the temple was burned; three years later the Jewish temple of Onias in Egypt was deprived of its treasures and permanently closed.[33] As for the funds formerly provided for the sacrifices at Jerusalem, Vespasian "imposed a head-tax of two drachmas on all Jews, wherever resident, to be paid annually into the Capitol as formerly contributed by them to the temple at Jerusalem."[34] Problems related to the payment of this tax had repercussions among both Jews and Jewish Christians. We find the problem touched upon in the Gospel of Matthew.

The setting for dealing with the problem is the story of the Coin in the Fish's Mouth. After Peter informs tax collectors, presumably Jewish, that his teacher Jesus does pay the tax, Jesus has a private conversation on the subject with him. He asks whether earthly kings receive duties or poll tax— evidently tribute is meant—from their own "sons" or from aliens. Peter answers, "From aliens." In that case, says Jesus, the "sons" are tax-free. In order not to cause scandal, however, Peter should get the tax money for Jesus and himself from a fish's mouth (Matt. 17:24–27).

What is the point of the story? It must have been modified in transmission even if it could perhaps go back to the time of Jesus, for the real temple tax was never collected by earthly kings. Such kings are now collecting the tax that goes to the Capitol. Christians or Jews who regard themselves as sons of God should be tax-free, but for convention's sake may pay. The point is best made in an article by Montefiore.[35] Presumably the advice given by Matthew was heeded by Jewish Christians. A strange story told by Hegesippus seems to point to this conclusion. He says that the emperor Domitian himself examined two grandsons of Jude in regard to their tax declarations and payments. They told him that they jointly owned farm property worth nine thousand denarii, and that from working it they supported themselves and paid "tribute money."[36] We know that the "Jewish tax" regulations were being enforced by Domitian around this time.[37]

Second-century Christians regularly insisted that they paid taxes. The apologists Justin, Tatian, and Theophilus agreed that this was the case,[38] while Tertullian argues that though temple revenues were declining, tax payments directly to the government were increasing because Christians filed honest tax returns.[39] Indeed, one of the first martyrs of Africa informed the proconsul that though he did not acknowledge "the empire of this age," he paid the market tax on whatever he bought just because he acknowledged his true master, the Ruler over all.[40]

On the other hand, Christians were not enthusiastic about some of their fellow taxpayers. Justin complains that the emperors receive wages and contributions and taxes from prostitutes female, androgynous, and male. Apparently he has in mind the tax levied by Caligula on the earnings of prostitutes.[41] Tertullian is appalled to think that the taxes of Christians are noted in the inspectors' books along with those paid by tavernkeepers, doormen, thieves in the baths, dice players, and pimps.[42] Some apologists criticized the gods on the ground that their temples paid taxes. This showed that they recognized the emperor as their superior.[43] Theophilus mentions the "mother of the so-called gods" as paying taxes and making contributions; Tertullian speaks of the temples of Serapis and other gods as similarly taxed.[44]

By the end of the third century the financial problems of the Roman state were more severe than ever before, and Diocletian turned to taxation and price control as the obvious solutions. He could not deal with such basic matters as the cost of maintaining the tetrarchy with its four bureaucracies, or the cost of continuing an elaborate building program, or the cost of the bonuses regularly paid to the soldiers. A papyrus of the year 300 shows how expensive the last item was, with bonuses in the millions of denarii.[45] In 301 the crisis deepened. Boldly claiming to act in favor of justice and equity, the emperors decreed that "from 1st September, A.D. 301 all new debts and assignments were to be paid in current *pecunia* with a doubled face value."[46] The result could have been anticipated: prices began to soar. Toward the end of the year, therefore, came the famous edict on maximum prices. The emperors claimed to be acting against avarice and in favor of low prices. They provided the death penalty for violations of the edict. Fragments of it have been found in no fewer than forty-one locations, ranging from Libya through Egypt to Asia Minor, Greece, and Italy.[47] One consequence of the edict may have been that goods tended to disappear from the market and were confiscated. The *Paschal Chronicle* says that in 302 Diocletian distributed "army bread" at Alexandria,[48] perhaps because the soldiers could not buy it. (The persecution of Christians began in the spring of 303.)

It is generally agreed that for several years the edict proved effective. The price of wheat, set at 333⅓ denarii per *artaba*[49] dropped to three hundred at Oxyrhynchus in 304/5 and held at 333⅓ as late as 311.[50] Two Christian writers denounced the legislation. The rhetorician Arnobius, obviously writing after the beginning of the persecution in 303,[51] expressed the viewpoint of the "very rich" Christians who had benefited from high grain prices. Nowadays, he said, lack of farm produce and scarcity of grain have a relentless grip on us. He denied that Christians should be blamed for high prices. During the past three hundred years goods had often been cheap and abundant. Indeed, in his opinion, there had been "so many periods of low prices and abundance of commodities as to cause an amazing paralysis of all business undertakings by the low price level."[52] Another rhetorician, Lactantius, denounced the avarice of Diocletian himself (he was writing a tract for Constantine). The tetrarchic system had multiplied armies and bureaucracies. Indeed, there were more on the public payroll than there were taxpayers. At the same time, the emperor's avarice led him to impose ever more burdensome taxes. He himself therefore caused the high prices which he proposed to cure by his edict. In consequence, much blood flowed and goods disappeared from the market, "until the law was abolished by necessity after the deaths of many."[53] Lactantius' comments on the economic policies of the other tetrarchs reveal nothing but a violent dislike for taxation and for tax collection as such.[54]

Another opponent of the tetrarchs was Eusebius, bishop of Caesarea in Palestine and a friend of Constantine. In his view the tetrarchs enjoyed complete prosperity until they persecuted the Christians. Then came famine and heavy taxation, aggravated by demands for payment in gold and silver and the activities of informers. Lactantius blamed the demand for precious metals and the rise of informers not on Maximin, as Eusebius did, but on his superior, the emperor Galerius. But Eusebius makes the same accusation in regard to Licinius.[55] It is clear enough that these writers, Christian and pro-Constantinian, are blaming the tetrarchs before him for their avarice. What they do not tell us is that Constantine followed in their footsteps.[56]

It seems likely that in the first years after Constantine's capture of Rome there was widespread prosperity. A panegyrist addressing the emperor in 313 claims that Maxentius wasted the wealth treasured at Rome for more than a millennium.[57] A more realistic picture is given by Julian in his panegyric on Constantius: "The tyrant's greed had worked like a drought, with the result that money was very scarce, while there were great hoards of treasure in the palace. He [Constantine] unlocked the doors and on the instant flooded the whole country with wealth."[58] According to Eusebius, he also remitted a quarter of the tax on land and appointed commissioners to equalize taxes; but this generosity may have been part of his twentieth-anniversary celebration, temporary rather than permanent.[59] He certainly introduced two new taxes: a sales tax payable in gold and silver every five years, and a graduated but very modest tax that fell on senators and their landed property.[60] The emperor was eager to improve the position of the rich. A panegyrist speaking in 321 insisted that the rich should rejoice over his reign not only because their holdings were secure but also because their hopes for increasing them were good.[61] Possibly what he had especially in mind was the abolition of the 5 percent inheritance tax, perhaps terminated under Constantine.[62] According to Julian, Constantine's ambition was "to amass great wealth and then to spend it liberally so as to gratify (his) own desires and the desires of (his) friends." In other words, he had wanted to be a banker.[63] Therefore, when Julian praises his son Constantius, saying that "you have made their wealth more secure for the rich than a father would for his own children," he is not offering unmixed praise.[64] The anonymous author whom E. A. Thompson called "a Roman reformer and inventor" (probably between 366 and 375) also argued that the rich got richer and the poor got poorer under Constantine and his immediate successors, and he found graft among tax collectors everywhere.[65] Ammianus Marcellinus depicts the same situation.[66] And by the fifth century it was possible for the Christian pamphleteer Salvian of Marseilles to cite inequitable taxation as one of the main causes of the collapse of Rome.[67]

EXEMPTION AND IMMUNITY

As taxes increased under the Roman empire, along with compulsory public services known as "liturgies," pressure for exemption from taxes and immunity from public services steadily increased also. Exemptions were provided for citizens in particular geographical areas or occupations, sometimes for private individuals. The basic ground for exemption, at least in theory, and often in practise, was social usefulness, present or past.

The province of Achaea, for example, was given tax-exemption by Nero in a moment of ill-advised enthusiasm for things Greek. The more frugal Vespasian restored the payment of tribute.[68] Among the groups exempted were veterans, thus aided from the time of Augustus onward.[69] According to Dio, after Augustus was cured by a Greek physician he and the senate paid for the cure and in addition gave tax exemption to all physicians present and future. If this situation ever existed it cannot have lasted long, for in the year 74 Vespasian offered exemption to physicians along with teachers.[70] Of course, exemptions and immunities were not always honored. We have a rather pathetic petition of a physician in 140 who has been forced to perform public services for four years.[71] Later in the reign of Antoninus Pius the emperor tried to keep down the number of tax-exempt physicians and teachers, certainly in Asia Minor and probably elsewhere. The emperor told the assembly of Asia that smaller cities could offer immunity to five physicians, three rhetoricians, and three teachers of grammar; larger cities could do so for seven, four, and four; the largest cities could have ten, five, and five.[72]

Another class of persons often exempted, at least locally, was made up of priests. Egyptian documents allow us to see something of the struggle that went on between the priests and the governments of that country, first under the Ptolemies, then under the Romans, Diodorus Siculus, who visited Egypt in 59 B.C., described the situation of temporary equilibrium between priests and king. He thought the priests owned a third of the land in the country, and with the income from it they per-

formed all the sacrifices throughout Egypt and maintained the
priestly order. They were held in great veneration because
they were in charge of the worship of the gods and because
they were more intelligent than other people. They paid "no
taxes of any kind" and were second only to the king.[73]
Diodorus did not understand the struggle between "church
and state" and naturally he did not anticipate that temple
properties and rights would be lost, first to Cleopatra as she
fought against the Romans and then to the Romans themselves.

After Cleopatra VII became involved with Mark Antony and
he lost the battle of Actium in 31 B.C., she returned to Egypt
and, in quest of funds, looted the temples.[74] (She was following
Antony's example: he had even sent Asian statues to Egypt.[75])
Since the queen had taken the temple treasures first, the
Roman victors could claim that they "committed no sacrilege
when they added them to their spoils."[76] Everything that had
belonged to the Ptolemies, for whom Egypt was a private estate, now belonged to Octavian and his successors, who ruled
the country through a personal representative, the prefect of
Egypt.

It seems that until the eleventh year of Augustus, or 20/19
B.C., the temple lands of Egypt were not disturbed again. In
that year, however, the Roman prefect confiscated them, offering in return either a fixed income *(syntaxis)* or a lease of the
confiscated lands back to the temples.[77] Rostovtzeff has pointed
out how such confiscations were to the advantage of "rich
Alexandrian landowners."[78] The priests were not idle, however. We know that very soon another prefect was receiving
priestly petition for exemption from poll tax. His response was
to order the priests and other temple officials to be enrolled on
census lists.[79] Two or three years later, another prefect received reports from priests about the income of each temple.[80]

Just at the end of Claudius' reign in the year 54, the prefect of Egypt gave a favorable response to a petition from the priests of the crocodile god at Arsinoe. They had asked not to perform compulsory labor in the fields, and he explicitly released them from it.[81] Exemption like this was not universal or, it appears, very common. The documents we possess, almost exclusively from the second century, reflect the struggle over exemption between the priests and the Roman administration.

Under Hadrian, priests in the Fayum asked for exemption on the ground that they wanted time to devote themselves to the education of their sons—undertaken "for the rise of the most holy Nile and the continuance of the eternal reign of the Lord Caesar."[82] Other grounds were mentioned by other priests. Perhaps about 140 a Roman administrator wrote officials of two regions in the Fayum, telling them that he was receiving petitions from "many priests and many hereditary prophets." These petitioners were claiming exemption from compulsory work in the countryside in accordance with "the sacred laws" and because of decisions made by prefects of Egypt. The papyrus letter breaks off here.[83] We do not know what decision was made at this point. Roman administrators usually paid more attention to Roman precedents than to "sacred laws," and the number of precedents available may not have been great. The traditional religious basis was mentioned in a plea for exemption offered in the year 140: "so that the worship of the gods may no longer be hindered."[84]

Such claims were repeated and further developed during the reign of Marcus Aurelius. In 171 the priests of the crocodile god at Bacchias complained that they were being forced to work on dikes far from their temple. They insisted that they had to stay near the village so they could perform the rites which were "for the continuance of our Lord Emperor Aurelius Antoninus Caesar and the full rise of the most holy Nile."[85]

Priests believed that their rites were important enough to merit exemption. A second-century letter from a priest to a priestess instructs her to "go to the temple of Demeter and perform the customary sacrifices for our Lords Emperors and their military success and the rise of the Nile and the increase of the crops and the mildness of the weather."[86] Presumably credit could be claimed for divine favor in any of these areas.

On the other hand, emperors like Hadrian did not suppose that priests made the Nile rise. In 135/136 a rescript of Hadrian recognized that for two years the rise of the Nile had not been "full," even though before that it had been greater than ever. He was aware that tax adjustments had to be made, averaging payments out over periods from three to five years. In the long run "the nature of things" would balance up good and bad years.[87] (The cult of "the rise of the Nile" was very elaborate, to be sure,[88] but when Constantine disbanded the androgynous priests the river rose higher than ever.[89])

As the second century wore on, the arguments raged over rights and privileges, not over religious magic. Even in 171 the presbyters of Bacchias had reported that they provided for the illumination of the temple from their own funds; they paid poll tax; they actually did work on the dikes and cultivate public land.[90] A letter from the village secretary of Nilopolis in 177 shows that villagers favored the priests, no matter what Roman officials might think of them. Between 175 and 177 the villagers had agreed "to discharge the compulsory public services imposed upon the priests." The letter was written to make sure that a priest remained free of the services. Outside the village there was less enthusiasm for exemption.[91] In 193 the situation of two presbyters in a Fayum village was unusual. They could point not only to their services for various deities but to their exemption from poll tax and "all other taxes."[92] Presumably the other temple attendants were not exempt. A complaint

from Bacchias in 198 seems typical. The priests paid poll tax at
eight drachmas a head. They conducted the worship of the
gods and did not work on the irrigation canals. Now, however,
they were being ordered to perform such menial tasks.[93]

Other documents reveal that the priests were trying to keep
or gain exemption. They suggest that during the second century their rights were eroding as the priesthoods lost even the
vestiges of the power they had held under Pharaohs and
Ptolemies.[94] Perhaps the priests were responsible for claiming
that when the Nile failed to rise adequately it was the Christians' fault. Writing in 197, Tertullian refers to the charge.[95]

By and large, these Egyptian priests were not immune from
public service, and thus they lacked the privileges generally
shared by priests in the Greek cities of the Roman east and by
members of the Roman priestly colleges.[96] The difference was
partly due to the general Graeco-Roman view that Egyptian
religion was rather contemptible because so often it involved
the worship of animals. The contempt was reinforced by the
numbers and low social status of the priests themselves. When
they tried to obtain exemption they claimed a social usefulness
that was by no means obvious.

During the last persecution of the Christians, the question of
social utility was often brought up. When the provincials of
Lycia and Pamphylia urged the emperor Maximin to persecute
the Christians in 312 they noted that the emperors had been
"seriously concerned with the divine worship on behalf of the
eternal safety" of their reign. They also urged that all should be
ordered to "devote themselves steadfastly to the worship of the
gods . . . on behalf of your eternal and indestructible majesty,
the extent of whose benefits to all your people is manifest."[97] In
his reply (at least to the citizens of Tyre), Maximin insisted that
the gods had inspired the petitions, for the gods welcomed
worship and responded to it with providential care.[98] It was

this viewpoint, held more or less firmly by all the tetrarchs, that made it difficult to bring the persecution to an end. Galerius justified his edict of toleration by arguing that persecution had resulted in the decline of pagan as well as Christian worship and by insisting in the edict that the Christians must pray for the welfare of the emperors, the state, and themselves.[99] The document issued by Constantine and Licinius in 313 states that toleration is offered "both to the Christians and to all" so that "all the divine and heavenly powers may be favorable to us and all those living under our authority."[100]

Privileges were expressly provided for Christian clerics in a letter sent by Constantine to the proconsul of Africa in April of the same year. The emperor informed him that it would be very dangerous for the state if worship of "the most holy and heavenly one" were to be neglected. In order to maintain "the performance of divine worship" it was therefore necessary for the performers to "receive the rewards of their own labors." What this meant was that "those who provide their service for holy worship, i.e., those who are called clerics, are once and for all to be kept absolutely free from all public offices, lest they be drawn away by any error or sacrilegious fault from the worship due to the Deity." The proper service of God would result in the maximum benefit for the state. Six years later the exemption was renewed and extended to other areas of Constantine's empire, perhaps in consequence of his brief campaign against Licinius and the resulting stalemate.[101]

One precedent for the kinds of tax privileges the clergy enjoyed was of course provided by the Egyptian priests we discussed earlier, especially if we bear in mind the social utility on which the priests insisted. Another might have been given at the Museion in Alexandria, with its free meals and tax exemptions for scholars, and a priest in charge.[102] But scholarship and clerical office were not always closely related. For a society more international than the Egyptian priests, we may turn to the associations of athletes or musical and dramatic artists. These societies carefully preserved dossiers listing the various emperors who had originally offered such privileges as freedom from public services and taxation. Thus an Oxyrhynchus letter of the year 289 includes Claudius' confirmation of privileges granted by Augustus, the summary of a decree by Hadrian providing exemption from services and taxes, Severus' reconfirmation, and Severus Alexander's reiteration of earlier grants.[103] The tetrarchs wrote to such a society (or to such societies in general) to state that traditional exemptions would be maintained but that abuses would have to be checked.[104] A foundation created by such a society at Rome in the year 313 may not have possessed exemption; the inscription is silent on the matter.[105]

Henry Chadwick has suggested that such societies offered precedents for the Christian church in regard to terminology (the expression "ecumenical synod" is found among them) and concern with exemption from taxes.[106]

Certainly clerical privileges multiplied during the reign of Constantine and especially under his sons. Many members of local city councils tried to escape from taxes and other civic obligations by seeking ordination to the Christian ministry. By 326 Constantine had to forbid their "taking refuge in the name and the service of the clergy."[107] Three years later, with the abuse apparently unchecked, he spoke again. "Great numbers shall not be added to the clergy rashly and beyond measure, but rather, when a cleric dies, another shall be selected who has no kinship with a decurion [city council] family." The emperor concluded that "the rich must assume secular obligations and the poor must be supported by the wealth of the churches."[108]

A papyrus letter addressed in about 336 to an official at Oxyrhynchus by "Dionysius, bishop of the Catholic church of the same city," reflects the trend. The bishop seems to be trying to be exempted from managing an estate and acting as guardian of some children.[109] The same official received a petition from a local "priest of the temple of Zeus, Hera, and the associated great gods, celebrant of the divine images and their advancing victory." The priest had been asked to state in writing where his priesthood came from, and he replied under oath that it had come from his father.[110] Why he thought there was "advancing victory" remains unclear. If he paid any attention to the growing privileges of the Christian clergy he would not have been so confident.

Toward the end of the reign of Constantius, clerical privileges flourished along with constant pressure on pagan worship. In 355 accusations of bishops in secular courts were prohibited, "lest there should be an unrestrained opportunity for fanatical spirits to accuse them."[111] The next year, pagans who offered sacrifice or worship to the gods were subjected to the death penalty, while the temples were closed and access to them was forbidden.[112] Christian clerics, on the other hand, were exempted again from menial public services, and the range of exemption was strikingly widened. "Wives of clerics and also their children and attendants, males and females equally, and their children, shall continue to be exempt forever from tax payments and free from such compulsory public services.[113] The Synod of Ariminum, meeting under Constantius' auspices in 359, was emboldened to ask "that the taxable units of land that appear to belong to the Church should be relieved of any compulsory public service and that all annoyance should cease." Apparently they actually did become tax-free for a very short time.[114]

With benefits of this sort provided for them, it was not surprising that some clerics were notorious for their acquisitive characters. Such was apparently the case with George of Cappadocia, the Arian bishop of Alexandria from 356 until murdered in 361. He is said to have got possession of the carbonate of soda monopoly and to have tried to acquire the marshes of papyrus reeds, as well as the salt lakes in Egypt. In addition, he hunted for inheritances and deprived heirs of what their parents left them; he created a monopoly in burials.[115] This is what the Christian writer Epiphanius reports. Part of it is corroborated by the pagan Ammianus Marcellinus. In Cilicia, George had "profited through the ruin of many people"; at Alexandria he accused many persons of rebellion against Constantius and even informed the emperor that all the buildings in the city were public property. In consequence, as Ammianus says, "All men without distinction burned with hatred for George."[116]

Christian clerics and others were clearly evading their responsibilities as members of local senates, and when Julian came to the throne one of his first actions was to insist that "decurions who evade their compulsory public services on the ground that they are Christians [i.e., clerics] shall be recalled."[117] His insistence on the responsibilities of this class, whether Christian or pagan, did not make him popular.[118]

Julian must have won more enemies by virtue of the amnesty he provided for clerics exiled by Constantius. He had allowed them to return and had restored property previously confiscated, but he did not allow them to sit as judges and draw up wills "and appropriate the inheritances of other men and assign everything to themselves."[119] After his death, however, the bishops and other clerics regained almost all their privileges. Through the centuries they were able to acquire still more.[120]

We should not imagine, however, that the clergy were alone in their pursuit of privilege. An edict issued shortly after Constantine's death in 337 provided a list of thirty-five kinds of skilled workmen (including physicians) who were to be immune from all compulsory public services, "since their leisure should be spent in learning these skills whereby they may desire the more to become more proficient themselves and to instruct their children."[121] The power to tax involved not only the power to destroy but also the power to promote social utility.

IV

Work and Occupations

WORK

Hesiod was not a Graeco-Roman work despiser. His *Works and Days* is like the practical Jewish book of Proverbs. Toward the beginning he praises the kind of strife that leads neighbors to compete in their pursuit of wealth. In the golden age men did not have to work (and they were not very bright either), but in the present age of iron, work became necessary. Indeed, "both gods and men are angry with a man who lives idle." Finally, "if your heart within you desires wealth, do these things and work with work upon work" (381f.). These passages show that not every Greek looked down on labor.

Eight centuries later we find the Roman historian Tacitus blaming the Jews for encouraging idleness. They not only rest every seventh day but also are idle, at least the farmers among them, every seventh year.[1] Josephus responds to charges like this and has to insist that the Jewish law provides for periods of strenuous labor as well as periods of rest; indeed, it "banishes idleness and teaches men self-sufficiency and love of labor."[2] Certainly there are familiar passages to this effect in the Mishnaic tractate *Pirke Aboth*. The maxim of the "father" Shema'iah, perhaps from the first century B.C., begins with the simple counsel, "Love work." Rabbi Gamaliel, son of Rabbi Jahudah ha-Nasi, said, "Excellent is Torah study together with worldly business, for the practise of them both puts iniquity out of remembrance; and all Torah without work must fail at length and occasion iniquity."[3]

With the rise of Christianity the same charge, with the same lack of point, was applied to the Christians. "We are said to be unprofitable in business," writes Tertullian. He replies by pointing to the common use of forum, meat market, baths, shops, factories, inns, market-days, "and the rest of business life." Christians like others, and with others, sail ships, serve in the army, work in country and city. There is nothing to the accusation.[4]

Indeed, if we look back to the early days of Christianity, we find Jesus described as a carpenter (Mark 6:3), Paul as a leather-worker or saddler (Acts 18:3).[5] And it is quite evident that both persons were deeply concerned with work. Sherwin-White has pointed out that the picture of social and economic life in the synoptic Gospels fits the Palestinian setting.[6] Others have indicated the extent to which the parables of Jesus reflect his environment. It is a world of fishermen and farmers who look not unsympathetically at the problems of hired hands and estate managers but have nothing to do with the exotic world of the royal families or the estate owners. Idleness is no virtue or pleasure. In the parable of the Laborers in the Vineyard we learn that the men to be hired are idle simply because no one has hired them; they might stand idle all day long. And then the Unjust Steward, about to lose his stewardship, meditates thus: "What shall I do . . . ? I am not strong enough to dig; I am ashamed to beg."[7] In both stories, manual labor (and managerial work, as well, in the second one) is a fact of life.

The apostle Paul makes even more of the fact of work. First, he praises work according to the book of Acts. In Paul's farewell address to the elders of Ephesus, he insists that he has coveted no one's silver or gold or clothing. "You yourselves know that these hands ministered to my necessities, and to those who were with me. In all things I have shown you that by so toiling one must help the weak, remembering the words of the Lord Jesus, how he said, 'It is more blessed to give than to receive.'" Conzelmann claims that Luke is giving concrete expressions like those in I Thessalonians a timeless character.[8] In Acts, Paul clearly regards himself as a model for the elders. But this is hardly surprising. His letters show that he did so regard himself. We now turn to them.

It is probably significant that almost all Paul says about work is to be found in letters written from or to Corinth. This was the home of the proto-Gnostics or Cynics, who were not eager to confront the realities of the world of work. They were happy to view themselves as wise men, rich and even kings because of their wisdom. It is clear from I Corinthians 4:8–13 that Paul insists on the reality of suffering and work, and in this passage even treats work as suffering, because of the lofty Corinthian attitude. They think of themselves as kings. "Would that you did reign, so that we might share the rule with you!" But the life of an apostle is not regal. "To the present hour we hunger and thirst, we are ill-clad and buffeted and homeless, and we labor, working with our own hands."

Whatever Paul's opponents made of this, it is a fact that later Gnostics resolutely resisted the meaningfulness of work. According to them, the creator-god or demiurge was inferior to the perfect Father who, as Tertullian commented, lived in idleness. The demiurge who "by nature is a work-lover," is no master-craftsman but is ignorant of the patterns of the things he made. One could go so far as to call him ignorant and stupid, for he does not know what he is doing. His angels dig up the ground in frost and rain with toil and sow the spiritual seeds (unwittingly); through the winter they continue looking after them, using the hoe and pulling up weeds. Such angels will not reap the harvest, for work has no relation to reward. Convinced that Paul cannot have resembled the demiurge or his angels, some Gnostics claimed that when he spoke of "working with his hands" he had masturbation in mind.[9]

It is conceivable that, as on other occasions, Gnostics appealed to sayings of Jesus like those in the Sermon on the Mount. There they could find counsel not to be anxious about the necessities to be acquired through work. God will feed and clothe you, and you do not need to sow, reap, or gather into barns anymore than birds do, or toil and spin anymore than lilies do.[10] Such sayings would appeal to Corinthians who thought they were already "filled, rich, kings" (I Cor. 4:8)— presumably also to Thessalonians who liked to eat but not work (II Thess. 3:10).

Given this insistence on work, Paul was naturally unable to receive gifts from the Christians at Corinth, whether or not they wanted to offer him any. His discussion in the ninth chapter of I Corinthians suggests that he had to insist upon the right to support from the congregation. And of course his idea that he always rejected congregational offerings is contradicted by his statement about the funds rather steadily sent him by the church in Philippi (Phil. 4:10–20). But he keeps on thinking about work. "By the grace of God I am what I am, and his grace toward me was not in vain. On the contrary, I worked harder than any of them [the other apostles], though it was not I, but the grace of God which is with me" (I Cor. 15:20). These other apostles worried him. "I think that I am not in the least inferior to these superlative apostles. . . . I am not at all inferior to these superlative apostles, even though I am nothing. The signs of a true apostle were performed among you in all patience, with signs and wonders and mighty works" (II Cor. 11:5, 12:11–12). And so we are not surprised to hear him ask, "Are they servants of Christ? I am a better one—I am talking like a madman— with far greater labors, far more imprisonments, with count- less beatings, and often near death" (II Cor. 11:23). Anton Fridrichsen long ago found the key to passages like this. Paul is listing his achievements in the manner of Graeco-Roman kings, generals, or emperors.[11] The difference is that whereas they win by exercising active power, he wins, so to speak, pas- sively. He wins by endurance, as described by the Stoics or exemplified in the life of Diogenes or the labors of Hercules.

The Corinthians were not the only ones to receive Paul's admonitions. From Corinth he wrote to the Thessalonians, who seem to have neglected work on other grounds. They simply laid undue emphasis on the nearness of the return of Jesus from heaven, without using the Cynic–Stoic paradoxes about the wise man. Paul's approach to their problem was therefore somewhat different. The first three chapters of I Thessalonians contain virtually nothing but reminiscences of Paul's mission to Thessalonica. They include a statement about this work there which, in the light of Philippians, is hardly ingenuous. "You remember our labor and toil, brothers; we worked night and day, that we might not burden any of you while we preached the gospel of God to you." Later on in the letter he praises their brotherly love and urges them to increase it by (a) living quietly, (b) minding their own business, and (c) working with their hands, as he has already told them. The purpose of all this is "that you may command the respect of outsiders and not be dependent on anyone" (I Thess. 2:9; 4:9–12). He himself is obviously their model. They are to re- spect the work done by other Christian leaders as well. "We beseech you to respect those who labor among you and are over you in the Lord and admonish you, and to esteem them very highly because of their work" (I Thess. 5:12–13).

In II Thessalonians, whether genuine and written under special circumstances for a special audience or not, the work ethic is expressed with full clarity. "We command you in the name of our Lord Jesus Christ that you keep away from any brother who is living in idleness and not in accord with the tradition that you received from us. For you yourselves know how you ought to imitate us; we were not idle when we were with you, we did not eat anyone's bread without paying, but with toil and labor we worked night and day, that we might not burden any of you. It was not that we have not that right, but to give you in our conduct an example to imitate. For even when we were with you, we gave you this command: If any one will not work, let him not eat. For we hear that some of you are living in idleness, mere busibodies, not doing any work" (II Thess. 3:6–11). He then goes on to say some of this over again, in case they have missed the point.

Two factors seem to have influenced the Thessalonians. The first is more important. They seem to have been deeply concerned with Paul's eschatological predictions and to have misunderstood them—if he really spoke clearly—to mean that the "day of the Lord" had already arrived and that they were living in the reign of God or at least so close to it that there was no point in working any more. Paul explicitly denounces this notion in the second chapter of II Thessalonians. It is not unlike what the Corinthians held about having already been filled and having become rich and royal. Both Thessalonians and Corinthians were anticipating what would come at the end of the age. Both groups felt it unnecessary to work in the apostolic manner.

The second factor is their failure to live up to ordinary human standards of self-support. It is hard to be quite so specific as Deissmann was when he wrote that "St. Paul was probably borrowing a bit of good old workshop morality, a maxim applied no doubt hundreds of times by industrious

workmen as they forbade a lazy apprentice to sit down to din-
ner."[12] Maybe so, maybe no. We do know that Paul, or whoever modeled II Thessalonians after I Thessalonians, shared
the belief expressed in Genesis 3:19: the right to eat is based on
work.

Similarly in Galatians there is a strong emphasis on testing
one's own work and bearing one's own load. Indeed, the Christian bears a double load, for as he fulfills the law of Christ
concerning love of neighbor he bears the neighbor's load as
well as his own. There is a reward for all this, described as
reaping the crop one has sown (Gal. 6:1–10). Naturally the
language is largely figurative, but the attitude underlying it is
what matters for our investigation.

In Paul's view, labor is not to be "vain" or pointless labor, as
he repeatedly states.[13] Instead, it is related to a reward or
"pay," sometimes spoken of as a crop and sometimes as
wages.[14] Indeed, one has a right to payment for work, and this
point is elaborately worked out in regard to the work of ministry in I Corinthians 9:4–14. When Paul implies that he and
Barnabas should have "the right not to work" he refers to work
other than the ministerial work to which as an apostle he was
called (I Cor. 9:6).

His zeal for work knows no limits, for he is extremely com-
petitive, especially when he is impressing the Corinthians. He
competes with the other apostles. "I worked harder than any of
them, though it was not I, but the grace of God . . . ." But this
was nothing new. Long before his conversion to Christianity he
was a hard worker. "You have heard of my former life in
Judaism, how I persecuted the church of God violently and
tried to destroy it; and I advanced in Judaism beyond many of
my own age among my people, so extremely zealous was I for
the traditions of my fathers." Then came his conversion due to
election and grace (Gal. 1:13–14). Just the same point is made

in Philippians, where he explains that he was "a Hebrew born of Hebrews; as to the law a Pharisee, as to righteousness under the law blameless." Having set up this standard of achievement, he then knocks it down: "whatever gain I had, I counted as loss for the sake of the Christ." Credits became debits in his business metaphor. And he speaks momentarily of faith rather than of achievement. Once more, however, his figure of speech changes, and we are in a race, straining forward to what lies ahead and pressing on toward the goal (Phil. 3:5–16). Justification by faith or grace is quite obviously only one side of Paul's complex religious personality. Indeed, he even competed with his Corinthian converts in the matter of "talking in tongues" (I Cor. 14:18).

This is not to say that he was always content to think of himself as farmer or soldier, as in I Corinthians 9. Instead, he could regard himself as a planter whose function was obviously more highly skilled than that of a waterer. Or he could speak of himself as "a skilled master-builder," one capable of laying a foundation and making plans for a whole building, no matter what anyone else might build on the foundation and with what sorts of materials. Long before, Aristotle had commented on the superiority of master-builders to manual laborers. The master-builders know the causes of what they are doing, and are capable of teaching others.[15] Finally, Paul could go a little higher and speak of himself as a servant of Christ and a trustworthy steward of the mysteries of God.[16]

Sometimes it is supposed that Paul and Christians after him were the only enthusiasts for work in the ancient world. Such a notion comes from taking rhetoricians and philosophers too seriously, especially Plato. "Why," Plato asks, "are mean employments and manual arts a reproach? Only because they imply a weakness in the higher principles. . . ."[17] By "mean employments" Plato meant nonintellectual pursuits. So did the

Stoic Zeno when he said that "nothing ought to be thought
sacred, or of great value, and holy, which is the work of build-
ers and artisans." Plutarch, Clement of Alexandria, and Origen quote this statement; the anti-Christian Celsus has a similar idea.[18] But all these authors share the Platonic attitude, and
it was not the only one there was. Paul's view can be paralleled,
as is often the case, among Stoics, especially Romans.

Indeed Cleanthes, head of the Stoa after Zeno, earned his
living by digging and drawing water in gardens, and he was
proud of his work. He praised a Spartan youth for asking him
if labor was a good thing; in his view the answer was obviously
Yes.[19] When we reach the Stoic moralists of Paul's time and
later, we find strong emphasis laid on the virtue of hard work.
Musonius Rufus wrote: "The teachings of philosophy exhort
the woman to be content with her lot and work with her own
hands." But "all human tasks . . . are a common obligation and
are common for men and women." Dio Chrysostom,
influenced by the Stoics, held that poverty "affords many opportunities of making a living that are neither unseemly nor
injurious to men who are willing to work with their hands."
The Stoic Hierocles, in his *Economics*, apparently followed
Musonius in extolling the virtues of hard work. Epictetus
agreed.[20] Marcus Aurelius was grateful to his tutor for the
lesson "to bear pain and be content with little; to work with my
own hands, to mind my own business, and to be slow to listen to
slander."[21] This is just what Paul said to the Thessalonians:
mind your own business and work with your hands.

Moreover, the same lesson is drawn from hard work by
Musonius as by Paul. Speaking of hard work in the country, he
asks:

> Do you think it is more fitting for a free man by his own labor to
> procure for himself the necessities of life or to receive them from
> others?

And he rapidly supplies the answer.

> But surely it is plain that not to require another's help for one's
> need is more noble than to ask for it.

The Stoic ideal of self-sufficiency, which Paul shares, is to be
achieved through hard work.[22]

Even the Platonist Maximus of Tyre, writing toward the end
of the second century, does not straightforwardly advocate the
contemplative life as contrasted with the life of action, but
provides two essays, one on each side of the question. The one
favoring action seems more convincing; it contains the statement that Heracles must labor constantly because he is the son
of his father, Zeus, who labors constantly to maintain the
universe.[23] New Testament critics have not failed to note the
resemblance to John 5:17, where Jesus criticizes sabbath observance by saying, "My Father is working still, and I am
working."

To some extent this attitude to work can be described as
Roman. It is set forth in stories of Cato, the hard-working
Roman statesman, and his attachment to the land.[24] We see it in
Plutarch's *Life of Cato*. We see it in what the younger Pliny said
to Trajan in his *Panegyric*: "you took delight in work and you
still do."[25] We see it in the inscriptions cited by MacMullen.[26]

Early Christians were encouraged to work too. We might
expect such counsel in relation to slaves. "Slaves, . . . whatever
your task, work heartily, as serving the Lord and not men,
knowing that from the Lord you will receive the inheritance as
your reward; you are serving the Lord Christ." Christian slaves
are to work especially hard for Christian masters. In I Clement
free workmen are also encouraged to do their duty. "The good
workmen receives the bread for his work with boldness, while
the bad and careless one does not look his employer in the
face."[27] (Obviously this employer is not of the kind denounced

in James 5:4, who defrauds laborers of their wages.) "The greater the toil the greater the gain," Ignatius writes to Polycarp; presumably he is quoting a proverb.[28] And in the Jewish-Christian books of Barnabas and the Didache the point is reiterated. Barnabas attacks those who steal rather than earning their food with sweat. The Didachist is much concerned with wandering Christians who ought to earn their keep. "If he wants to stay with you and is an artisan, let him work and eat. If he has no skill, look after him intelligently so that no one may live idle with you as a Christian. If he does not want to do thus [i.e., work at something], he is a Christian for gain; keep away from such persons."[29] Two Christian writers of the second century use the expression "manual laborers and untrained persons" when describing their co-religionists.[30]

The apologist Justin tells how he was converted to Christianity. An old man asked him embarrassing questions when he was still a budding Platonist. The old man accused him of loving words more than work or truth, of being a sophist rather than a practical man. Justin tried to defend philosophy as differentiated from what we might call "ditch-digging."[31] But when he became a Christian himself he was willing, at least for apologetic purposes, to find the cross imaged in such workaday tools as a ship's mast, a plough, and a shovel. (This is not to say that he was not pleased to find it hinted at in the *Timaeus* of Plato.)[32] Manual labor, *autourgia,* is treated enthusiastically by Clement of Alexandria, presumably because he has found it approved by Musonius. All the examples (eight of them) but one are to be found in chapters III through XI of the third book of the *Paedadogus,* where the influence of Musonius is conspicious. The one exception comes when Clement discusses frugality and hard work among the ancient Greeks and claims that such traits were not confined to untrained persons but were found among leaders like Odysseus.[33] At this point Clement's enthusiasm seems based on his literary model, for as a Platonist of sorts he does not really like the work of artists and he criticizes such work as mean because it uses materials and influences the senses.[34] Manual craftsmanship lacks understanding of primary causes and is obviously inferior.[35] Clement was far more devoted to contemplation.

This is what we should expect from a teacher of philosophical theology at Alexandria. Probably Tertullian was a better representative of the general Christian attitude. He was much distressed when he heard pagans complain that Christians were idle. He hastened to list the kinds of activities in which they vigorously participated.[36] Certainly the church order known as the *Didascalia apostolorum* shares his view: "Be occupied in the things of the Lord or engaged upon your work, and never be idle." From the book of Proverbs the author picks up the examples of the ant and the bee for imitation and then passes on to Paul: "Always be working, for idleness is a blot for which there is no cure. 'But if any man among you will not work, let him not eat': for the Lord God also hates sluggards; for it is not possible for a sluggard to be a believer." In addition, you as Christians are to "teach your children crafts that are agreeable and befitting to religion, lest through idleness they give themselves to wantonness."[37] All these injunctions are repeated in the fourth-century *Apostolic Constitutions,* where one chapter is entitled "The Idle Believers Must Not Eat," and the injunction is justified by apostolic models. Peter and others were fishermen; Paul and Aquila were leather-workers; the descendants of Judas, son of James, were farmers.[38] On the other hand, when preaching on II Thessalonians, Chrysostom says that after the injunction about working and eating, Paul went on to tell the congregation not to be weary in doing good "for fear that they would perish in the famine." The rest of his sermon is on almsgiving and helping others, not on the work ethic.[39]

One should add just a few words about the problem of work in relation to unemployment, since the ancients were quite aware of its existence. Suetonius tells a story about the emperor Vespasian and his rebuilding of the Capitol after a fire. "To an engineer, who offered to convey some lofty columns up to the Capitol at a small expense, he gave no mean reward for his device, but declined his services with the remark: 'You must allow me to feed the populace.'"[40] Labor-saving devices were rejected in favor of employment—although by the end of the century sophisticated equipment was in use, as we see from a bas-relief on the tomb of the Haterii.[41] In Jerusalem a few years earlier a similar problem had confronted the authorities. Work on the Herodian temple had been completed, and eighteen thousand craftsmen faced unemployment. The group that Josephus calls "the people"—presumably the Sanhedrin—was concerned not only about the living of these workmen but also about the funds on deposit in the temple treasury, preferring to spend the money on public works rather than have it confiscated by the Romans. They urged King Agrippa to raise the height of a stone portico, but he refused because it would take too much time and money. What he did instead was pave the city with white stone.[42]

An especially interesting feature of the work on the temple as it was nearing completion was that "if anyone worked for but one hour of the day, he at once received his pay for this."[43] The word "this" is ambiguous, but it probably refers to "day" rather than "hour." We thus have a remarkable parallel to a Matthaean parable ascribed to Jesus. According to the parable, a "householder" hires workmen at various hours of the day; all work until the twelfth hour, and even those hired at the eleventh receive the day's wage, a denarius. Difficulties arise when those who worked longer complain about the others. The employer answers that: *(a)* he is keeping his contract, *(b)*

he can do as he pleases with his money, and *(c)* some are be-
grudging his generosity (Matt. 20:1–15). The parable seems to
make sense if it is related to echoes of the Jerusalem situation
just before the revolt. It is hard to imagine that Jesus really
supposed that money entitles one to absolute freedom of
choice.

A. T. Geoghegan exaggerates when he says that Christianity
brought "a complete change in the opinion of physical work."
He claims that the Greeks and Romans who favored work were
not able to change "the general attitude," while "the Jewish
attitude towards work was nationalistic."[44] What is true is that
nonworkers were not encouraged in the early church. There
were few adherents of the Messalian group, denounced by
Epiphanius, who claimed to be following the words of Jesus:
"Do not labor for the food which perishes." Epiphanius had no
difficulty in citing countertexts. We must not be idle or sluggish
or even eating at unseasonable times, or like the drone bee.
Instead, we must work with our own hands as Paul said, and if
not, not eat. Abraham was a herdsman, supplying food to
angels; Elijah provided for a poor widow and her son; the rich
Job worked constantly at doing good; and this is what Paul
commended in Ephesians. So, too, the book of Proverbs warns
against idleness.[45] Such is the generally accepted Christian
teaching about work.

CLASS AND OCCUPATIONS

There was a good deal of subjectivity in ancient ideas of
social class, especially one's own, just as there is now. "We do
not originate from the lowest levels of society," wrote Minucius
Felix, in response to the claim that Christians are "from the
lowest dregs."[46] He was writing an apology in the manner of
other second- and third-century apologists, proving that by

pagan standards Christians are not such a bad lot. Later on, however, when Jerome wanted to show how authentically evangelical he was in contrast with the philosopher Marius Victorinus, he insisted that "the church of Christ was gathered not from Academy or Lyceum but from the worthless populace."[47]

Thus when Seneca wrote, "See how much larger is the number of the poor" than of the rich, we cannot be quite certain what he meant. He went on to "pass over the wealth that is nearly poverty" and turned to the "really rich."[48] One would suppose he had himself in mind.

We do not deny the existence of economic and social realities behind the talk about class and economic groups. We are simply concerned with the question of attitudes. In passing we note that if women can be urged not to wear gold, pearls, or expensive clothing (I Tim. 2:9) they are not far down on any social ladder. This is not to say that they stood close to a Lollia Paulina, who when engaged to Caligula wore forty million sesterces' worth of emeralds and pearls.[49]

Let us consider the question of socially approved and, more important, disapproved occupations, bearing in mind what Ramsay MacMullen calls "the lexicon of snobbery."[50] The theory behind the attitudes is fairly consistent and is well expressed by two representatives of the Middle Stoa, Panaetius and Posidonius. The former, as rendered by Cicero, differentiates trades and other pursuits suitable for a free man from those merely "low" *(sordidi)*. Low businesses involve animosity; the examples are tax collecting and usury. Manual labor is in the same category unless artistic skill is involved. So is retail trade, since it involves lying about what is sold. Manufacturing is no fit for the free. Worst of all are occupations related to meals or entertainment.[51] Seneca, in turn, gives us the thought of Posidonius. He has four classes of activities. First come those that are vulgar and sordid, manual labor and manufacture. Second, occupations related to providing pleasure for eye and ear. Third, the education and upbringing of children. Fourth, and of course at the top, the liberal arts concerned just with virtue.[52]

If we take MacMullen's "lexicon," it is worth noting that the terms expressing contempt for various occupations can be arranged in relation to the classifications of Panaetius or, better, those of Posidonius. We might think ourselves in the eighteenth century, whether in England or in France. Occupations having to do with money or "trade" are looked down on. No one puts it better than Cicero. "Trade if on a small scale is to be considered vulgar; but if wholesale and on a large scale, importing large quantities from all parts of the world and distributing to many without misrepresentation, it is not to be greatly disparaged, and indeed it seems to deserve the highest respect. . . ."[53] All Cicero means is that "money talks." Among the least favored occupations, as one might expect, is tax collecting. We shall return to this presently. Manual labor, trades having to do with food, drink, shelter, clothing, entertainment, and even the care and upbringing of children—all were often despised in literary circles, and even beyond in the Graeco-Roman world. Perhaps this is not altogether surprising. What is more surprising is that identical attitudes turn up in groups where we should not expect them. These groups are first Palestinian and Babylonian Jews, and second, leaders of the Christian church.

In regard to Judaism we are fortunate enough to have three lists assembled by Joachim Jeremias from the Talmud.[54] The first comes from about A.D. 150 and in Danby's translation it reads thus: "A man will not teach his son to be an ass-driver or a camel-driver, or a barber or a sailor, or a herdsman or a shopkeeper, for their craft is the craft of robbers."[55] Just so, aristo-

cratic Romans called their enemies "muleteers."[56] It might sur-
prise you to know, said Dio Chrysostom, that not even dealing
with an ass or a sheep is a matter for inexperienced persons.[57]
Sailors were not regarded highly. When Tertullian snipes at
the heretic Marcion, he calls him a shipmaster.[58] Barbers had a
bad reputation. No one had a good word for shopkeepers, as
MacMullen's many examples show. Paul called opponents
"peddlers of God's word" (II Cor. 2:17).

The second list from Jeremias includes many occupations
characteristic of women and having to do with clothing and
cleaning. Suffice it to say that these are just the occupations for
which the pagan critic Celsus taunted the Christians. Among
the most devoted adherents of Christianity, he said, were
wool-workers, cobblers, and laundry-workers. They persuaded children to disregard the admonitions of their father
and their teachers.[59]

The third list is especially interesting. It seems to revolve
around fraud and trickery. The first part of it also occurs in the
Mishnah tractate *Sanhedrin*, where we find that those not qualified to be witnesses or judges include dice-players, usurers,
pigeon-flyers, and traffickers in Seventh Year produce.[60] The
pigeon-flyers are obviously likely to cheat in the races, while the
Seventh Year produce is not supposed to exist at all. What of
dice-players and usurers? It is significant that just the same two
occupations are mentioned in an early Christian attack on the
presumption of the Montanist prophets. "Does a prophet dye
his hair? Use eye makeup? Love jewelry? Play at tables and
dice? Lend money at interest?"[61] It is to be assumed that the
Jewish-Christian Montanists would find such questions embarrassing. And Roman laws, on the books in the third century
A.D., absolutely forbade gambling with dice, even though the
laws were widely disregarded, not least by the emperors.[62] The
Gnostic Heracleon, commenting on Jesus' cleansing of the

temple, says he drove out "the dicing traders and all wickedness."[63] A third-century Christian denounced dice-players; their game was both illegal and immoral. But it was not until the synod of Elvira, early in the fourth century, that a church council forbade the game.[64]

Usurers were feared and despised in the Graeco-Roman world generally, but an early Roman prohibition of usury became a dead letter as early as the second century B.C. Plato and Aristotle had condemned the taking of interest on loans, but the ordinary rate was 12 percent. Cicero found a rate of 48 percent rather horrifying.[65] Among Jews the taking of interest on loans to other Jews was forbidden but not on loans to gentiles.[66] On the other hand, in a parable of Jesus, getting a return on money by charging interest is taken for granted, while in two different forms of the Apocalypse of Peter either interest or compound interest is condemned.[67] With the passage of time, however, Christians came to be much more critical of usury.[68]

In the Babylonian version of *Sanhedrin* three more activities are denounced: those of shepherds, tax collectors, and customs collectors. Why shepherds? Musonius Rufus commends their way of life; Dio Chrysostom presents an idyllic picture in which poverty presents no obstacle, but he seems aware that his audience will find his thoughts surprising.[69] Were shepherds associated with tax collectors because of what they did to the sheep?

Any society complains about tax collectors. In the synoptic Gospels tax collectors—especially customs collectors—and "sinners" are often mentioned together, even though one of Jesus' twelve principal disciples had been a collector.[70] In one Gospel passage (Matt. 21:31–32) we hear that "the tax collectors and the harlots" have precedence in the kingdom of God, ahead of the religious authorities. The pairing of these two occupations must have been fairly common, at least in the minds of authors. We find both called "shameful and disgraceful" by Dio Chrysostom, associated by Artemidorus the writer on dreams, and mentioned along with shopkeeping and dancing by the emperor Julian.[71] The anti-Christian Celsus mentions tax collectors with sailors because he has read about the apostles, but he names their occupations in tones of contempt.[72] And Philostratus mentions tax collectors along with various hucksters and usurers concerned with trivial amounts of money.[73] They are retailers, not wholesalers.

We have seen that the occupations criticized by Jews were in essence the same as those criticized by Greeks, Romans, and Christians. The criticism was not related to religious principles as much as to attitudes widespread in the Mediterranean world. But now let us see if the Christians greatly modified the attitudes present in their society. We begin by quoting a sentence from Cicero to which we have already referred: "Least respectable of all are those trades which cater for sensual pleasures: 'fishmongers, butchers, cooks, and poulterers, and fishermen,' as Terence says; add to these, if you please, the perfumers, dancers, and the burlesque shows."[74] This is our text, which we shall gloss with Christian examples.

Our first witness is Clement of Alexandria, who denounces the idle rich for keeping so many different kinds of cooks in their "labor for gluttony."[75] This is not to say that a Christian could not be a cook. And later on, when John Chrysostom denounces the new rich he tells one of them, "Go back beyond your parents and grandparents, and you will undoubtedly find bakers and ass-drivers and cooks."[76] (His own status was higher than that.[77])

More obviously, perfumers were viewed without favor.[78] So were dancers, even though some Christians danced or thought that Jesus and the apostles had danced.[79] As for theatrical shows, we can of course refer to Tertullian's treatise *De spectaculis,* a vindictive attack on all performances. Perhaps its high point is reached when we learn about one woman who was possessed by a demon when she went to the theater, another who died soon after a recitation by a tragedian.[80] The tradition of hostility lasted a long time.[81] Cyprian kept a retired actor from teaching dramatics by putting him on the church pension fund.[82]

Christian lists of unacceptable occupations, which first occur in the early third century, move in a somewhat different direction from the ideas of their contemporaries. It is clear that in the *Didascalia apostolorum* a list of prospective donors whose gifts are not to be accepted is based on moral grounds. It begins with the mention of "rich persons who keep men shut up in prison or ill-treat their slaves or behave with cruelty in their cities or oppress the poor." Then it turns to various kinds of immoral persons, much in the manner of the Old and New Testaments. Indeed, one might suspect that the list has been "moralized," so to speak; for in sequence we find "painters of pictures, *makers of idols,* workers of gold and silver and bronze *who are thieves, dishonest* tax-collectors."[83] The italicized words give the moral explanation for condemning the occupations, and at the same time they make the condemnation less than universal. The list is very specific as it goes on with the mention of "those who alter weights or measure deceitfully, innkeepers who mix water (with their wine), soldiers who act lawlessly, murderers, spies who procure condemnations,[84] any Roman officials who are defiled with wars and have shed innocent blood without trial." These denunciations clearly show the concern of Syrian Christian leaders for the questions of social ethics. More than a century later, the author of the *Apostolic Constitutions* used the *Didascalia* but left out the dishonest innkeepers, the spies, and the Roman officials. Changed political conditions probably account for the last two omissions. Had innkeepers become more honest? The author added mention of forgers and executioners. Had both become more common?

Around the time of the *Didascalia* there is a list of crafts and professions forbidden to Christians. It is found in the *Apostolic Tradition* traditionally ascribed to Hippolytus of Rome, and named on his headless statue found at Rome in the sixteenth century. This list begins with procurers, whose occupation, like that of the women associated with them, was looked down upon by most Greeks and Romans, condemned as immoral by some.[85] Next come sculptors and painters, traditionally associated with the manufacture of idols. They are followed by people connected with the theater. More surprising is the mention of one who teaches children "worldly knowledge." He can continue in his work only if he has no other craft. Is this a specifically Christian attitude? No, Seneca had indicated how inferior the teacher of preliminary subjects was to the real philosopher—and had mentioned painters, sculptors, and marble-workers as servants of luxury.[86] Similarly Juvenal, denouncing clever Greeks, lists all these among their unworthy occupations.[87] And Dio Chrysostom says one should not sneer at a man whose father was a schoolmaster or a tutor.[88] The Christians are not so different from others, though their reasons for action may differ. But this passage on teachers was left out when the author of the *Apostolic Constitutions* revised Hippolytus' list. In any case it was an intrusion, oddly placed between the theater and the racetrack.

Both *Tradition* and *Constitutions* reject charioteers and gladiators as well as others connected with games or even attendants at games. *Constitutions* goes into more detail, listing participants in the Olympic games (a condemnation unnecessary after the end of the fourth century), flutists accompanying a chorus, and lyre players, not to mention dancers. With just

the same intensity both documents denounce those who practice sexual aberrations, astrology, and magic.[89]

Christian lists of undesirable occupations do not include socially useful arts or crafts. Presumably, Christians supported
the exemption of their practitioners from compulsory public
services, as outlined in a decree of Constantine published in the
summer of 337.[90] Christian influence can be seen in the legislation finally formulated in the Theodosian Code of 438, especially in Book XV. Title 5 deals with the regulation of shows,
Title 6 specifically with the show of the Maiuma, much
criticized by Christian authors, Title 7 with "men and women
of the stage," Title 8 with procurers, Title 9 with expenditure
on shows, Title 10 with chariot horses, Title 11 with the chase
of wild beasts, and Title 12 with gladiators. Here we find the
same subject matter as in the Christian lists.

This was also the period when Christians took pride in the
wide distribution of occupations among them. Theodoret
speaks of men who are cobblers, coppersmiths, and wool-
spinners, as well as of women who spin on a daily basis or are
seamstresses or handmaids. Such people live in the city, but
there are Christians in the country too, including diggers, cat-
tle drivers, and gardeners.[91] There is a marked difference between the fifth-century Theodoret and the third-century Origen in regard to some of these occupations. When Origen
found Celsus attacking the Christians as "wool-workers,
cobblers, laundry-workers, and the most illiterate and bucolic
yokels," he simply argued that Christian doctrine was not
taught by such persons.[92]

There is a similar difference between attitudes toward the
poor. Early in the second century Pliny as an outside observer
was a good witness to the presence of all classes among the
Christians of Pontus,[93] but at Alexandria the theologians had
little enthusiasm for the poor. Clement explained that what

mattered was spiritual poverty. Jesus did not bless "the poor without qualification" but those who volunteered for poverty.[94] Origen insists that "not even a stupid person would praise the poor indiscriminately; the majority of them have very bad character."[95] This is not the view of Chrysostom a century and a half later. He says that the poor have to put up with "countless slanders and criticisms and accusations of idleness and curses and insults and ridicule." The ordinary middle-class church member, when asked for alms, will reply, "But nothing is more impudent than a poor man." The bishop does not agree.[96]

Whether or not there actually was a middle class in the late Roman empire, Christian writers supposed that there was, and that most Christians belonged to it. In the longer version of Eusebius' *Martyrs of Palestine* we are told of martyrs who were members of the nobility and of others who belonged to "the middle and ordinary class in life." Some were even slaves.[97] But it is Chrysostom who gives us a schematic picture of the three classes at Antioch toward the end of the fourth century. In his opinion, 10 percent were rich and 10 percent were so poor that they had nothing. The remaining 80 percent belonged to the middle.[98] We may wonder, of course, whether Chrysostom is describing the situation or stating an ideal. Aristotle regarded the most viable society as one in which the middle class was bigger than either the rich or the poor, or rather, than both put together.[99] Certainly Chrysostom's Antioch should have been stable, if Aristotle was right.

Chrysostom gives us a little more information when he starts using his figures, as he ordinarily does, in preacherly fashion in order to get funding from the rich. It is true that the church has an income equal to that of a moderately rich man, but with the income it supports three thousand widows, orphans, and others. The capital fund is not touched. So if ten men were to spend their income in the same way, there would be no poor. Perhaps he means that if ten men spent some of their income thus, there would be no poor. It is clear enough from other sermons that there was no likelihood of their doing so.

According to A. H. M. Jones, prices in relation to the gold *solidus* remained fairly stable from the fourth to the sixth century, in spite of fluctuations due to the nature of harvests.[100] This stability may suggest that we can take as maximal the eighty pounds of gold a year set aside by Gregory the Great "to feed 3000 refugee nuns in Rome,"[101] and then apply the figure to Antioch. If we should imagine the income of the church of Antioch to be a hundred pounds of gold a year, or two or three times that in view of the support of clerics and the maintenance of buildings, we could see that Chrysostom was right when he compared it with that of a moderately rich man. For the early fifth century the historian Olympiodorus of Thebes tells us about households at Rome with incomes of four thousand, fifteen hundred, and one thousand pounds of gold.[102] But the concentration of wealth at Rome was notable. The income of the endowments provided just for the upkeep of Roman churches by Constantine amounted to more than four hundred pounds of gold a year.

At the other end of the social scale from the Roman senatorial aristocracy stood the slave class with which Christians have often been identified. The expression "slave of God" or "slave of Christ," however, reflects Semitic religiosity, not social rank in the Graeco-Roman world. The idea of remaining in slavery rather than seeking emancipation presumably reflects the expectation of the end of the world, whether generally or for individuals. It was certainly not the view generally held in the Roman world, where emancipation was common and the expectation of it was widespread among slaves.

In the Gospels, and chiefly in Matthew, we find emphasis laid

on the inferiority of slaves to masters and on the slaves' responsibilities.[103] There is not a trace of the view ascribed to the
Essenes by Philo.[104]

> They denounce the owners of slaves, not merely for their injustice
> in outraging the law of equality, but also for their impiety in annul-
> ling the statute of nature, who like a mother has borne and reared
> all alike as genuine brothers, not in name only but in reality.

For the apostle Paul, "everyone should remain in the state in
which he was called," and though his syntax is not fully clear in
I Corinthians 7:21, the context shows that he meant for slaves
not to seek emancipation. The letter to Philemon guarantees
the expenses of the runaway slave Onesimus but returns the
slave to his master. Whether Paul or another Christian wrote
the letters to the Colossians and the Ephesians, the former
contains fifty-six words of counsel to slaves on obedience, eighteen to masters on fair treatment; in the latter the proportion is
thirty-nine to twenty-eight. In three other passages counsel is
given only to slaves or servants.[105] One might suppose that this
means that only slaves are in the congregation. It is equally possible that much of the author's own emphasis is being laid on
the need for submission. Admittedly the Christian situation is
different from that of the Stoic ethicists described by Seneca,
who hold that philosophy deals with ethical duties such as the
right way for a master to rule his slaves.[106] But the presence of
slaves in Christian congregations did not mean that the church
was slave-oriented. Two Jewish-Christian writings instruct
masters not to give orders in a bitter manner, at least to slaves
who are fellow Christians. More important, the slaves are told
to obey the masters "as a copy of God."[107]

Ignatius of Antioch considers it necessary to tell Polycarp,
the younger bishop of Smyrna, not to look down on either male
or female slaves. At the same time, he is not to let them get

puffed up. They are to work all the harder as slaves for the glory of God, so that they may obtain "better freedom" from God. The trouble is that some evidently want to be set free at the church's expense. Polycarp is not to permit this, for it would make them "slaves of lust."[108] How so? Once they became emancipated, they might well desire to become rich. They might want to acquire honors in order to conceal the lowness of their real ignobility.[109] Beyond that, popular poets such as Euripides and Menander had already pointed out how irritating slaves were when they thought too highly of themselves.[110]

Slaves, unlike free men, were liable to torture when under investigation, and according to Justin it was only under extreme torture that household slaves or their children or wives could be compelled to testify to Christian immorality, since the immorality was nonexistent.[111] Justin assumes, but does not state, that the slaves were not Christians themselves. At Lyons about 175 pagan slaves were frightened by the tortures actually applied to Christian masters and therefore hastened to make accusations against them.[112] The contemporary apologist Athenagoras was misinformed when he wrote his defense.[113]

> We have slaves, some many, some few and it is impossible to escape their observations. Yet not one of them has ever told such monstrous lies about us.

At Alexandria both Clement and Origen advocated treating slaves as equals, while Origen once referred admiringly to the Old Testament law "which prohibits any Jew from being the slave of a fellow-believer for more than six years."[114] (He did not propose to have it adopted by Christians, however.)

At Carthage the attitude of Tertullian was quite different. He imagined pagan slaves as peeping through cracks and holes at their masters' assemblies, and held that they were "by nature" hostile.[115] His comparison of demons with rebellious slaves is quite startling.[116]

> When, like resisting or rebellious slaves, confined in work-houses or prisons or mines or quarries or suffering any other penal servitude of this kind, they break out against us, in whose power they are, knowing full well both that they are ill-matched and that they are thus all the more losers, we resist them against our will as equals and attack them in return. . . .

Tertullian's antipathy toward slaves has carried his simile far beyond what he needed. In attacking women who wear gold and silver ornaments he touches on the deplorable circumstances under which slaves worked in the mines, but he is concerned far more with the morality of women's attire than with the situation of the miners.[117] With his lack of concern we may contrast the comments made by Diodorus, Strabo, and Pliny the Elder when discussing the dangers and misfortunes of slaves in the mines.[118] Across two hundred years, however, his attitude finds echoes in some comments or stereotypes expressed by Jerome. Jerome's thought does not advance far. In 384 he tells us that if a monk's tunic is not spotlessly white, bystanders proclaim him an impostor and a Greek. Eleven years later he explains how much slaves hate frugality. "What they do not get they think is taken from them, and they consider only their wages, not your income." Therefore when they see a Christian they cry out: "The Greek! The impostor!" They spread scandal about Christian households. The bystanders have become slaves. Another eight years, and in another letter we hear that slaves always complain that what they get is too little; "they do not consider how much you have, but only how much they get"; they spread scandal.[119] Such was Jerome's prejudice, maintained and developed for nearly twenty years.

Some of the local synods were fairly conservative. At Elvira, early in the fourth century, the bishops decided that if an enraged mistress whipped her maidservant so badly that she died within three days, "and it is a question whether she killed her on purpose or by accident," she was to do penance in order to be readmitted after five or seven years, depending on the circumstances.[120] Antonine constitutions had restricted the severity of masters, but under Constantine the old moderation was abandoned. Two constitutions in the Theodosian Code make this clear.[121] At Gangra in Cappadocia, about 340, this rule was set forth: "If anyone teaches a slave, under pretext of piety, to despise his master, to forsake his service, not to serve him with goodwill and all respect, let him be anathema."[122]

The last quotation shows, of course, that some people were encouraging slaves to leave. An expression of "leveling" occurs in the semi-Gnostic Acts of Thomas early in the third century. The apostle informs the slaves who are bearing the litter of a noblewoman that Jesus was speaking of them when he said, "Come unto me, all ye that labor and are heavy-laden."[123]

> Though you are men they lay burdens on you as on unreasoning animals, while those who have authority over you suppose that you are not men such as they are.

This is like the old Graeco-Roman view as expressed, for example, by Seneca: "We maltreat slaves, not as if they were men but as if they were beasts of burden."[124]

An odd story told in the martyr-acts of Pionius, perhaps about 300 but referring to events half a century before that, shows Christians helping a slave to run away, though not just because she was a slave. She had belonged to a woman who tried to convert her to paganism and then had her bound and banished to the mountains. There she was secretly given supplies by Christians, who managed to get her freed from her bonds and from her owner.[125] She lived with the presbyter Pionius at Smyrna until they were arrested as Christians.

Among Christian leaders of the late fourth century we find

little encouragement of voluntary emancipation on the part of masters. There seems to be less than what existed at Rome in the first two centuries of the empire. Groups like the Circumcellions in North Africa encouraged a ruder revolt, but their influence did not amount to much.[126] Christian society within the Roman world was not ready for egalitarian emancipation, though few Christians would have shared the petulance expressed by Symmachus when twenty-nine Saxon gladiators strangled one another rather than take part in the public games he was providing.[127] Gregory of Nyssa preaches on the emancipation of slaves at Easter, but the context shows that the emancipation is from sin, not slavery.[128] Jerome comments on the emancipation of Hebrew slaves under the old law. "How much more in the gospel!" But he adds no details to this pious generalization.[129] Theodore of Mopsuestia criticizes egalitarian-minded contemporaries and contrasts Paul with them. Social distinctions would not exist had God not willed them.[130] Theodoret explains that in I Corinthians 7:21 Paul was arguing that one should not flee from slavery on the pretext of religion.[131]

The basic Christian attitude seems to have involved practical improvement. To be sure, Chrysostom is quite clear about the need for discipline. A master must not tolerate any blurring of the lines of division by insult or disloyalty. He must use threats and actual punishments. If he tells them they will not be punished, is this a mark of goodness? Not at all; rather of ultimate cruelty—toward the master's wife, his children, himself. It can be called "untimely gentleness."[132] Other Christians insisted that Christian slaves should have as holidays both Saturdays and Sundays, not to mention all the major festivals of the lengthening church year.[133]

Chrysostom goes so far as to criticize the rich for owning one or two thousand slaves.[134] He upholds the monastic-Pauline ideal of self-support by manual labor, and argues that a Christian should not have slaves at all, or at most one, or perhaps two. In his opinion slaves should be taught trades so that they can support themselves and then they should be freed. "When you beat them or put them in prison, this is not an expression of brotherly love." He is aware that, as usual when he touches upon social issues, his audience finds his remarks oppressive. But he feels it is his duty to make them.[135]

Once more, however, we must avoid canonizing any one of Chrysostom's sermons. When he discusses the content of Philemon he insists that Paul urged slaves to remain in slavery. Christianity did not enter the world in order to overturn everything and require masters to free their slaves.[136]

And in his homily on Hannah, Chrysostom provides a singular argument for maintaining the existence of poverty. "If you eradicated poverty you would eradicate the whole structure of living; you would destroy our life. No sailor, no pilot, no farmer, no builder, no weaver, no shoemaker, no carpenter, no coppersmith, no leather-worker, no miller—none of these craftsmen or others would exist. . . . If all were going to be rich, all would live in idleness, and so everything would be destroyed and perish."[137]

By "rich," then, Chrysostom usually means "idle rich," and he condemns them not because they are rich but because they are idle. This is exactly the point he makes in his homily *In inscriptionem altaris.*[138] He attacks not the rich but those who use wealth badly. To use it badly is to be idle. He praises the poor, for they keep busy. They necessarily lack leisure, they are concerned with their daily labor, they are making a living with their hands. They are concerned with bringing up a family. "I say this not to provide a defence for them but to show how much greater an accusation the rich deserve."[139]

V

Private Property

ALL THREE synoptic evangelists tell the story of a man who addressed Jesus as "good master" and asked him what to do to inherit eternal life. After Jesus rejected the appellation "good" and reminded him of the basic Old Testament commandments about human relations, the man said that he had kept all of them since his youth. "One thing is lacking for you," said Jesus. "Go, sell what you have and give to the poor, and you will have treasure in heaven; and come, follow me." The man could not accept this counsel, for he had many possessions. The Gospel materials include sayings about wealth as an impediment to entrance into the kingdom of God and end with the promise of great rewards for disciples who leave possessions and families behind. So the story goes in Mark 10:17–31. In Luke 18:18–30 it is copied nearly word for word.

Matthew (19:16–30) modifies the account. First, he does not want to allow Jesus' goodness to be questioned. Next, he adds the requirement of love toward neighbor to the laws Jesus cites. The man, now a "youth" (perhaps less prone to sin?), claims to have kept all of them and Jesus says to him, "If you wish to be perfect, go, sell what you have. . . ." This is often called a qualification added to Mark by Matthew, but since according to the later evangelist all disciples of Jesus have to be perfect (5:48) and have already abandoned their property, it is hard to see what is qualified. Origen, who raised no questions about giving property up (as we shall see), found in Matthew's version the idea that perfection lies beyond love of neighbor. He thought that the scene in Matthew was different from the one in Mark and Luke.[1]

What qualifications there are seem to occur in the tradition before Matthew and long after him. Thus in the setting Mark supplies for the story, Jesus is described as commenting, "How hard it will be for those who have money to enter the kingdom of God." The disciples are amazed at these words, and he then offers a generalization: "How hard it is [for anyone] to enter the kingdom of God." With this saying is associated the dramatic hyperbole, "It is easier for a camel to go through the eye of a needle than for a rich man to enter the kingdom of God." The hyperbole was spoiled by later Christians, ever eager to conciliate the rich, who pretended that there was a "camel gate" at Jerusalem through which a camel could pass only on its knees(!) or, to little effect, invented the meaning "rope" for the Greek word "camel." In the synoptic account the disciples are even more amazed at this. They inquire, "Then who can be saved?" The answer is that renunciation will bring great rewards both in "this time" and in "the age to come." It need hardly be said that Origen was convinced that here was proof that the allegorical method was right. Jesus could not possibly have promised crass rewards of houses and fields to his disciples, especially not in "this age."

What the promises indicate, at any rate, is that the context of story and sayings is the coming kingdom of God, in which family ties and property will be done away and what will count will be nothing but one's own relation to Jesus in disciple-

ship—or rejection. There is no trace of social teaching or
doctrine, for there will be no recognizable social structure.
The whole emphasis is laid on the response of the individual to
Jesus' counsel. And in connection with this response-relation
the later Christians had to construct whatever would come to
be their teaching on private property.

The Gospel of Luke and the companion Acts of the Apostles
contain a high proportion of the New Testament teaching on
property and its use and abuse. Luke "often represents Jesus as
drawing his illustrations from finance," and he is concerned
with such mundane matters as "poverty and wealth and the
generosity of the rich toward the poor."[2] In his Gospel we find
a tax collector commended because he gives half his property
to the poor (Luke 19:8–9). In Acts there are descriptions of the
practices and even the procedures of the early communities in
regard to such matters.

Luke's most striking statements about Christian life at
Jerusalem are to be found in passages he created as summaries
of his materials. The first example is Acts 2:42–47, where we
read that "all who believed were together and had all things in
common; and they sold their possessions and goods and distributed them to all, as any had need." The second is Acts 4:
32–35.

> Now the company of those who believed were of one heart and soul,
> and no one said that any of the things which he possessed was his
> own, but they had everything in common. . . . There was not a
> needy person among them, for as many as were possessors of lands
> or houses sold them, and brought the proceeds of what was sold
> and laid it at the apostles' feet; and distribution was made to each as
> any had need.

Luke obviously has two points in mind in both instances. First,
the charitable activities of property owners; second, the com-

mon ownership of property, along with some system of distribution. The distribution system is discussed later, in Acts 6:1–6, where we find that the apostles were accused of neglecting Hellenist widows in "the daily distribution" and therefore recommended the appointment of seven deacon-prototypes.

In regard to charitable activities, Luke knows, or at any rate uses, only one story about a prominent Christian donor. This was about the Levite Barnabas from Cyprus, who sold a field and did bring the money and lay it at the apostles' feet (Acts 4:36–37). Presumably he is mentioned because he will later play a prominent role in the Christian mission, and in the book of Acts. It is not clear whether or not other early Christians followed Barnabas' example, and whether or not the practice was compulsory.

In regard to common ownership and imperfect charity, Luke gives us the story of Ananias and Sapphira (Acts 5:1–11). This couple had some land. When they sold it they decided to withhold part of the proceeds. Ananias brought the balance and laid it at the apostles' feet. The apostle Peter immediately criticized him, not for refusing to share but for making a false return, explicit or implicit, to the Holy Spirit. As Luke tells the story, Peter asked two questions, which presumably explain the situation more fully. "While it remained unsold, did it not remain your own? And after it was sold, was it not at your disposal?"[3] If these questions are to be taken seriously, they suggest that the procedure for making private property public had not been fully worked out, or that it was not clear in Luke's mind. Or perhaps he is indicating that freedom of choice and the opportunity for moral failure remained open until the funds were actually handed over. Certainly in the rather similar situation at Qumran there were those who made false declarations.[4] After the sudden death of Ananias, his wife Sapphira confirms his lies and, like him, falls down dead.

This is all Luke has to say about the so-called communism of the early church in Jerusalem. In what historical direction do his accounts point? The very first sentence in the second summary shows us what he has in mind. "The company of those who believed were of one heart and soul, and no one said that any of the things which he possessed was his own, but they had everything in common." "One heart and one soul" sounds biblical, but in fact "one soul" was used to describe the life of Pythagorean communities. In such communities no one considered anything as his own property, but everything was held in common.[5] Luke is presenting the Jerusalem community to readers who, he expects, will understand his allusions to the Pythagorean parallel. He is placing Jerusalem in the context of Hellenistic–Roman communal sharing.

If we look at the accounts of Pythagorean groups we may be able to understand better what Luke had to say about Ananias and Sapphira. In the first century B.C. Diodorus Siculus describes their sharing as originally quite voluntary. "Whenever one of the companions of Pythagoras lost his fortune, the others would divide their own possessions with him as with brothers."[6] Later on things seem to have become more systematic. We find trainees called Pythagorists who sell their property and give it to Pythagoras in trust; at the end of the training period the trust terminates. If they become full-blown Pythagoreans the property goes to the group; otherwise they take it back.[7] Perhaps Ananias and Sapphira had not fully entered the Christian community when they made their gift.

And then if we look at a community which was close geographically to Jerusalem—the sectarians, probably Essene, of Qumran—we find that according to Josephus their lifestyle came from Pythagoras.[8] At least it was like that of the Pythagoreans. Here, too, there were two kinds of members. Full members, regulated in accordance with the *Manual of Discipline,* were expected to turn over all their property to the community but, as among the Pythagoreans, this was done only gradually. There was a period in which the funds were still kept separate even though under community control. On the other hand, those who integrated themselves less fully into community life were instructed by the *Damascus Rule,* or "Zadokite document." They had to turn in their wages for at least two days per month, and if they lied about property matters they had to do penance for six days.[9] Neither Philo nor Josephus mentions the "diaspora" Essenes, preferring to extol the more heroic inner group. Josephus, however, does state that "they occupy no one city, but settle in large numbers in every town."[10] This suggests that he knew of both kinds of groups.

In ancient times yet another group of Jewish ascetics, the Therapeutae, was compared with the primitive church of Jerusalem. It was Eusebius of Caesarea who made the comparison, early in the fourth century. Indeed, he believed that when Philo described this group in his treatise *On the Contemplative Life* he was actually describing early Christians.[11] But the attitude of the Therapeutae was much more theoretical and spiritual than that manifested in Acts. Prospective Therapeuts gave their money to "sons or daughters or other kinsfolk," not to the community, even though they held that inequality was injustice, equality justice.[12] Eusebius glosses over the difference.

Finally, that such notions as those set forth in Acts lingered on into the second century seems clear from the satirist Lucian and his description of Palestinian Christians defrauded by the Cynic philosopher Peregrinus. These Christians "despise all things indiscriminately and consider them common property," Lucian writes.[13] And indeed the apologist Tertullian states that "among us every thing is common property except our wives."[14] The situation Luke described in Acts was not just the product of his imagination.

The Jerusalem Christians were not the only Christians there

were. It would be wrong to neglect their great benefactor, the apostle Paul, who after promising to bail them out (Gal. 2:10) tried to raise money for their support in Galatia, Achaea, and Macedonia—successfully in the last two areas.[15] Paul's ideas about property were quite different from those of the Jerusalem Christians. The Corinthians were to save from their individual earnings so that contributions would be ready for Paul when he visited them (I Cor. 16:2). Their abundance should supply the want of the Jerusalemites as a matter of equity or fair treatment (II Cor. 8:14). But what they offer is to "be ready not as an exaction but as a willing gift" (9:5); "each one must do as he has made up his mind, not reluctantly or under compulsion" (9:7). And God will repay them for their generous contributions (9:10). In Romans we learn what is meant by "equity." The gentiles have shared in the spiritual blessings of the Jerusalem church and therefore ought to provide material blessings in return (Rom. 15:27).[16] Paul's idea of equity is like fairness in business dealings. It is what we should expect from one who likes commercial and legal analogies and considers it self-evident that "children ought not to save for their parents, but parents for their children" (II Cor. 12:14).[17]

On the other side, there were those at Corinth who espoused the Cynic–Stoic–Pythagorean ideal and spoke excitedly about being wise, strong, well born, "filled," rich, kings (I Cor. 1:26–27; 4:8–10). Most of these points seem based on early Christian teaching about the kingdom of God, now reinterpreted in the light of the "wise man" ideal. According to philosophers, the wise were the only possessors of any good or significant attributes, and such ideas passed into both Hellenistic Judaism and Christianity. We need look only at the use of the maxim, "Among friends everything is common property." Fused with thoughts about wise men, this led to a fine Cynic–Stoic paradox. All things belong to the gods; the wise are friends of the gods; among friends everything is common property; all things belong to the wise. So it goes in Diogenes Laertius.[18] For Philo of Alexandria the wise man par excellence is Moses. Thus we read in his *Life of Moses* that "if as the proverb says what belongs to friends is common, and the prophet is called the friend of God [Exod. 33:11], it would follow that he shares also God's possessions, so far as it is necessary." The difference between God and any man at this point is that God needs nothing while man needs what God gives him. Philo concludes by urging others to imprint the image of Moses in their souls.[19] Something like a mixture of these traditions, combined with thoughts about reigning with God, led the Corinthians to their own affirmation: "All things are ours" (I Cor. 3:21). Everything belonged to them because they were wise.

Paul's basic problem, confronted in the first four chapters of I Corinthians, was that some Corinthians used their unrealistic self-portrait to differentiate themselves from other Christians. They claimed to be wise, filled with God's gifts, rich, even kings. "Would that you did reign," writes the apostle, "so that we might share the rule with you" (I Cor. 4:8). According to Lucian, the aspiring wise man thought of himself as the only rich man, the only king, while others were slaves and "scum."[20] Probably this is why Paul identifies himself with "garbage" and "scum" at the end of his attack on their pretensions. It is why he lists his own very real sufferings (I Cor. 4:9–13). "The kingdom of God does not consist in talk but in power" (4:20).

On the specific issue of whether or not everything belongs to them, and presumably is being shared by them, Paul agrees with them in part. Surely everything belongs to God. But for Paul the full sharing comes in the future, not the present; it is eschatological. And Paul could never have referred to himself or to any other Christian as a "friend of God."[21] Such an expression occurs in John 15:14–15 (disciples of Jesus), James

2:23 (Abraham), and I Clement 10:1 and 17:2 (Abraham).
Paul prefers to call Christians "brothers" and himself God's
slave, and he speaks of the love of God, not friendship. He
could never have accepted the Cynic-Stoic-Philonic syllogism,
though we note that Clement of Alexandria could and did.[22]
For equality and communalism Paul substitutes a hierarchical relationship. Yes, everything belongs to the Corinthians,
everything there is. But they belong to Christ, and Christ belongs to God (I Cor. 3:23).[23]

Like Paul, Ignatius of Antioch thought hierarchically, and
while he urged Polycarp of Smyrna not to be haughty toward
slaves, they were to endure their slavery to the glory of God.
"They are not to want to be emancipated out of the common
fund, lest they be found slaves of lust."[24] There is a common
fund, obviously under the bishop's control. Some slaves evidently believe that the common fund should be used to promote common equality. Ignatius, following what was probably
Paul's view, held that what counted was equality spiritual, not
political. There were very few early Christians who agreed with
the Therapeutae described by Philo, that slavery was contrary
to nature.[25]

The second century witnessed little enthusiasm for the
socializing of private property, with one exception to which we
shall presently turn. The socializing of women may have been a
more popular fantasy. Apart from the widespread rumors
about Gnostic and Christian licentiousness,[26] Epictetus tells us
that "at Rome the women have in their hands Plato's *Republic*,
because he insists on community of women." The philosopher
argues that they misunderstand Plato.[27] Yet he himself, as reported by Arrian, conceded that women were common property by nature. He then went on to restrict licentiousness by
giving two analogies. The first elegant analogy compares a wife
to a portion of the common meal served at a banquet. Since it

has been assigned to one guest, another must not take it. The second is based on Chrysippus. "Is not the theatre the common property of the citizens?" But the individual citizen should not be deprived of his seat.[28] As for private property in general, Epictetus does not speak of its socialization, only of its transient nature.

The complete sharing of property, and of women regarded as property, seems to have been advocated only by a precocious author who died at the age of seventeen and was venerated as a god on the island of Kephallenia, west of the Greek mainland. The youth, son of the Gnostic haeresiarch Carpocrates, was named Epiphanes. Clement of Alexandria gives extracts from his book *On Justice*.[29] Apparently Epiphanes began with a definition of justice as equal sharing *(koinōnia met' isotētos)*, a definition apparently borrowed from the Platonic Academy.[30] The idea of sharing or fellowship was prominent in early Christianity, but one meets it also among philosophers, especially Stoics.[31] Equality raised a few more questions. Ever since the times of Plato and Aristotle, philosophers had joined kings in the view that the best kind of equality was proportional, not arithmetical. A speaker in Plutarch's *Table Talk* denounces arithmetical equality. It is "the equality which the mob seeks, in reality the greatest injustice of all," and "God eradicates it as far as is feasible."[32]

The young philosopher Epiphanes, however, advocated arithmetical equality and justice. He first mentioned the sky, circular and therefore universally equidistant. Then he pointed out that at night one can see that the stars are equally bright (actually this is not true, and Paul spoke more correctly in I Corinthians 15:41). By day the sun pours forth its light equally upon all, rich and poor, people and ruler, fools and wise, females and males, free men and slaves, even upon irrational animals. It seems fairly likely that behind Epiphanes' statement there lie some aspects of the Christian tradition, for according to Clement he was a Christian Gnostic. We venture to compare what he has said with Jesus' words about the heavenly Father who "makes his sun rise on the evil and on the good, and sends rain on the just and on the unjust" (Matt. 5:45). And it was the apostle Paul who at least sometimes insisted on the overcoming of distinctions not only in the future but in principle now. "There is neither Jew nor Greek, there is neither slave nor free, there is neither male nor female; for you are all one in Christ Jesus" (Gal. 3:28).

At this point Epiphanes, as reported by Clement, takes several leaps of faith, or at any rate logic. The sun, he says, makes foodstuffs grow to be shared by all animals; all alike have the instinct for reproduction; all alike have eyesight, and this shows that equality was intended by the creator. So far, so good. As Epiphanes said, "God made all things for man to be common property."[33] But then "the laws," he says, referring to human or even diabolical laws, "were unable to punish human ignorance, and they taught men to act illegally. Thus the specific character of the laws cut up and destroyed the sharing required by the divine law." There was a primordial law of God and nature, requiring equal sharing. Later came the individual laws, which gave instruction in illegal acts. The instruction they gave was based on the terms "mine" and "thine."[34]

The bad laws actually caused theft. In addition, they did violence to the situation at the creation, when God made everything for man to share, brought the female to the male (cf. Gen. 2:22) for sharing, and similarly united (cf. Gen. 2:24) all the animals. It is difficult to follow Epiphanes' exegesis. Presumably he was emphasizing the fact that Eve was shared by all the men there were at the beginning; but since there was only one Adam, the Genesis text seems to point more toward monogamy than polygamy. In his view, however, the most important feature of the union was desire, implanted in the males for the continuation of the species. "No law or custom or any other existing thing can make it vanish; for it is a thing decreed by God."[35]

Now, therefore, Epiphanes is ready for his final assault upon the Ten Commandments. Since God implanted this desire in nature, the legislator's phrase "Thou shalt not covet (or desire)" is absolutely ridiculous. We may be reading a secularized version of Paul's words: "I should not have known what it is to covet if the law had not said, 'Thou shalt not covet.' But sin, finding opportunity in the commandment, wrought all kinds of covetousness in me" (Rom. 7:7–8). Epiphanes is quite blunt about what he means. "Thou shalt not covet what belongs to thy neighbor" is ridiculous, since neither you nor your neighbor should possess private property. And "thou shalt not covet thy neighbor's wife" is still more ridiculous because she belongs to you as well as to him.

It is surprising to find such advocacy of communism just beyond the edge of what was coming to be orthodox Christianity. But there was a good deal of overlapping between Christian and Neopythagorean ideas and ways of life. We have already encountered the overlap in Luke's account of the Jerusalem Christians. In the second century something like it comes back in the *Sentences of Sextus*, a collection of Christian and Pythagorean moral maxims. In these greed and the lust for possessions are vigorously condemned. The philosopher or the Christian was to count no possession his own. Those whose common father was God had to treat their possessions as common too. But we do not find any denunciation of private property as such, much less of marriage. Instead, there is a strong emphasis on almsgiving.[36] This attitude was shared by Clement, the famous teacher at Alexandria at the end of the second century.

In Clement's view, equity *(isotēs)* was an attribute of God and of Christ, expressed in the divine dealings with mankind.[37] Thus as creator, God supplied necessities like water and air to all humanity, while he concealed what men did not need—gold in the ground, pearls in the sea. Everything necessary is, or should be, common property. God made the human race for sharing and usage in common. It is absurd for one person to live in luxury while many suffer from poverty.[38] Elsewhere, however, he takes a different line. Stoics had held that the wise man was the only rich man, for he alone knew how to limit his needs. Clement makes a similar point. Good things belong to the good alone. The Christians are good. Therefore good possessions belong only to the Christians.[39] This is nothing but an abstraction based on a paradox. Again, in a discussion of Pythagorean passwords he claims that equality or equity *(to ison)* is justice and that for a Christian to become "like children" (Matt. 18:3) means becoming equal to others.[40] But he does not carry the idea very far.

A more significant treatment occurs in his late treatise called *Who Is the Rich Man Who Is Being Saved?* This is basically a defense of the rich Christians of Alexandria, based on allegorical interpretation of Jesus' command to sell possessions and give the proceeds to the poor (Mark 10:17–31). Clement was unable to believe that the story in Mark meant what it said. He himself could see no virtue in poverty or in the general idea of renouncing wealth. In his view wealth was an instrument for producing fellowship and sharing. We must not fling away the funds with which we could have helped our neighbor. Thus giving away great wealth is bad because it limits one's opportunities to do good, while giving away small amounts is merely trivial.

Where did property come from? To see the importance of Clement's view we must look back at Irenaeus, whose work he knew and used. Irenaeus said that Christians' possessions came either from preconversion acquisitions due to avarice, or ultimately in consequence of injustice, by gift from pagan parents, relatives, or friends.[41] Compare this with what Clement said on the same subject. Property is legitimate, he held, if before conversion to Christianity one strove for wealth and by thrift acquired a modest competence. Alternatively, God "the distributor of fortune," may have placed one in a rich family.[42] It is quite clear that at this particular moment Clement ascribes to thrift what Irenaeus ascribes to avarice, to God what Irenaeus assigns to injustice. It also is clear that Clement's attitude was ambivalent. When Jesus spoke of "the mammon of unrighteousness," he wrote, he was showing that "all possessions are by nature unjust, when a man possesses them for himself as absolutely his own and does not set them in the common fund for those in need."[43]

The right of private property thus depends upon the use made of it. There is a right of private property, but it is limited by the needs of our fellow men, first Christians and then probably others.

Clement's balanced presentation did not appeal to the puritanical allegorizer Origen, eager to impose ascetic practices on all. In his *Commentary on Matthew* Origen criticized anyone who did not take the Gospel commandment literally and sell his possessions for the poor. It was meant literally, and there were real examples of persons and groups who had lived in voluntary poverty. The philosopher Crates offered one example; the community in Acts, another.[44] In two sermons Origen made the point even more plainly. First, citing Luke 14:33 on renunciation, Origen says that "Christ denies that a man is his disciple if he sees him possessing anything."[45] Second, "The law of Christ, if we follow it, does not permit us to have possessions on earth or houses in cities. Why mention houses? It does not permit us to have several tunics or much money. 'Having food and clothing,' it says, 'let us be content with these.'"[46] We should be clear as to what his point is. Origen is appealing for voluntary poverty. He is appealing for Christian asceticism. There is no theory about property involved.

Similarly at Carthage, Tertullian speaks of the usefulness of riches for philanthropy, and Cyprian, while emphasizing God's equal justice, does not question the legitimacy of private property.[47] Later on at Alexandria the bishop Maximus does not seem to have shared Origen's ideas about renunciation; he was too busy acting as financial agent for up-country Christian traders.[48] It is true, as we look back on Roman history from many hundreds of years later, that there was some kind of crisis in third-century political and economic life. But to criticize Cyprian for not having a definite political-economic program, as G. Alföldy criticizes him,[49] is to take a God's-eye view of the historical situation. A more limited and human picture is given us by Dionysius of Alexandria, who includes "seizure of possessions" among what he suffered in time of persecution, and rejoices over the restoration of the emperor Gallienus. "The empire has shed its skin [like a snake], as it were, and cleansed itself from its former wickedness; now it flourishes more vigorously, is seen and heard more widely, and spreads forth everywhere."[50]

It is sometimes thought that utopianism and millenarianism went hand in hand. When Christians expected the end of the world immediately, private property meant little to them. On the other hand, when eschatology cooled they became more worldly. There is some evidence for this notion, but not much; and like most theories in this area it fits only some of the facts. We do learn from Hippolytus of Rome about a couple of bishops in the early third century who somehow reached the conclusion that the end was near. In Syria a bishop persuaded his congregation to abandon their possessions. With him they wandered in desert and hill-country until the provincial governor almost had them executed as a band of robbers. Fortunately the governor's wife happened to be a Christian. She could explain their behavior as harmless. Again, in Pontus another bishop had visions which made him have his followers sell their possessions and leave their lands and fields. He proposed a wager entirely in his own favor. "If it does not take place as I said, believe no more in the scriptures, but let each one of you do as he pleases." No further belief in the bishop would have been more to the point, as Hippolytus is quite aware. After a year there was much confusion. Virgins married; men returned to farming, or if they had sold their property, entered upon a life of begging.[51] Unfortunately this is the only direct evidence we possess for a link between utopia and eschatology in the early church.

In the new age under Constantine we do not expect, and we do not find, a new attitude toward private property. Indeed, our chief witness, the rhetorician Lactantius, sets forth what might seem to be three different views on the subject; but perhaps we can treat them as thesis, antithesis, and synthesis. First, he explains that "private property contains the matter of both vices and virtues, but *communitas* [communal sharing] holds nothing but license for vices." Something like this thought, but more moderately expressed, had already been set forth by Aristotle.[52] Later on in his principal treatise, Lactantius happens to mention the view of the Stoic poet Aratus, that in the golden age land was held in common. He agrees, but insists that "we should not suppose that there was absolutely no private ownership at the time."[53] Finally he states that perfect justice is the use of wealth not for personal enjoyment but for the advantage for the many.[54]

Only in the later years of the fourth century, as the empire entered into troubles far more severe than those of the century before, do we find a more vigorous attack by some of the fathers not so much on private property as on its excessive accumulation in the hands of the rich. The tax system was actually breaking down. Graft and corruption were said to be everywhere.[55] And some of the fathers, all influenced by Christian monasticism and pagan rhetoric, very boldly discussed the abuse of private property. Traditional Christian ascetic motifs were important; so were the Pythagorean elements thereto related at least since the second century. First, the Pythagoreanizing *Life of Antony* by the influential Alexandrian bishop Athanasius spread the ideas in the east and introduced them to the west.[56] Second, the hermit Basil took the Pachomian monasteries as his models when he produced his monastic rule between 358 and 364. Like his friend Gregory, he went from the monastic life to the episcopate: Basil at Caesarea in Cappadocia; Gregory at Nazianzus, then at Constantinople. Basil's homilies on property were enthusiastically welcomed in the west by Ambrose of Milan. John Chrysostom was first a Pachomian monk, then a presbyter at Antioch, finally bishop at Constantinople. Third, Theodoret, educated in monastery schools at Antioch, entered a monastery but emerged to be a Syrian bishop in 423. All these writers discuss the evils of private property. Their upbringing must have had something to do with what they thought.

Their training was pagan as well as Christian, at least for the most important of them. Chrysostom was certainly trained in law and rhetoric at Antioch by the famous orator Libanius.[57] Both Basil and Gregory probably studied with the same teacher.[58] There they would certainly have heard the proverb, "The property of friends is held in common." According to a modern dissertation, Libanius cited it six times in letters, once in a speech.[59] More than that, Libanius gave addresses on such topics as "avarice," "that unjust enrichment is worse than poverty," and simply on "poverty." He also provided rhetorical exercises on themes including "denunciation of wealth." In that one we read that "the mother of wealth is avarice and not loving equality for equals." Wealth produced both wars and robberies.[60] These lessons show how simple it was for disciples of Libanius, once they had become bishops, to use his teaching. And if occasion demanded, they could also use the exercise on "denunciation of poverty."

Beyond this lies the fact that the Cappadocian Fathers were members of the curial class, the richer citizens of the Cappadocian towns. The father of Ambrose was praetorian prefect at Trier. Chrysostom's father was a general. Only Augustine, who had more respect for private property, was the son of "a poor freeman."[61] Augustine's philosophical quest led him to Academic Skepticism, indeed, but never to the Cynicism affected by Gregory of Nazianzus, or to his foolish confidence in the Cynic trickster Maximus.

We see, then, that the attitude of these fathers toward private property was based on Christian asceticism, pagan rhetoric, and upper-class disdain for mere wealth. But it is not possible to find in their voluminous writings any advocacy of compulsory communal sharing. Private property remains private, though the Christian authors urge its owners to use it to express their love of their neighbors.[62]

Gregory of Nazianzus has rather more to say, if not to do, on the subject. He could speak of an "original equality" or "the ancient freedom" and urge the rich to imitate God's equity as shown in his gift of rain for the just and sinners alike. Earth, springs, rivers, forests, air, and water are common property by nature. Later than the natural state, envy and strife entered the world, as did law itself.[63] Evidently Gregory is fusing ideas of the golden age and natural law with the Jewish-Christian doctrine of the fall. Similarly, in another oration he asks, "What is more beautiful than air, fire, water, earth [i.e., the four elements], rains, fruits cultivated and wild, a roof, clothing?" And he explains that "there is common sharing in these, in some absolutely, in some partially." The sun rises impartially for all; rain falls upon rich and poor alike. And for all there are night and day, health, even death.[64]

For a long time Gregory flirted with Cynicism. Modern scholars have found many Cynic echoes in his works.[65] But the flirtation ended when at Constantinople Gregory discovered that Maximus the Cynic, his friend and indeed idol, was having his shaggy locks cut so that he could usurp Gregory's place in a truly cynical power-play directed by the patriarch of Alexandria.[66] And in any case, Gregory had not handed over his inherited estate to the church or to the poor. His father, sometime bishop of Nazianzus, had not been able to give it away because he had children. Gregory himself simply kept it until he no longer needed it.[67]

The most famous patristic economist, so to speak, was John Chrysostom, renowned preacher at Antioch from 386 until he was made archbishop of Constantinople in 398. Within five years he was ruined. Whoever wrote the article on him in the *Oxford Dictionary of the Christian Church* described the causes well. "His combination of honesty, asceticism, and tactlessness, . . . joined with the hatred of Theophilus, the unworthy Patriarch of Alexandria, his disappointed rival, and of the Empress Eudoxia, who with some reason took all attempts at moral reform as a censure of herself": these led to his deposition and exile. Presumably his attitude toward the rich contributed something. In his twelfth homily on I Timothy, probably delivered at Constantinople, Chrysostom begins with a dialogue between himself and a more or less imaginary rich man. His adversary defends wealth by pointing to the Old

Testament. Was Abraham's wealth unjust? What of Job's? The
bishop replies by stating that their wealth was God-given;
it came by natural increase, not injustice. In other words,
the ideal is rural, not urban. Then he turns to question the
defendant.[68]

> Tell me, where did your wealth come from? From whom?
>
> From my grandfather and my father.
>
> Would you be able to go back in your family and show that the
> acquisition was just? No, you couldn't. The beginning, the source,
> *must* be from someone's injustice. Where did it come from? From
> the beginning did God make one rich, another poor? Did he guide
> one and show him many treasures of gold, but deprived that other
> of the search? No, he provided the same earth to all. Since it was
> common property, how is it that you have so and so many acres,
> while your neighbor has not a spoonful of earth?
>
> My father handed it on to me.
>
> From whom did he get it?
>
> From his ancestors.
>
> But it is absolutely necessary to go back and find the beginning.
> Jacob was rich [Gen. 30:43] but from the reward for his labors.
> Suppose we allow that your ancestor was not a robber but had gold
> which somehow gushed up from the earth. What then? Did this
> make the gold good? Not at all.
>
> But not evil either.
>
> If he was not greedy, then not evil; if he gives to those in need.
> But if not, then evil and treacherous.
>
> If a man does not do evil, he is not evil, even if he does not do
> good.
>
> Right. But is this not evil, for some one person to have what is the
> Master's for some individual to enjoy what is common property? Or
> is not "the earth God's and the fulness thereof" [Ps. 24:1]? If what is
> ours belongs to the common Master, it belongs to our fellow-slaves;
> for all the Master's property is common property. Or don't we see
> that matters are arranged thus in great houses? Thus a quantity of
> bread is given to all equally, for it comes from the master's trea-

sures. The master's house is open to all. Similarly all imperial property is common property: cities, markets, arcades are common for
all; we all share equally. Now see God's world! He made some things
to be held in common, in order to put the human race to shame,
such as air, sun, water, earth, sky, sea, light, stars; he distributed
them all equally as to brothers. He made eyes the same for all, body
the same, soul the same, a like frame among all, from earth all, from
one man all humanity, in the same house all humanity. But none of
these put us to shame. And he made other things common, such as
baths, cities, markets, arcades. See how there is no conflict over
common property but everything is peaceful. But when someone
ventures to seize something and makes it his own, then jealousy
enters in, as if nature herself were displeased, because though God
gathers us together from everywhere, we compete in separating
and detaching ourselves when we make things our own and say
Thine and Mine—that frigid expression. Then comes conflict, then
disgust.

The power of the bishop's personalized rhetoric is obvious.
Less obvious, but not less important, is the depth of his concern
for this matter. He had long been convinced that "mine and
thine" was the cause of war.[69] And while we need not suppose
that he spent much time on strictly philosophical reading, he
had at least heard of the radical Cynic and Stoic discussions of
the ideal state, established in conformity with nature.[70] God's
making eyes the same for all comes ultimately from Plato;[71]
cities, markets, arcades as public property, from Panaetius.[72]

But although modern writers have often spoken of Chrysostom's "communism," he does not actually advocate it in this
sermon. We come closer in a sermon on the Jerusalem Christians, delivered at Constantinople.

Chrysostom starts with rather literal exegesis of the Acts
story. He points out that the Jerusalem Christians supported
the community, including themselves, not on the basis of private charity but in reliance on common funds to which they

had given all they had. They had made the apostles stewards and trustees of the common funds.[73]

From literal-historical exegesis he passes on to moral exhortation.

> If this were done now, we should live more pleasant lives, rich and poor, nor would it be more pleasant to the poor man than to the rich themselves. And if you will, let me now for a while depict it in words, and derive at least this pleasure from it, since you have no mind for it in your actions. For at any rate this is evident, even from what took place then, that when they sold their possessions they did not come to be in need but made the poor rich.

Some of Chrysostom's hearers, however, may have recalled that by Paul's time the saints of Jerusalem actually were poor and had to be supported by gifts from other churches.

> But let us now depict this in words [he repeats], and let all sell their possessions and bring them into the common stock. In words, I mean; no one should be excited, rich or poor.

What, then, if every Christian man and woman in Constantinople sold his or her possessions—not counting slaves, since in the Jerusalem model they did not have slaves?

> Probably they would collect a million pounds of gold, or rather two or three times that. Now tell me, how many acres does our city extend to? How many Christians do you suppose there are? Do you suppose a hundred thousand, apart from Greeks and Jews? How many myriads of gold would they collect? And what is the number of the poor? I think not more than fifty thousand.

For the background of these guesses we should recall that Constantinople at this time had a population of about half a million. In other words, it was about the size of Antioch, and Chrysostom was applying the same statistical grid there that he used in his old home town. He may well be right: the church historian Socrates tells us that originally there were eighty thousand on the grain dole at Constantinople but Constantius cut the figure back to forty thousand.[74] We should expect some increase by Chrysostom's time. When speaking at Antioch he claimed that the very rich constituted a tenth of the population, the poor another tenth, and the middle class 80 percent. The church's income was equal to that of one rich man.[75] In actual fact, however, the income was so large that congregational gifts were declining.[76] This makes Chrysostom's rhetorical statement hard to accept or assess. For example, if ten rich men gave away their income, no one would be poor. Or if the rich and the middle class contributed generously, the poor group would go down from 10 percent to 1 or 2.[77] Or if each Christian gave a loaf of bread or a tiny coin everyday for the poor, the problem would be solved.[78] Chrysostom's goal seems evident: he wants increased charity but he has no social program to be imposed by church or state.

His ideas are religious, not economic. After his suggestion that Constantinople imitate Jerusalem, he goes on to ask rhetorical questions. Someone may ask what happens after the money is gone.

> Do you think it ever could be spent? Would not the grace of God be ten thousand times as much? Would not the grace of God be richly poured out? What then? Would not we make heaven of the earth?

But he is still ready to answer practical objections. First, funds would surely be received from those outside the Christian community. (This seems unlikely.) Second, expenses would be less if there were common meals and housing. Third, the contemporary monasteries offer the life of the Jerusalem Christians then. In spite of all he says, he realizes that his words are in vain.

> But men fear this more than falling into a dread and endless sea. If we made a trial of it, we could boldly enter upon the matter.

But he knows his hearers are not going to do so.[79]

Augustine, too, was an enthusiast for the monastic life. Even before he became a Catholic Christian, he belonged to a little group at Milan which proposed to pool property so that the whole would belong to each and to all. The ten prospective members were led by the very rich Romanianus, Augustine's friend and patron, who like him had come from Carthage to Milan. Two "magistrates" elected annually were to take care of the community's business. But it all fell through when the ten finally realized that their wives, present or prospective, would not accept the arrangement. Augustine's later venture into community life at Cassiciacum did not involve any pooling of property. The estate on which he and his friends lived was borrowed from a rich professor named Verecundus.[80] And though like others of his time Augustine frequently criticized the rich, he did not question the right of private property. Even after the sack of Rome in 410, when he moralized in a traditionally Cynic manner on the vanity of riches that can be taken away,[81] he carefully insisted that it was the desire for riches that was bad, not the possession of them.[82]

We have now traced the general lines of ancient Christian attitudes toward private property. It is clear that when Christians encountered compulsory sharing of property they did not favor it. There were very few who shared the idea found in the pseudo-Clementine *Homilies,* that private possessions are immoral.[83]

At the same time, the fathers were certainly not ardent defenders of property as such, any more than most of them were defenders of the Roman empire. They took it for granted. More than that, the early expectation of the reign of God kept them from excessive love of worldly goods; so did the later development of asceticism and monasticism. Many of them liked the sound of the Pythagorean maxim about sharing. Few were aware of Aristotle's practical distinction between private ownership and common use.[84]

Moralists have rarely blessed the desire to accumulate property, whatever they may have said about possessing it. Of course, in a relatively static economy the property accumulated is likely to belong to someone else. The problem of limits also rises. How much is too much? What is one to think of concern for small sums? Jesus tells of a woman who turned her house upside down in her search for a lost drachma. When she found it her joy was like that of the angels of God over a repentant sinner. Theophrastus cites a similar case, though with a smaller coin, as an example of penuriousness, while Dio Chrysostom says that while losing a drachma is disturbing, it should make less difference than losing a day.[85]

Is acquisitiveness bad? Galen denounces the insatiability of the avaricious man who desires to double, triple, or quadruple his fortune, even when he knows that in Pergamum there are few richer than himself. According to Herodian, barbarians are naturally avaricious. But "the kingdom of heaven is like a treasure hidden in a field, which a man found and covered up; then in his joy he goes and sells all that he has and buys that field." Or it is "like a merchant in search of fine pearls, who, on finding one pearl of great value, went and sold all that he had and bought it."[86]

Death marks the most obvious limit, expecially if, as in the case of the Rich Fool, one has no heirs. This rich man decided to build larger barns and, with ample supplies, to take his ease. "But God said to him, 'Fool! This night your soul is required of you; and the things you have prepared, whose will they be?'" So Seneca tells of a man who could have said, "I will buy and build, loan and call in money, win titles of honor, and then, old and full of years, I will surrender myself to a life of ease"—only to die unexpectedly.[87] The basic point is that of Psalm 39:6: "Man heaps up, and knows not who will gather." In the epistle of James we find criticism of those who say, "Today or tomor-

row we will go into such and such a town and spend a year there
and trade and get gain." They do not know how long they will
live and therefore should be content with tentative plans.[88]

The influential *Shepherd* of Hermas insists that riches are
transitory. God will reduce them if the rich do not share with
the poor. What Hermas opposes most strongly is the business
of acquiring wealth. The rich deny God because of their wealth
and their business occupations. The ideal is to be poorer, not
richer, than anyone else. One should put away the extrava-
gance based on wealth and any needless food and drink. Instead, one should be concerned only with self-sufficiency.[89]
One should not touch or desire another person's wealth, for it
is generally wrong to desire what belongs to another person.[90]

Oddly enough, in his genuine letters the apostle Paul never
denounces love of money. Instead, his converts, at least at
Corinth, denounced him as a thief either actually or poten-
tially, and he had to defend himself from the charge that he
wanted their property for himself. "I will not be a burden, for I
seek not what is yours but you; for children ought not to save
for their parents, but parents for their children" (II Cor.
12:14). It is clear, however, that Paul's idea of saving money is
to save it for others. This is the point he makes toward the end
of I Corinthians when he is giving instructions for his collection
for the saints. And his insistence upon generous giving obviously excludes avarice.[91]

Other books ascribed to Paul make up for his relative si-
lence. In the Pastoral Epistles and the closely related letter of
Polycarp to the Philippians avarice is incessantly denounced.
Love of money is the root of all evil, and the bishops and
deacons are to be absolutely free of it. This is a general advice
to administrators; in the contemporary *Strategikos* of Onosander we are told that the good general must be free from avarice
so that he cannot be bribed. But this is not the only problem

related to money. Onosander advises against choosing as generals men who have been usurers, traders, or merchants. "These men must have petty minds; excited over gain and worried about the means of getting money, they have acquired absolutely none of the noble habits of a general."[92] The word for "worried" is the one found in the Sermon on the Mount.[93]

Attacks on avarice were sometimes, of course, aimed at particular individuals. Thus when Cicero criticized "the limitless desire for money" just after the death of Julius Caesar, he obviously had Caesar in mind; and he limited the range of his criticism by adding this: "I do not find fault with the accumulation of property if it hurts no one, but damage to others is always to be avoided."[94]

Inherited wealth was the most respectable kind, though Philo of Alexandria did not condemn gain. It was wrong for Caligula to confiscate the property of those who "inherited from their parents or relations or friends or, by choosing a business career, acquired it through their own efforts."[95] Indeed, Philo condemned Cynics who "without full consideration give up the business and financial side of the citizen's life."[96] Riches in themselves are morally neutral. What matters is what you do with them.[97] Christians, on the other hand, were likely to hear abuse of their business activities in sermons, at least in those preserved to us. Much of this was merely conventional, however, as we see from the "denunciation of wealth" by the rhetorician Libanius, friend of Julian and teacher of the Christian Chrysostom. "I think that the mother of wealth is avarice and not loving what is equitable for equals." Julian was even more contemptuous of "money-making," "trade," and "barter."[99] Chrysostom denounced not only the rich but those who tried to become so.[100]

The original eschatological outlook of Christianity made Christians indifferent to wealth, and as the eschatological en-

thusiasm waned the philosophical ethic that replaced it reinforced a conservative outlook. Christian sermons contain pro
forma denunciations of wealth, much more severe condemnations of avarice. This is to say that the rich could remain rich
but social mobility was not encouraged. We might expect this in
Eusebius, and we are not disappointed. Eusebius denounces
Maximin not just for confiscating property but for "taking
away from the wealthy the property they had kept from their
ancestors."[101] A century earlier, Hippolytus had criticized the
slave origins of Callistus.[102] And bishops in synod at Antioch in
268 virulently attacked Paul of Samosata, the local prelate, as
having enriched himself by fraud, "although he was formerly a
poor beggar who had received no wealth from his ancestors
and had not acquired it from a skill or any business activity."[103]
The bishops did not explicitly condemn the possession of
wealth, or even its acquisition, but their implicit attitude was
hostile to Paul's advancement. When they say that Paul "clothes
himself with worldly dignities," they find his ambition unworthy when contrasted with what Dionysius of Alexandria
suffered in the persecution: "sentences, confiscations, pre-
scriptions, spoiling of possessions, losses of dignities, despis-
ings of worldly glory. . . ."[104] To put it simply, the Christian
attitude toward property tended to be an aristocratic one, and
the criticism of avarice was an important aspect of it.

VI

The Organization
of Alms

A stork now nests on the column erected in honor of Julian
at Ancyra, but when the emperor visited the city in the summer of 362 he seized the occasion to reform and reconstitute
the pagan religion of Galatia. In a letter to the high priest
of the province he complained that pagans were not imitating
the virtues of the Christians. "Why do we not notice that what
has made godlessness grow is benevolence toward strangers
and care for the graves of the dead and moral character, even if
pretended?" To improve the situation, Julian ordered discipline for the priests and the development of charitable institu-
tions. "Establish numerous hostels in each city so that strangers
may enjoy our benevolence, not only our own people but also
others who may need money." In order to finance the new
scheme, Julian provided government allocations of thirty
thousand pecks of wheat and sixty thousand pints of wine per
year, to be used for the whole of Galatia. Only one-fifth of this

was to be used "for the poor who serve the priests." The rest
was for "strangers and beggars."[1] In another letter to a priest
the emperor returned to the same point: "I think that when the
poor happened to be neglected and overlooked by the priests,
the impious Galileans observed this and devoted themselves to
benevolence." In his view the Christians were like those who
get children to follow them by tossing bits of cake to them and
then ship them off into slavery. But he admitted that pagan
priests actually fell short in the matter of benevolence.[2] The
comments we have mentioned had to do with the administration of funds provided by the state, but Julian also went on to
urge private almsgiving in a manner strikingly reminiscent of
Christian exhortations. "We ought to share our money with all
men, but more generously with the good, and with the helpless
and poor so as to suffice for their need." He developed this
theme at considerable length.[3]

According to Julian, "no Jew ever has to beg, and the impious Galileans support not only their own poor but ours as well.[4]
Therefore, in tracing the development of Christian almsgiving
in the Roman world we should begin with Judaism—just as
Christianity did. The eighth-century prophets denounced the
rich for their treatment of the poor. They were primarily concerned with what they called justice rather than with charitable
giving. On the other hand, when the Deuteronomic Code was
formulated, we find the statement that "there will never cease
to be poor in the land," along with the conclusion that "therefore you must always be openhanded with your brother and
with anyone in your country who is in need and poor."[5] After
the exile and under continuing Persian rule, more emphasis
came to be laid on individual acts of almsgiving, and they are
fairly prominent in Proverbs and in Job.[6] The golden age of
almsgiving came in the second century B.C., when Sirach
claimed that "almsgiving atones for sins" and the whole book of

Tobit encouraged the practice as dear to God and rewarded by him.[7] This Hellenistic period was only the first golden age, however, for in the time of the Tannaitic and Amoraic rabbis, Jewish teachers virtually demanded charitable contributions.[8]

In the New Testament attitudes vary. The Gospel of Mark contains very little teaching on almsgiving. Jesus tells an inquirer to sell all he possesses and give the proceeds to the poor, but this seems to be an isolated case. Again, when a woman is criticized for pouring expensive ointment on Jesus, on the ground that it could have been sold for three hundred denarii, the proceeds given to the poor, Jesus replies with an allusion to Deuteronomy 15:10–11 and the additional comment that he, unlike the poor, will not always be with them and therefore the woman has done a "good work" by preparing him for burial (Mark 10:17–22; 14:3–9). In the Gospel of John the story is told of Mary, the sister of Lazarus, and it is Judas Iscariot who complains, "not because he cared about the poor but because he was a thief; he used to appropriate contributions" (12:1–8). This is all that is said on this topic in John.

Matthew and Luke report more teaching about giving. Thus Matthew tells of giving to anyone who asks for either a gift or a loan, of loving enemies, even of giving alms in secret.[9] The disciple is to lay up treasure in heaven, not on earth, and the means to do so can be provided by selling all possessions and giving to the poor. The anointing story is repeated, but great emphasis has been laid on Jesus' last words to his disciples, consisting of the parable of the Sheep and the Goats at the last judgment. The basis of the judgment will be the treatment of Christ, present in anyone who has been hungry, thirsty, a stranger, naked, sick, or in prison. Charitable behavior is evidently essential in Matthew's presentation.[10] It is not just Matthew's work, however, for many of the sayings, also presented by Luke, come from a common sayings-collection or tradition. Luke himself added teaching ascribed to John the

Baptist ("He who has two cloaks must give one to him who has none, and he who has food likewise"), beatitudes on the poor and woes on the rich, and the parable of the Good Samaritan.[11]

In the book of Acts we find two Jewish converts who were conspicuous for their almsgiving; we also find Peter offering a miraculous healing in place of the alms requested of him ("I have no silver or gold").[12] Christian charity soon comes to be rather systematic. Thus at Jerusalem there is a daily distribution of food for widows and possibly for others. According to Jewish precedent, there were two kinds of relief at Jerusalem. The resident poor received money every Friday for fourteen meals, while poor strangers received food and drink daily from a tray filled by three collectors going from house to house. Presumably the Christian arrangement came into existence as a split between Christians and other Jews gradually developed.[13]

A specifically Christian kind of charity seems to arise at the time of a famine in Palestine, apparently about the year 47, when the disciples at Antioch sent gifts to the elders of the church in Jerusalem "by the hand of Barnabas and Saul." Whether the visit thus mentioned is the same as that for the "apostolic council" cannot be determined. At this council Paul (Saul) was asked to "remember the poor," evidently those at Jerusalem, and many years later he came back to the city with what Luke has him call "alms for my nation and offerings."[14] This is the famous collection for the poor saints of Jerusalem, discussed in four of his major epistles. It was the occasion of a great deal of effort and a good deal of conflict (the Galatians evidently refused to contribute), not to mention the accusations of Paul as a thief. Finally the churches of Macedonia and Achaia made their contributions.[15]

Luke points to all this trouble but says nothing specific about it. Instead, when saying goodbye to the churches of Asia, Paul expresses himself thus:[16]

> I coveted no one's silver or gold. You yourselves know that these hands ministered to my necessities and to those who were with me. In all things I have shown you that by so toiling one must help the weak, remembering the words of the Lord Jesus, how he said, "It is more blessed to give than to receive."

As commentators have noted, the saying of the Lord Jesus is based on a Greek proverb, whether he said it or not. Thus Paul's message concludes with borrowing from Hellenistic ideas of charity.

Beyond comments on the collection, Paul has little to say about almsgiving. "Bear one another's burdens, and so fulfill the law of Christ"—a law "fulfilled in one word, 'You shall love your neighbor as yourself.'"[17] Or again, "contribute to the needs of the saints, practice hospitality." In Ephesians the thief is urged not to steal but to work "so that he may be able to give to those in need."[18] In Paul's view, however, "if I give away all I have, and if I deliver my body to be burned, but have not love, I am nothing." What matters for him is not "works" but faith, hope, and love (I Cor. 13:3, 13). In the non-Pauline letters not much is new. Charity and practical love are commended. There is strong stress on the need for doing rather than just saying. The rich, especially, are urged to give.[19]

An increased emphasis on almsgiving arises or, at least, is expressed in the "Judeo-Christianity" of the late first century and the early second. In II Clement (16:4) we are told that "almsgiving is as good as repentance from sin; fasting is better than prayer; almsgiving is better than either." Not surprisingly, there was a reaction against such teaching, and notably in Gnostic groups. Ignatius of Antioch complains about this reaction.[20]

> For love they have no care, none for the widow, none for the orphan, none for the distressed, none the prisoner or the ex-prisoner, none for the hungry or thirsty. They abstain from Eucharist and prayer. . . .

But we do not need to rely on the testimony of Ignatius. The Gospel of Thomas sets forth a remarkably similar view. According to this Gnostic book, Jesus' disciples asked him if they should fast and how they should pray and give alms. His response was that fasting produces sin, prayer condemnation, and almsgiving harm to one's spirit.[21] Clement of Alexandria ascribes rejection of prayer to the heresy of Prodicus.[22] Any number of Gnostic sects could have rejected almsgiving. According to Origen, those who reject prayer also "reject objects of sense and use neither Baptism nor Eucharist, and slanderously affirm that when the scriptures speak of 'praying' they do not mean this but teach something with quite a different meaning."[23] Origen is apparently thinking of philosophical-theological interpretations, but Clement tells us how some Gnostics did take a text about almsgiving. "One of them approached a beautiful virgin of ours and said to her, 'Scripture says, Give to everyone who asks you.'" She did not understand what the man had in mind (or did she?) and replied, "As for marriage, speak to my mother."[24]

Among more ordinary Christians almsgiving was firmly upheld, but occasional hesitation was expressed. The Didache provides fine examples. First, there is the prudential element. "If anyone takes what is yours from you, do not refuse it—for you cannot."[25] Practical problems are much in view. Second, while one should give to all and receive a blessing, the burden of guilt and woe is laid on the underserving recipient. Apparently at the last day, "he who receives alms without need shall give a justification of why he took it and for what, and being in prison he shall be examined for what he did, and he shall not come forth until he repays the last penny." We should note that as the Didache relates the judgment scene of Matthew 5:25–26 to the proper receipt of alms, naturally the Gnostic Carpocratians held that it referred to death and reincarnation.[26] In addition, the donor is really responsible too, for the Didachist has read somewhere, apparently in a version of Sirach 12:1, that one's alms should sweat into one's hands until the recipient is known (1:6). Elsewhere the teaching is more traditional: don't hesitate or grumble; give, share. Don't turn the needy away.[27]

At Rome there was some concern for the mutual benefits to be shared by rich and poor on the basis of almsgiving. Clement of Rome develops Paul's image of the body and recalls how its members are to work together. So in practical charity: "Let the rich man supply the needs of the poor and let the poor man give thanks to God because he gave him someone to supply his lack" (I Clem. 37–38:2). Hermas explicitly states that rich and poor work together. "When the rich man rests upon the poor and gives him what he needs, he believes that what he does for the poor man can find a reward with God, for the poor man is rich in intercession and confession, and his intercession has great power with God."[28] Like the Didachist, Hermas insists on almsgiving and on meritorious recipients as well.[29] Especially interesting are his comments on diet, fasting, and alms. The rich, he finds, get sick because of their overeating, while others who have nothing to eat are suffering too. "So this lack of sharing is harmful to you who are rich and do not share with the poor."[30] But Hermas does not leave his exhortations without practical planning. "When you have finished what is written [whatever that was], on that day when you fast you shall taste nothing but bread and water, and you shall reckon the amount of the expense of the foods you would have eaten on that day you are going to observe, and you shall give it to a widow or an orphan or someone in need, and you shall fast so that through your fasting he who receives may fill his soul and pray for you to the Lord."[31] Here fasting, alms, and prayer are firmly linked, in just the reverse of the Gnostic attitude.

The Roman apologist Justin shows us that by the mid-second

century Christian charity was rather highly organized and was connected not with fasting but with the Eucharist.[32] There are voluntary offerings, he tells us, and apparently they are collected once a week and desposited with the "president" or bishop. It is he who protects orphans and widows, those in distress for sickness or another cause, those in prison, and sojourners who are strangers. In short, he is the guardian of all who are in need.[33] The list given by Ignatius to the Smyrnaeans suggests that this kind of catalogue was at least a generation old. We find something quite like it, without explicit reference to episcopal involvement, in the *Apology* of Aristides, about 140. Christians, Aristides says, do not overlook the widow and do not grieve the orphan. He who has supplies the needs of him who has not, without grudging. If Christians see a stranger they bring him under their roof and rejoice over him as over a real brother.[34] Even the pagan satirist Lucian confirms this picture. When Peregrinus Proteus, supposedly a Christian, was arrested and imprisoned in Palestine, Christians flocked around him. "From the very break of day aged widows and orphan children could be seen waiting near the prison," perhaps to join with him in prayer. Christian "officials even slept inside with him after bribing the guards; then elaborate meals were brought in. . . ." Any charlatan or trickster, Lucian concludes, can get rich quick by imposing on such people.[35]

Such conditions, already hinted at in earlier times, made it necessary to take considerable care in almsgiving. Tertullian, for example, says, "I will give to everyone who asks in a situation of almsgiving, not in a shake-down." He refuses to be influenced by threats.[36] He is coming to be in line with the Roman Stoic tradition in which caution in giving was firmly advocated.[37] And thus he lines up both with Clement of Alexandria and with Seneca and their recommendation of "disciplined, charitable almsgiving."[38] Thus by the time we reach Origen's

Commentary on Matthew, written at Caesarea not long before 250, we find in it a significant citation of Psalm 41:1. In translation from Hebrew the text reads thus: "Blessed the man who cares for the poor and the weak." In Greek, however, it became, "Blessed the man who understands about the poor man and the pauper." This gave Origen the opportunity to claim that there ought to be careful social-service investigations of church relief clients. One ought to know the causes of their indigence, the original status of each and how he was brought up, how much is necessary for him to have or why he is indigent. You don't treat in the same way people who from infancy were brought up harshly and strictly and those who were fed bountifully and luxuriously and later fell. Treatment will be different in the cases of men and women, old and young, the young who are weak from lack of food and those who at least in part can help themselves. There must be an investigation to find out how many children there are. In short, says Origen, the administrator of the church's revenues needs much wisdom.[39] Perhaps he got his from rabbis. G. F. Moore gives an example of just the same teaching in his *Judaism,* though analogies occur elsewhere.[40]

More than a century later at Antioch we find John Chrysostom developing almost a mania on the subject of alms. O. Plassmann has provided an admirable survey and analysis of his comments.[41] Here we shall be content with two examples of his dealing with reluctant givers. First, based on general considerations. "You are not able to become propertyless? Give from your possessions. You cannot bear that burden? Divide your possessions with Christ. You do not want to surrender everything to him? Hand over even a half share, even a third."[42] Second, a more sophisticated criticism. The nondonor answers that the beneficiary "has the common fund of the church." But you yourself must give in accordance with the law of God, says Chrysostom. You have suspicions about the priest, that is, about his honesty? This, says Chrysostom, is an especially grave sin; but I am not going to quarrel over trifles; do everything for yourself and thus you will gain double the reward! He asks the critic to remember, when he sees the size of the church's estate, that it deals with "hordes" of poor people on the relief rolls.[43]

One should also mention Chrysostom's imaginary dialogue with those whom he wanted to leave bequests to the church. It runs thus. "Then what are our children going to inherit? The capital remains theirs, and the income increases, with property laid up in heaven for them. You do not want to do this? What about half, what of a third share, or perhaps a fourth, or even a tenth? I don't say (finally) to reduce your capital; use the income. —But I pay taxes.—Do you despise (the church's claim) because no one is making a demand?"[44] This is really no more than the interest on a deposit, Chrysostom argues. You owe it to God.[45]

In spite of such conflicts of interest, the church steadily pressed for alms for the poor. Tertullian claimed that the *agape*-meal, apparently separated from the Eucharist early in the second century, was intended for the feeding of the poor.[46] But there were many other opportunities for sharing food or funds. Cyprian has a whole treatise *De opere et eleemosynis*, in which he first argues that alms obliterate the pollution caused by sin after baptism, next gives many biblical citations, and then turns to particular problems. Will you use up your inherited wealth? Certainly not; more citations. Actually the accumulation of wealth is bad and so is being rich. If you have many children to look after, simply give more; give as the Christ; give as one who shares everything. Farther to the east, there was more emphasis on orderly giving. We read in the *Didascalia* that offerings should definitely be presented

through the bishop, who will distribute them justly.[47] "For the
bishop is well acquainted with those who are in distress, and he
dispenses and gives to each as is fitting for him, so that one may
not receive often on the same day or in the same week and
another receive not even a little." The more distress, the more
support, says this document. To be precise, whatever the
widow gets, the deacon is to get double, the bishop quadruple.
Or so it reads in the Syriac version. The Latin differs. Nothing
is said about what the widow is paid; the scale simply runs one
for presbyter, two for deacon, four for bishop.[48]

Before we leave alms and move to the more precise cat-
egories of gifts, first-fruits, and tithes, let us simply note what
Chrysostom says in his sixty-sixth homily on Matthew: "I am
ashamed to speak about alms, for though I have often discussed this subject I have achieved no results worthy of the
exhortation. A little more has come in, but not as much as I
wanted."[49] So a fund-raiser could speak in any generation.

GIFTS, FIRST-FRUITS, AND TITHES

Early Christian writers often insist on the voluntary nature
of gifts for church purposes. Paul tells the Corinthians that
"each one must do as he has made up his mind, not reluctantly
or under compulsion, for God loves a cheerful giver" (II Cor.
9:7). Justin says that the gifts are by free choice, and he says so
three times in one sentence.[50] Tertullian explicitly claims that
among the Christians there are no religious fees. Instead, each
member makes a modest gift once a month, or when he prefers. No one is forced to give.[51] Such monthly contributions
also existed in burial societies, but a burial society charter from
Lanuvium in the second century makes it clear that if you die
with your payments some months in arrears the society will not
pay for your funeral.[52] The church was more "charitable,"

even though the clergy were being paid monthly at least as early as the mid-third century. Most of the funds were used, at least in the early period, for "the support and burying of the poor, and on boys and girls deprived of property and parents, and on aged servants now unable to work, also on shipwrecked persons and any who are in the mines or on islands or in prisons, provided it be for the cause of God's religion, and become pensioners of their confession."[53]

Such gifts were not, of course, found only among adherents of the Christian religion. Much money was collected at various temples for the support of the public worship, and the begging priests of several oriental cults were famous for their activities.[54] Tertullian may have been right when he claimed that even pagans noticed temple revenues declining because so few persons contributed.[55] He may have misunderstood the usual money-raising problems of religious organizations, finding a trend where there was none. An inscription from the acropolis at Lindos in the first century shows that the problem is perennial and nonsectarian. The temple of Athena needed money, and therefore a committee to sell bronze and iron objects was being set up. In addition, it was hoped that rights to inscribe one's name on the bases of uninscribed statues in the sanctuary could be sold. Voluntary gifts were to be sought, and donors' names would be inscribed on a plaque. Finally, people were to be urged to take the office of sacrificing priest without charging for their services.[56]

What kept many temples going was a combination of endowment income, fees, locally levied taxes, and the gifts we have mentioned. These sources of funds should not be differentiated too sharply, however, especially when we consider "tithes" and "first-fruits" as found among Greeks, Romans, Jews, and Christians.[57]

Tithes were a common feature of religiously oriented giving

in antiquity. Nilsson defines the tithe quite adequately thus: "the tenth part of a revenue offered as a thankoffering to a god; the sense is often the same as that of votive offering, *aparche*."[58] In the Roman world tithes on booty acquired in war or profit obtained in business were especially common, and were usually paid to Apollo or Hercules.[59] Such was not always the case, however. For one thing, sometimes Apollo got as little as a twentieth.[60] For another, other gods were also the beneficiaries of such gifts. The comic poet Diphilus, in his play *The Merchant,* refers to valuable fish and addresses Poseidon thus: "If you had received a tithe from the price of these each day you would be by far the richest of the gods."[61] Aelius Aristides advocates treating Serapis not just as the recipient of tithes but as a full partner, as in the case of merchants and shipowners.[62] (Just so, Cyprian would urge Christians to make Christ a partner in worldly possessions so that he would make them co-heir in celestial kingdoms.[63])

Among the Jews tithes were especially prominent. Hecataeus says that the number of Jewish priests who receive the tithe is about fifteen hundred.[64] Josephus explains how there are tithes upon tithes for the support of the priests and Levites and for such women and children as widows and orphans.[65] Such matters are discussed in full detail in the division of the Mishnah entitled *Zeraim,* or "Seeds."[66] A Pharisee is described in the Gospel of Luke as tithing all he acquires, while in Matthew Pharisees and scribes are criticized for tithing "mint, anise, and cummin" while neglecting justice, mercy, and faith. The tithing as such is not condemned.[67]

In spite of conflicts over the tithes between the high priests, who even sent their slaves to the threshing-floors to take the tithes that belonged to ordinary priests, and the inferiors whose tithes were being stolen,[68] few questions were raised as to the propriety of the tithe system itself. In the early years of the Jewish revolt, Josephus went to Galilee with two other priests to collect tithes there.[69] And the language he uses about the Essenes suggests that they too collected tithes.[70]

Nothing is said about Christian tithes in the New Testament. Indeed, the story of the Widow's Mite points to the notion that one should contribute everything one has, one's "whole living."[71] Thus Irenaeus contrasts the tithes paid under the old law with the "whole living" which the widow contributed to the treasury of God.[72] Clement of Alexandria praises the payment of tithes, which he identifies with first-fruits.[73]

A more obviously agricultural form of donation for sacrificial purposes was "firstling" or "first-fruit" *(aparchē)*, a votive offering or thank-offering consisting of the first part gained, grown, or otherwise obtained. By Hellenistic times the first-fruit could be defined in cash terms. Thus at Magnesia on the Maeander under Attalus II (mid-second century B.C.) a particular *aparchē* for the goddess is defined as a hundred drachmas.[74] An annual *aparchē* for the crocodile god Soknopaios in the Fayum in 95 B.C. is set forth as 182½ measures of grain, or one-half for each day.[75] Papyri show that Jews in Egypt paid *aparchē*, probably for the support of the priesthood in Egypt or Jerusalem.[76]

The literal offering of first-fruits is not mentioned in the New Testament, and Irenaeus speaks of Christ as commanding his disciples to offer the first-fruits to God by means of the bread of the Eucharist.[77] Already in the Didache, however, there are rather detailed instructions about the offering of first-fruits for the support of Christian prophets. These instructions are based on Old Testament passages concerning first-fruits for priests.[78] Hippolytus gives exact rubrics for the blessing of fruits and flowers.[79] And Origen insists that first-fruits must be offered to "the priests of the gospel."[80] For the *Didascalia apostolorum* the first-fruits and tithes of former times are now offerings made through the bishop for the remission of sins.[81] The *Apostolic Constitutions* make a clear distinction of uses between first-fruits and tithes. The former are for bishop, presbyters, and deacons; the latter are for other clerics, virgins, widows, and attested paupers.[82]

The most important example of Christian firstfruits is to be found in the Didache. The situation reflected in the earlier sections on the ministry has to do with an itinerant ministry of apostles and prophets. They are allowed to settle in communities but under restrictions. If a wandering apostle asks for money, "he is a false prophet." Any itinerant who "in the Spirit" asks for money "or anything else" is not to be given a hearing unless it is for others who are in need. If itinerants settle, they are to "work and eat" (in agreement with II Thess. 3:10–12). And the author either insists or concedes that authentic prophets and teachers who settle in a community "deserve their food."[83] Beyond this comes a section in which the prophets are regarded as equivalent to the Old Testament high priests.

> You shall take every firstfruit of produce—
>   the winepress and the threshing-floor, oxen and sheep—
> and shall give it to the prophets,
>   for they are your high priests.
> (If you have no prophet, give to the poor.)
>   If you make bread
> take the firstfruit
> and give in accordance with the commandment.
>   Similarly when you open a jar of wine or oil
> take the firstfruit
> and give to the prophets.
> Take the firstfruit of money and clothing and every possession
>   however it seems good to you
> and give in accordance with the commandment.

These regulations are based on the Old Testament law set forth in Numbers 15 and 18 and Deuteronomy 18 and summarized in Nehemiah 10:36–40 and Sirach 7:31–32; in the last-cited passage giving to the poor is mentioned too. The Old Testament passages say nothing about money, clothing, and other possessions, but in Deuteronomy 14:22–27 there is some discussion of converting produce into cash, and this is presumably the point involved in the Didache. One would not expect to find a capital levy here, any more than in the Jewish discussions of the subject.[84]

Along with the establishment of fixed places of worship and definite orders of ministers came clearer definition of the financial responsibilities of the communities toward the ministers. In the first period the wandering apostles could be described as carrying nothing but a staff—no bread, no bag, no money in their belts (Mark 6:8–9). "The laborer deserves his food" (as in the Didache) or "wages."[85] As the wandering tends to come to an end, the relationship to the community—accepting pay from it—remains constant. Thus Paul could speak of not muzzling the ox on the threshing floor and of the command given by the Lord "that those who proclaim the gospel should get their living by the gospel" (I Cor. 9:9, 14). In I Timothy, as in the Didache, the itinerant ministry has come to an end. The presbyters who rule well are to receive double pay, especially if they teach as well as preach. The author of the Pastoral Epistles then quotes the Old Testament on not muzzling the ox and the Gospel of Luke on the workman's wages (I Tim. 5:17–18).

No definite figure is quoted for the amount of the Christian minister's wage, and in Carthage as late as the third century the bishop and the presbyters were paid monthly on "the dividend principle."[86] In other words, the presbyters shared alike in part of the offerings of the faithful, while the bishop received a larger share, presumably double that of a presbyter in accordance with I Timothy 5:17. Jones agrees with the "conjecture that such a system was general in the primitive churches." Now we should examine the evidence for the dividend and for the introduction of another system.

Whether or not the Parable of the Laborers in the Vineyard originally had anything to do with the payment of Christian ministers, in its present position in Matthew (20:1–16) it follows a discussion of what the disciples of Jesus should expect to receive, and it ends with a similar "parabolical conclusion" (19:30; 20:16). The parable does not point to the dividend principle as such, for the laborers receive a denarius apiece. But it does point to equality of payment, no matter how the amount of work varies.

The apostle Paul vigorously argued that the apostles had the right to be supported by the communities in which they preached the gospel. The analogical examples he gives do not generally show how the rate of support should be fixed (I Cor. 9:7), but there is one exception: "Those who serve at the altar," he writes, "have shares in the sacrificial offerings." Here the dividend principle is clearly present, and it *may* be implied for the church. Certainly Paul invoked the principle of equity in appealing for gifts to the poor saints of Jerusalem. "As a matter of equality your abundance at the present time should supply their want, so that their [spiritual] abundance may supply your want, that there may be equality."[87] General equity *may* imply local dividend. And whether or not the resident prophet of the Didache has to share with anyone, it is evident that his own pay, derived from "first-fruits," is not fixed but varies in relation to the agricultural produce of various seasons.

With such precedents, then, we can understand the late second-century objections to fixed "salaries" for sectarian clerics. An anti-Montanist writer denounces Montanus for "appointing collectors of funds, contriving present-taking under the title of 'offerings,' and supplying salaries for those who preach his doctrine."[88] The three charges are interrelated. In order to pay salaries it was obviously necessary to have collectors and to encourage collections as "offerings." It is more surprising that in a millenarian movement there was such a down-to-earth financial arrangement. To put it in modern terms, the Montanist salesmen were not on commission, like their Catholic competitors. According to the anti-Montanist, their rewards were sufficient for the prophets to accumulate gold and silver and to lend money at interest.[89] Was the rate high in view of the impending end of the age?

Toward the end of the century a banker named Theodotus was one of the leaders of a minority group within the Roman church, and he and his friends subsidized a certain Natalius as their own sectarian bishop, paying him a salary of one hundred fifty denarii per month. A Catholic critic waxed indignant, apparently complaining about both the amount and the fixity of its payment.[90] The complaint seems to prove that in the Catholic church of Rome the dividend principle was being followed.

Around the same time Victor of Rome provided a monthly stipend for the ex-banker Callistus, in retirement at Antium (Anzio). Hippolytus says that he "set for him a certain monthly sum for his support."[91] This seems to mean a monthly sum exactly determined in advance rather than a monthly share or dividend.

What we have seen thus far is that the idea of a fixed salary for clerics arose toward the end of the second century and not in Catholic circles. The greatest inequality was said to exist in Gnostic circles, where individual teachers delivered the mysteries to those who could pay the most.[92]

G. E. M. de Ste Croix complains about the vagueness of

Christian criticisms of avarice and he denies that almsgiving could provide a solution for the problem of poverty. He does not mention gifts for the support of the clergy, but it is clear that he could not favor them.[93] With a more severely historical purpose in view, we simply point out that the Christian ideas about avarice were nothing new but were shared by almost all moralists. As for their emphasis on almsgiving, we have an excellent pagan witness, the emperor Julian, who commended it strongly and wished that his pagan priests were concerned with others half as much as they were concerned with themselves.

Before concluding our discussion of almsgiving we must consider the important area where the church's economy overlapped with that of the state, and clerics served as administrators for the social program of the state. This is the area of the grain distribution in the fourth century.

From the second century B.C. onward there were distributions of grain by the Roman state to Roman plebeians. The grain dole, called *frumentum,* was often abused by various persons or groups illegally enrolled. Julius Caesar, for example, reduced the number of recipients from 320,000 to 150,000 in 46 B.C., but the figure was higher than that under Augustus.[94] The basic question for us concerning this Roman distribution is: was it shared by right or on the ground of need? Appian clearly supposed that it was for the poor alone; he said that the idle, beggars, and vagrants of Italy went to Rome to participate.[95] On the other hand, Philo of Alexandria claimed that the Jews of Rome enjoyed Roman citizenship and because of it they participated in the monthly distributions of "money or grain." (Philo also speaks of the imperial "favor" and "the common benevolence," terms which will reappear when we look at Roman church charities.) He had no intention of referring to impoverished Jews at Rome, and he insisted that the distribution was for the whole Roman people.[96] We should agree with those scholars who have rejected need as the criterion for the distribution.[97]

The distribution at Rome was the most important one, but the practice was widespread. Thus under Claudius or Nero we find an inscription in Greek mentioning a Bithynian "steward over the grain."[98] From the same reigns comes the record of privately endowed foundations to provide *frumentum* for the children of the citizens of Atina until they are of age.[99] Especially under Trajan such foundations flourished, and especially in Italy. The capital was invested in real-estate mortgages; the interest was paid to towns or to state administrators, usually at the rate of 5 or 6 percent. Under Antoninus Pius there was certainly a "distribution of loaves" at Antinoopolis in Egypt, presumably related to an official list of those "on the *frumentum*" and "off the *frumentum*."[100]

Early in the third century, Septimius Severus added an oil ration to the wheat, and the most Syrian of emperors, Elagabalus, extended the dole to noncitizens.[101] From the middle of the century we possess the statement of Cornelius of Rome about the number of officers (155) and "widows with those in straitened circumstances" (1500) being given support by "the favor and benevolence of the Master" in the Roman church. The terms Cornelius used were the same, as we have already indicated, as those used by Philo in regard to the *frumentum*.[102] Less than a decade later, Dionysius of Alexandria provides valuable testimony concerning the grain dole at Alexandria. Discussing the effect of plague and famine on the population, Dionysius states that the number now enrolled for the distribution, including all from fourteen to eighty years of age, is less than the "elderly" in former times, those who were from forty to seventy years.[103] A whole dossier of documents from Oxyrhynchus between A.D. 268 and 272 shows that careful scrutiny was given the qualifications of those, aged thirteen and up, who were admitted by citizenship or special privilege. Citizens of Rome and Alexandria were also admitted. The distribution was made once a month.[104] Perhaps, as at Rome, bread was substituted for wheat about 275.[105]

By the time Constantine inaugurated the dole at Constantinople in 332, bread rather than grain was used for the daily provision. The original number of recipients was eighty thousand.[106] According to the Byzantine chronographer Theophanes, there was a famine the following year, and Constantine donated the grain ration in various cities to the churches for the continuing support of widows, hostelers, the poor, and clerics. In Antioch, Theophanes says, the church received thirty-six thousand measures of grain—apparently enough to support a thousand persons for about a year.[107] Naturally the clerics involved in the distribution were careful to see that the grain or bread reached Catholics, no Arians.[108] Athanasius looked out for the food supply of Egypt rather than that of Constantinople; perhaps such a concern underlies the accusation against him that he was threatening to hold up the flow of grain to Constantinople.[109] On another occasion his enemies said he sold the grain intended for Libyan and Egyptian widows and kept the funds.[110]

It looks rather as if the clerics were being paid administration fees in relation to that portion of the general grain dole that was being transmitted to Christians. Typically, such administrative costs increase and come to be commingled with the main body of funds. It is hard to believe that the church historians give us reliable accounts of just how generous the emperor was. Eusebius says that he gave the churches grain distributions for the support of poor men, orphan children, and pitiable women (no mention of clerics here),[111] while Theodoret states that he instructed governors to provide annual grain supplies for perpetual virgins, widows, and clerics, in relation to rank rather than need.[112] Each author is laying emphasis on what he likes.

The pagan reaction at Ascalon and Gaza under Julian suggests that some pagans felt deprived of such donations. They cut open the stomachs of a few Christian presbyters and virgins, stuffed them with grain, and fed them to pigs.[112] This looks like a symbolic protest against the administration of the dole. Julian himself took the dole administration away from Christian clerics and transferred it to pagan priests, as we have seen. After Julian's brief reign was over, his successor, Jovian, restored the dole to the offices of the church but, since there was a famine at the time, set the rate at a third of what it had been before. The end of the famine was supposed to permit the rate to be restored in full, but apparently this never took place.[114] The church had to rely on private donations or on other forms of state aid.

Thus ended an interesting experiment in mixed economy, in which, as in universities and colleges today, state funds were administered by a private group for the benefit of both public and private sectors. It reflected the rapid expansion of the church in the early fourth century and the failure of private giving to keep pace with the church's needs. An odd "separation of powers" doctrine was intimated by Constantine in 326. "The rich must assume secular obligations and the poor must be supported by the wealth of the churches."[115] It is odd because, unless the churches were to be made superlatively rich, they obviously could not support all the poor of the Roman world.

VII

Temples, Churches, and Endowments

GROWING RELIGIONS need expanding space for their assemblies. We recall "the upper room" in Jerusalem, along with other houses and halls mentioned in the book of Acts. Presumably Paul's own "rented dwelling" at Rome should be included among them.[1] Churches in various people's houses are mentioned in Paul's letters.[2] Indeed, the house-church was the normal church building during the first two centuries of Christian expansion. Even the church at Dura-Europus on the Euphrates was a house-church, created by throwing together quite a few rooms. Christians were slow to build permanent and distinctive church buildings.[3] Perhaps their primitive eschatology had something to do with this. Why build if the end of the world is at hand? The slowness was also due to their lack of funds, their uncertain legal status, and their desire to spend what money they had on practical charity.

Before regarding their situation as unique, we should consider the case of the worship of Serapis on the Greek island of

Delos. An inscription of the late third century B.C. supplies a sixty-five-line hymn on the way the worship of Serapis was introduced, as well as a prose account prepared by a priest. The prose account explains how the priest's grandfather, "an Egyptian of the priestly class," brought the god with him. His father "succeeded him and continued in the service of the gods." But it was only the priest Apollonius himself who received a dream oracle and removed the cult to permanent quarters. The god said that "he must have a Serapeum of his own dedicated to him and that he must not be in hired quarters as before, and that he would himself find a place where he should be set and would show us that place." Unfortunately, as Nock suggested, it is likely that "Apollonius had not obtained from the popular assembly the authorization necessary for buying land for a foreign worship." In consequence, a lawsuit was brought against the new temple and its priest. Priest and people defended themselves against it, and the god himself promised, in another dream, that they would win. In fact, they did.[4] So the priestly family passed from being tenants—over three generations!—to being owners.

Another example is the god of the Tyrian coast, Helios Saraptenos, who came by ship from Tyre to Puteoli near Naples about two months before the eruption of Vesuvius in A.D. 79. The inscription, now at the University of Michigan, points out that Elim (presumably a priest) brought him in accordance with a command. Nearly a century later, another inscription contains a letter from the Tyrian community at Puteoli. They cannot afford to keep up the national worship and want more of the expenses borne at Tyre or Rome.[5] Once more, the question of rent comes up. Originally Tyrians resident in Puteoli were numerous and wealthy; by 174 there were few, and they claimed that "since we pay the expenses for the sacrifices and services to our ancestral gods consecrated here in temples, we do not have the means to pay the agency's annual rent of 250 denarii." (This was the Tyrian commercial agency of Puteoli.) One may wonder about the number of ancestral gods, the number of temples, their size, and perhaps whether the Tyrian community owned any of them.

We have mentioned the Christian house-churches. It should be noted that the Christians' competitors, the Mithraists, also had sanctuaries in members' houses, notably at Rome but at Ostia as well.[6] Since they wanted darkness and privacy for their liturgy and met only in small groups, the use of parts of houses, large or small, was chiefly a matter of convenience. Cumont long ago noted inscriptions on the subject of Mithraic temple-building and the provision of various sacred objects. Members would pay for land, the cost of digging, and the decoration of the shrines. As among the Christians before Constantine, there was no state support.[7]

Closer to Christianity was the Jewish synagogue, itself a "community house" being developed toward a basilica in the early imperial period.[8] Krautheimer has noted the religious sects that used adaptations of the basilica form from the second century onward: worshipers of Isis and Osiris at Pergamum; Neopythagoreans and "Tree Bearers" at Rome; probably Jews for synagogues in Galilee.[9]

Support for these religious groups was derived from several sources, none of which should be sharply differentiated. One might speak of kings and emperors, but they had both private and public accounts and it is often hard to tell which kind they are using. There were local gifts both private and public or mixed. And there were endowments provided by funds set apart by living donors or bequeathed by the dead. At the beginning of any religion there are, of course, normally no endowments. They were rather characteristic of the Graeco-Roman world, however, and in the studies of B. Laum and A. R. Hands we find many examples. Laum provides examples of endowments for the support of priests and temples, since Hands does not treat these as evidence for "charities and social aid."[10] The endowments for priests and temples are especially important to us because they provide precedents for the endowments given to Christian churches by the emperor Constantine.

We possess little evidence for the endowment of oriental cults in the Roman world, but first-century inscriptions from Amorion in Phrygia indicate that "initiates of the tribe of Zeus" provided vineyards from whose income annual votive offerings were presented to Mithras.[11] From the second century comes an Alexandrian inscription referring to a shrine of Aphrodite and the shops connected with it, probably as income property. It has had tax exemption from former times to the present. A would-be donor is "desirous of adding a brewery for the support of the shrine," and requests tax exemption for it as well.[12]

In early Christianity there were neither endowments nor church buildings, and the eastern teacher Justin met with other Christians only "above the bath" of someone or other, where he lived. The name of the bath has been corrupted in the manuscripts. Perhaps it referred to Novatianus and Timotheus, traditionally hospitable to Christian visitors at the site of what is now Santa Pudenziana.[13] Other evidence makes it plain that there were philosophical-theological objections to the idea of templelike buildings. The nonlocal God, who needed no sacrifices, could not be worshiped in a special sacred place and the church consisted of believers, not buildings.[14] There was probably no change from the earlier house-churches at the time of Gallienus, about 261, and his edict restoring "worship-places" to the Christian bishops. These were probably house-churches like the buildings restored to Christians by Maximin and Constantine in 313.[15] But Eusebius does insist that before 303 there were so many Christians that "they were no longer satisfied with the former buildings but would erect from the foundations churches of spacious dimensions in all the cities."[16] Even allowing for exaggeration, it is clear that there were at least some church buildings, probably basilicas, before Constantine's time. None can be precisely identified at Rome, however, and there are no definite examples elsewhere.

The destruction of house-churches in the early fourth century and the consequent need to rebuild gave Eusebius and other bishops a great opportunity to develop their ideas about the church building as the new temple of Solomon, with the emperor or other donors as new Solomons, and we find such thoughts in Eusebius' sermon for the consecration of the new Christian church at Tyre, probably in the year 315.[17] He himself says that "the temple in Tyre," as he calls it, surpassed in splendor all the others in Phoenicia. It had been built by the zeal of the local bishop, who "eagerly desired to spare no expense."[18] To judge from a somewhat similar passage in the *Life of Constantine,* the expense was not his but the emperor's.[19]

The church historians Eusebius and Lactantius claim that by June 313 Constantine and Licinius took a significant step when they restored confiscated property to the Christian church. Their step was less significant than these Constantinian loyalists made it, for in most areas of the empire various other rulers had already restored such property. Maxentius had led the way in 310, while on their respective deathbeds Galerius in 311 and Maximin in 313 had done the same thing. Galerius had explained his move as based on social and religious utility: the Christians, permitted to assemble and build churches, were expected to pray to "their own god" on behalf of the emperors, the state, and themselves. Maximin described his edict as an act of indulgence, and he claimed that it proved his religiousness and concern for his subjects. He increased his indulgence by adding that houses or lands formerly owned by "the Christians"—presumably church properties—were to be restored even if later transfers had taken place. Constantine and Licinius held that both pagan and Christian worship brought about the favor of whatever deities there were, and that the restoration of church properties was especially likely to be propitious. This time the practical question of indemnification was considered. Repayment would be provided by the state. The emperors also wrote to the proconsul of Africa with orders to restore all the properties of the churches, including "gardens and buildings."[20]

The lands, gardens, and buildings mentioned in various pieces of legislation may well have constituted endowment properties held by the various churches, even though it is difficult for us to see how organizations supposedly illegal could be endowed. Against this we note that Greek foundations possessed lands, gardens, vineyards, and houses (especially shops), while among Latin records one can note income from apartment buildings, gardens, vineyards, and buildings in general.[21] Furthermore, the government evidently assumed that churches could hold property. In 304 an Egyptian declaration insists that a village church never had any gold, silver, money, clothing, animals, slaves, lands, or other properties derived either from gifts or from bequests.[22]

More important was the new construction and endowment provided by Constantine, especially at Rome. There were seven Constantinian churches at Rome. Two means for dating them are known. First is the obvious pursuit of archaeological evidence. Second is the less obvious consideration of the location of the endowment properties listed in the *Liber Pontificalis.* Properties located in lands ruled by Licinius between 313 and 324 cannot have been given to the churches before the latter date.[23]

Constantine's largest and best-endowed basilica, underlying the present S. Giovanni in Laterano, owed its location to the military-political situation of the early fourth century. His rival Maxentius had ruled at Rome because he had been hailed as emperor by the praetorian guard in 306; many of the praetorians died defending him six years later. Constantine disbanded the survivors.[24] Closely related to the praetorians were the *equites singulares imperatoris,* or horse-guards. An inscription from their barracks, under S. Giovanni, shows that the barracks were dedicated in 197.[25] This building, now useless after the praetorians and the *equites* were disbanded, served as the foundation for the emperor's *Basilica Constantiniana.*[26]

Nearby, probably just to the north, was a villa of which Constantine also took possession. He presented it to his wife, Fausta, and in turn she permitted Miltiades, bishop of Rome, to use it for a conference on the Donatist problem in October 313.[27] It seems unlikely that Fausta, who was not a Christian, transferred the villa to the church. More probably the emperor gave it to the church after Fausta's death.

His gifts of gold and silver ornaments to the church were extensive, as the *Liber Pontificalis* reveals.[28] In addition, he provided—both for the basilica and for a baptistry connected with it—an endowment in lands in Italy, Africa, Crete, and Gaul which yielded more than fourteen thousand solidi a year, or more than two hundred pounds of gold. All these areas were in his control by 317.

The next Constantinian church was probably the basilica of St. Peter on the Vatican. The Constantinian church was built over a shrine honoring the memory of Peter and dating from about 160. Building began between 319 and 322, because inscriptions in honor of the nearby cult of the Phrygian goddess end in 319, while one set up in 349 says that her worship has been resumed after an interval of twenty-eight years.[29] The endowment, however, came a little later. It was derived from the diocese of Oriens, taken from Licinius in 324, and consisted of revenues from properties in and near Antioch, in Egypt (mostly from gifts made to Constantine), and in the province of Euphrates.[30] The place-names reflect a double process of confiscation. Originally all belonged to Maximin Daia; then to Licinius; finally to Constantine.

Constantine promised Silvester of Rome that he would erect basilicas for both Peter and Paul. He kept his promise in regard to the second apostle only about 326, and the church he built was much smaller than St. Peter's. The original endowment came from Tarsus in Cilicia, appropriately enough—and inexpensively. As in the case of St. Peter's, the properties had belonged first to Maximin (now buried at Tarsus), then to Licinius. To pass the income on to the church cost Constantine little.

His mother, Helena, died in 329, and her death had important consequences for Roman churches and mausoleums. First, her palace—the Sessorian—was utilized for building the Basilica Sessoriana. Next, the Church of SS. Marcellinus and Peter was erected close to the mausoleum of Helena, the Tor Pignattara, and endowed from an imperial domain stretching from the Sessoriana northward beyond the mausoleum. The mausoleum, along with the cemetery of Marcellinus and Peter, seems to have been intended by Constantine for his own use. The warlike decoration of the sarcophagus, now in the Vatican, is far more appropriate for Constantine than for his mother. But by the time she died he had nearly finished building Constantinople. He had no desire to be buried at Rome. He therefore honored his mother by respecting and carrying out her legacies and by burying her in his own sarcophagus.

Finally, around the same time, when Constantinople was being dedicated, the emperor gave another church to Rome.

This was the Basilica of St. Laurentius (outisde the walls), honoring an important martyr of the third century. The endowment, all Italian, amounted to little, since the emperor's attention was now turned eastward.

Rome owes one more church to the family of Constantine. This is St. Agnes (outside the walls), built and modestly endowed by Constantine's daughter Constantia between 337 and 350. In the latter year a circular mausoleum was built for her nearby. Her sarcophagus, now in the Vatican, may have been originally intended for Helena.[31]

In Italy Constantine also endowed churches at Ostia, Alba, and Naples, and he handed over the palace of Maximian at Aquileia for use as a church. Either he or his successors similarly disposed of the mausoleum-temple of Galerius at Thessalonica and the mausoleum of Diocletian at Split. His Christian basilica at Trier was erected over a royal palace. One emperor needed fewer palaces than four had required.

After 325 Constantine's building activities in the east paralleled what he had done in the west. His new city of Constantinople was adorned by two basilicas: the Church of the Twelve Apostles, in which he was to be buried, and the extant, though heavily restored, Church of Peace. At Nicomedia he rebuilt the church destroyed under Diocletian. At Antioch the Golden Church, begun in 327, was not completed until 341. In the same city the so-called old church was restored by the bishops.[32] In 327 and 328 the emperor's mother was on pilgrimage in the east, and one imperial personage or the other was responsible for building churches commemorating the birth, death, and ascension of Jesus, as well as the appearance of the Trinity to Abraham at Mamre. In most of these cases the building of the churches involved the destruction of already existing pagan shrines. According to Epiphanius, a convert from Judaism and friend of Constantine was involved in the building of churches at Tiberias, Diocaesarea (Sepphoris), and Capernaum in Palestine.[33]

It is obvious that the extension of Christianity during the early fourth century could not have proceeded without the aid provided by the emperor.

Constantine took part in the dedication of the city of Constantinople on May 11, 330, and aspects of religious observance there became important for his policy in other areas of the eastern empire. First, the city was adorned by treasures taken from temples throughout the east. Eusebius specifically mentions the Pythian Apollo and the Sminthian, the tripod from Delphi, and the Muses of Helicon.[34] This transfer of temple treasure seems to have led to the confiscation of the revenues of three pagan temples in Constantinople itself[35] and to the destruction of a few temples in the eastern empire. Eusebius names the temples of Aphrodite at Aphaka in Lebanon, Asclepius at Aegae in Cilicia, and Aphrodite at Heliopolis (Baalbek) in Phoenicia.[36] In his *Chronicle* Jerome says that in the year 331 "by an edict of Constantine (the) temples of the gentiles were overthrown." The *Chronographia* of Theophanes is more detailed and, one would suppose, exact: "in this year Constantine the Pious undertook to destroy the idols and the temples, and in various places they disappeared; and their revenues were given to the churches of God."[37] Apart from the temples already mentioned there is no evidence for Constantine's destroying temples on a large scale or even closing them;[38] instead, the emperor Julian agreed with his friend the orator Libanius that Constantine's moves were directed against temple revenues.[39] Similarly, the anonymous author of *De rebus bellicis* speaks only of Constantine's confiscation of temple gold, silver, and precious stones.[40]

We begin to wonder if Constantine destroyed any temples at all, especially when we note that the troubles of the temple of

Asclepius at Aegae seem to have occurred under his son Constantius. The evidence on Aegae does not confirm Eusebius' notion that the temple was razed and thus "the celebrated marvel of the noble philosophers" (he means Apollonius of Tyana) was overthrown by a soldier.[41] Libanius says it was destroyed by Constantius.[42] Perhaps the year was 355, when a dedication at Epidaurus was made to the Asclepius of Aegae "in accordance with a dream."[43]

The other two temples were more natural targets for reform. Lucian had described the temple of Aphrodite at Aphaka in Lebanon as founded by a certain Cinyras, and the Christian Clement of Alexandria explained that he was famous for having introduced sacred prostitution.[44] According to Eusebius the prostitutes were castrated males wearing women's clothing.[45] Likewise the temple of Aphrodite at Heliopolis (Baalbek) in Phoenicia was well known for sacred prostitution. According to Eusebius, Constantine arranged for a large church to be built, manned by clerics including a bishop; he gave poor-relief funds as well. But nothing is said of the destruction of the temple, and Heliopolis was later a stronghold of paganism.

No matter who was attacking the temples, not everyone, either Christian or pagan, was in sympathy with the imperial program. Julian makes this clear in a letter describing his visit to Troy in the autumn of 355. The Christian bishop there became his guide on a tour of the closed temples. He volunteered to show Julian the temple of Athena of Ilios, opening the locked door for him. "As though he were producing evidence he showed me all the statues in perfect preservation." He also had the tact to refrain from making the sign of the cross or hissing at the demons. The bishop later claimed that he had merely pretended to be a Christian so that he could save the temples of the gods.[46] Presumably there were others like him. When Julian became emperor in 361 he relied to some extent on ex-Christians or crypto-pagans like the former bishop of Troy as he tried to restore paganism.

As part of his revival, he gave orders to open the temples, provide sacrifices for the altars, and restore the worship of the gods.[47] Naturally such a venture was expensive. The money was to be provided, basically, by restoring the revenues stolen by Constantine and Constantius and by transferring the administration of the government grain dole from Christian clerics to pagan priests (see Chapter VI). In addition, Julian took away the swollen exemptions enjoyed by clerics and assigned them to the decurions, whose status he was determined to improve.[48] As for the temple buildings, Libanius tells us that "people who had built houses for themselves from the stones of the temples began to pay money." He adds that "one could have seen pillars carried by boat or wagon back to the pillaged gods."[49] The emperor took a personal interest in restoration. On his way to Persia in 363 he was at Tarsus when he learned that Christians had robbed the temple of Asclepius at Aegae, using its columns to build a church. He ordered the columns returned at the Christians' expense.[50]

Somewhat earlier he enjoyed taking action against the Arian church at Edessa. The Arians there had attacked some of the few surviving Valentinian Gnostics and produced civic disorder. "Since by their most admirable law they are instructed to sell their possessions and give to the poor so that they may more easily enter the kingdom of the skies, in order to assist these persons we have ordered that all the money of the church of the Edessenes be given to the soldiers and that its properties be confiscated to the [imperial] privy purse."[51]

After Julian perished in the Persian campaign, the general Jovian succeeded to the throne for a short time. He restored the bread ration to the churches, though only at a third of its former rate. A famine, he claimed, prevented him from restoring it in full; but it never came back to the Constantinian rate.[52] After Valentinian and Valens obtained power in 364, they made every effort to take back the temple properties. "All property which was transferred from our patrimony and placed in possession of temples by the authority of the divine Julian, we order to be restored with full legal title to our privy purse."[53] Valentinian tolerated paganism, including the practice of divination (if not done "harmfully"), though he forbade nocturnal rites.[54] After Valens uncovered conspiracies in 371–372, often said to involve magic, sacrifices were generally prohibited.[55]

The parlous state of paganism became evident at Rome in 376, when Gratian, son of Valentinian and co-emperor with him, visited the city. The next year saw the urban prefect Gracchus, intent upon baptism, destroy a shrine of Mithras in proof of his devotion.[56] And at some undeterminable date after 364 the vestal virgin Claudia, lauded in an inscription still extant in the Forum, became a Christian; in consequence, all but two letters of her name were erased.[57] Devoted pagans multiplied dedications to the gods, but trouble was at hand.

As the eastern emperor Theodosius was finally achieving a settlement with the Goths of 382, the western emperor Gratian, deeply influenced by Ambrose of Milan, took a decisive step against paganism. He terminated state support of the temple rites and the priesthoods. In consequence, the Roman senate, still largely pagan, sent a delegation to the imperial court at Milan in an attempt to have the payments restored. Damasus, bishop of Rome, sent Ambrose a petition signed by Christian senators; they insisted that they would have nothing to do with the attempt to restore the revenues.[58] Ambrose kept the pagan delegation from presenting its case, and no change was made. Before his death in 383 Gratian also rejected the title pontifex maximus, held by emperors since Augustus.[59]

There were two kinds of problems involved in the whole controversy. First, the altar of Victory in the senate-house, already removed when the Christian emperor Constantius visited Rome in 357 but later restored,[60] was now definitely taken away. This action obviously had a severe effect on the morale of the pagan religious leaders, perhaps comparable to the rejection of prayers in the American public schools. Second, measures were taken against the rights and privileges of pagan priests. What Symmachus and Ambrose say about these measures is not in complete agreement, but it is clear enough that the state no longer was willing to pay for sacrifices and other rites or for the maintenance of the vestal virgins and other priestly colleges. Whatever exemptions priests possessed were abolished. Landed estates left to priestly colleges were to be confiscated.

Apart from the exemption question (see Chapter III), this legislation simply put pagans on the same footing as Christians. The state obviously did not pay directly for Christian rites or support Christian priests and, since 370, clerics and monks had not been allowed to receive legacies. Jerome noted in a letter that unlike clerics, "idol-priests, actors, charioteers, and prostitutes receive legacies." Since he was writing in 394 his news was a bit out of date.[61]

: When Symmachus protested to the emperor Valentinian II in 384, he insisted upon the damage imposed upon the vestal virgins, part of the Roman tradition from time immemorial. According to Livy financial support for the vestals went back to the legendary reign of Numa.[62] It was said that Augustus himself had assigned lands in Lanuvium for their maintenance.[63] During the third century the cult had been popular,[64] and an anonymous *Description of the whole World*, perhaps under Julian, says that the seven virgins were noble and illustrious; they performed the rites of the gods for the benefit of the state in accordance with the tradition of the ancients.[65]

Symmachus himself was what we should call a trustee of the vestals. In 380 we find him writing to his brother, then vicar of Africa, to help the treasurer of the vestals retain possession of an estate at Vacca (now Béja).[66] We do not know the dates of his most important letters related to the virgins. In any event they show that vestal morale was low. He had to write to one of them to ask about the rumor he had heard that she wanted to be released from her vows before the statutory period of twenty years. A second letter to her tells of his relief upon learning that the rumor was false. Another case was more serious. A priestess of Vesta at Alba confessed her guilty relationship with a certain Maximus; Maximus, too, admitted the offense. Symmachus wrote two letters to dilatory officials who obviously had no intention of punishing the couple. He had hoped that she would suffer the traditional penalty of being buried alive.[67] These letters reflect his complete failure to grasp the political situation, not to mention the religious one. One of the pontiffs investigating vestal morality three centuries earlier became so upset that he died in the senate chamber.[68] It is unlikely that even Symmachus would have suffered thus toward the end of the fourth century.

Ambrose, bishop of Milan, heard of Symmachus' address to the emperor. He obtained a copy and answered it in two letters, addressed to the emperor and read in the consistory. The emperor's advisers counseled inaction. An imperial constitution of December 23 warns against questioning imperial judgments, and Symmachus himself may have been banished from Milan.[69] In the east the rhetorician Libanius, devoted to paganism and to the memory of the emperor Julian, addressed the emperor Theodosius late in 386 to ask him to protect the temples against the attacks by mobs of monks. He claimed that although Constantine made use of "the sacred funds," he did not disturb any lawful rites. There was poverty in the temples, but apart from that everything went on as before. Constantine's successors, except for Julian, kept applying pressure, but even Theodosius himself had "neither closed the temples nor forbidden access to them," and had prohibited "neither fire nor incense, nor the other offerings of perfumes." But the monks were very destructive. They did not bear in mind the sacrifices in the temples at Rome, carried on for the good of all, or the rites for the rise of the Nile at the Serapeum in Alexandria. Even Constantius, hostile to paganism, protected the temples; and, after all, they were the property of the emperors. Erected with toil and time and skill and great expense, they contributed brilliance to the cities and were the principal adornment after the royal palaces. In the east a great temple once formed part of the Roman defense system, but it too had been smashed. If the emperor so wished, he could proscribe paganism altogether. Since he had not done so, he should protect the ancient monuments.[70]

The imperial answer to Libanius' religious arguments was given five years later. On February 24, 391, the urban prefect at Rome was ordered to terminate sacrifices and forbid access to the temples. On June 16 the same order was extended to Egypt.[71] In the west Roman senators hastened to visit Valentinian in Gaul, mistakenly believing that now they could recover the vanished pagan privileges. Ambrose did not even write a letter to the emperor. He knew that he would reject the new petition.[72]

Valentinian mysteriously died in 392 and his chief minister, Arbogast, promoted the nominally Christian courtier Eugenius, once a teacher of rhetoric, to the imperial throne in the west. Neither Ambrose nor Theodosius was willing to deal with him, and he therefore welcomed the usual delegation from the Roman senate. He restored the altar of Victory to the senate house but was unable to replace the temple lands and subsidies confiscated under Gratian. As a beginning, however, he authorized payments to the senators themselves; they were to hand the funds over to priests for the temples. Since this procedure was sure to arouse Christian ire, he also allotted funds to the Italian bishops for charitable purposes. When Eugenius entered Italy from Gaul, Ambrose withdrew to the south and wrote a letter reviewing the religious case and, at least implicitly, excommunicating the new emperor—who had not been recognized by Theodosius.[73] The pagan revival lasted no more than a year. In September 393 Theodosius defeated Eugenius and had him beheaded. He then informed the senate that "the treasury was burdened by the expense of the rites and the sacrifices, he wanted to abolish them, and furthermore military necessity called for additional funds." In spite of the counterclaim that "the ceremonies could not be rightly performed except at public expense," the pagan religion was now abolished.[74]

Theodosius' supreme commander in the west visited Rome not long thereafter. His wife observed a necklace on the image of the Great Mother in the Palatine temple and took it to wear herself. An old woman, the last of the vestals, rebuked her and, while being ejected from the temple, laid a curse upon her which, according to Zosimus, was later fulfilled.[75]

The temple revenues were handled in the treasury by a new bureaucratic agency dealing with the *fundi iuris templorum*.[76] (An obvious precedent had been given by the diversion of the Jewish temple tax after 70.) During the fifth and sixth centuries the Christians, now secure from pagan attempts at restoration, were able to appropriate many temple buildings or sites. Among the best-known examples are the Parthenon at Athens, the Pantheon at Rome, the temple of "Concord" at Agrigento, and the temple complex at Baalbek.

The Christian population was steadily growing. Persecutions by the state were no more. All that remained politically was to bind church and state together in matters of detail, for example by having the patriarch crown the emperor. Christians loyally paid taxes and the clergy loyally received exemptions.

Approved occupations, along with the duty to work, were assiduously promoted by state and church alike, and the state protected private property, especially that belonging to the church. Charitable relief was largely in Christian hands and private almsgiving reduced social tensions.

Any idea that paganism could be socially useful had been rejected by the Christian emperors when they stopped sacrifices, closed temples, and confiscated temple endowments. Church buildings took the place of temples; church endowments replaced temple lands and funds. Such is the history of the early Christian economy before its full flowering in the Middle Ages.

Notes

I. THE CHRISTIAN POPULATION OF THE ROMAN EMPIRE

1. Rom. 13:1; I Cor. 2:6; John 19:12, 15.
2. J. Crook, *Consilium Principis* (Cambridge, 1955), 148–190 (Prosopographical Index), nos. 10, 168, 169, 18.
3. Tacitus, *Ann.* XV 44 (cf. *Hist.* V 5–9); R. Syme, *Tacitus* (Oxford, 1958), II 467–469; 532–533.
4. Crook, *Consilium*, 53 and 179 (no. 263).
5. Pliny, *Ep.* X 96; A. N. Sherwin-White, *The Letters of Pliny* (Oxford, 1966), 692; cf. 705.
6. Suetonius, *Claud.* 25, 4. Suetonius too may have been an *amicus* of Trajan; cf. Crook, *Consilium*, 185 (no. 311a).
7. Suetonius, *Nero* 16, 2.
8. Lucian, *Alex.* 25; *De mort. Peregr.* 11–13.
9. Tertullian, *Apol.* 37, 4. 8; translated by J. E. B. Mayor, *Tertulliani Apologeticum* (Cambridge, 1917), 109.
10. Tertullian, *Ad Scap.* 4, 3–6; 5, 2. Cf. G. W. Clarke, "Two Christians in the Familia Caesaris," *HTR* 64 (1971), 121–124.
11. Theophilus, *Ad Autol.* II 32; Tertullian, *De anima* 30, 2–4, with the notes of J. H. Waszink, *Tertulliani De Anima* (Amsterdam, 1947), 370–375.
12. Eunomius in Nemesius, *De natura hominis* 17.
13. E. Hennecke and W. Schneemelcher (trans. R. McL. Wilson), *New Testament Apocrypha* I (Philadelphia, 1963), 491.

14. Origen, *C. Cels.* III 8.
15. G. E. M. de Ste Croix in *HTR* 47 (1954), 101–102.
16. H. J. Lawlor and J. E. L. Oulton, *Eusebius* (London, 1928), II 160; cf. O. Hirschfeld in *Sitzungsberichte der preuss. Akad. der Wiss.* (1895), 381–409 (followed by H. Quentin in *Analecta Bollandiana* 39 [1921], 113–138).
17. Modern guesses on martyrs, as by L. Hertling in *Gregorianum* 25 (1944), 103–129, seem too large generally.
18. Eusebius, *H.E.* VI 43, 11.
19. A. v. Gerkan in *Mitteilungen des Deutschen Archaeologischen Instituts, Roemische Abteilung* 55 (1940), 149–195; supplemented ibid. 58 (1943), 213–243; cf. J. E. Packer in *JRS* 57 (1967), 80–89.
20. Dio LXXVI 1, 1. ·
21. Cf. M. Durry, *Les cohortes prétoriennes* (Paris, 1938), 88.
22. On lists and the grain dole, see Chapter VI.
23. Eusebius, *H.E.* IV 23, 10.
24. Ibid., VII 11, 3.
25. Josephus, *Bell.* II 80 = *Ant.* XVII 300.
26. Julian, *Misopogon* 357D.
27. Chrysostom, *Act. hom.* 11, 3 (PG 60, 98). On Constantinople, cf. D. Jacoby in *Byzantion* 31 (1961), 81–110.
28. Chrysostom, *Matt. hom.* 85, 4 (PG 58, 762–763); cf. G. Downey, *A History of Antioch in Syria* (Princeton, 1961), 582–583.
29. Chrysostom, *I. Tim. hom.* 10, 3 (PG 62, 551).
30. L. von Hertling in *ZKTh* 58 (1934), 243–253; 62 (1938), 92–108; A. Lehmann in *Die Religion in Geschichte und Gegenwart* (ed. 3) I (1957), 1705–12.
31. Origen, *C. Cels.* VIII 69.
32. Zosimus I 26. 36. 46.
33. Eusebius, *H.E.* VII 21, 9.
34. J. C. Russell, *Late Ancient and Medieval Population* (*TAPS* 48, 3, Philadelphia, 1958), 78.
35. Ibid., 6.
36. Edition, introduction, and commentary by H. Grégoire and M. A. Kugener, *Marc le Diacre: Vie de Porphyre* (Paris, 1930).
37. Ibid., vii and c. 41.
38. A. H. M. Jones, *Cities of the Eastern Roman Provinces* (Oxford, 1937), 502–540, esp. 534; Ammianus Marcellinus XIV 8, 11.
39. Cf. Peter Brown, *Religion and Society in the Age of Saint Augustine* (New York, 1972), 161–182.

II. CHRISTIAN DEVOTION TO THE MONARCHY

1. Forms of states: Polybius VI 3–10; on Rome, VI 11–18.
2. Josephus, *Ant.* XVI 294. 355.
3. Ibid., XVIII 53 (cf. Tacitus, *Ann.* II 42).
4. Tacitus, *Ann.* II 42. 56.
5. Josephus, *Bell.* I 169–170 (contrast *Ant.* XIV 77–78).
6. Ibid., I 282–285. 387–393 (paralleled in *Ant.*).
7. Ibid., I 646. 664 (paralleled in *Ant.*).
8. Ibid., II 57. 62; *Ant.* XVII 272. 285.
9. Ibid., II 93–94; *Ant.* XVII 318.
10. Ibid., II 118; cf. *Ant.* XVII 355; XVIII 4.
11. *C. Ap.* II 164–165.
12. Ibid., 185.
13. Josephus himself was a priest (*C. Ap.* I 54; *Vit.* 1–2).
14. Mark 6:14. 26; Josephus, *Bell.* II 181–183; *Ant.* XVIII 240–255.
15. Dio Cassius LIX 24, 1.
16. Cf. Suetonius, *Jul.* 79, 2; Dio XLIV 10, 1 (11, 3); LIII 17, 2; LVI 43, 4.
17. I Pet. 2:13–14; I Tim. 2:2.
18. F. C. Grant in *The Sacral Kingship* (Supplements to Numen IV, Leiden, 1959), 443.
19. Cf. esp. Josephus, *Bell.* II 223 = *Ant.* XX 106; Mark 14:2.
20. Josephus, *C. Ap.* II 106: *nec vas aliquod portari licet in templum.*
21. On Zechariah and the New Testament cf. *JBL* 67 (1948), 297–303.
22. Josephus, *Ant.* XII 316–318.
23. Josephus, *Ant.* XIV 73.
24. Josephus, *Ant.* XV 380 (*Bell.* I 401 is probably wrong in mentioning the fifteenth year).
25. Ibid., 388.
26. Cf. Mark 8:15; 13:13; Luke 13:32.
27. Josephus, *Ant.* XVIII 116–119.
28. Mark 15:2ff. with parallels.
29. Josephus, *Ant.* XIV 9; XV 273. 409; XVI 291–311.
30. Josephus, *Bell.* I 648–655; II 5–13; *Ant.* XVII 149–163. 206–218.
31. Josephus, *Ant.* XVII 161–164.
32. Rom. 14:17; I Cor. 4:20; 6:9–10; Gal. 5:21; I Thess. 2:12.
33. I Cor. 15:23–28; cf. 15:50.

34. Did. 8; 2; cf. 9; 4; 10:5–6; II Clem. 5:5; 6:9; 9:6; 11:7; 12:1, 6.
35. Early good period: Eusebius, *H.E.* II 22, 8; 25, 1–26, 1; Lucan I 33–35 *(aeterna regna);* O. Murray in *Historia* 14 (1965), 41–61.
36. Philo, *Leg.* 22–113 (Caligula); 143–158. 309–318 (Augustus); 141–142 (Tiberius); cf. G. Delling in *Klio* 54 (1972), 171–192.
37. H. A. Wolfson, *Philo* (Cambridge, Mass., 1947), II, 384–387.
38. Ibid., 388; 420–425.
39. *The Roman Revolution* (Oxford, 1939), 9; Appian, *Bell. civ.* I 6; Lucan I 670.
40. Cf. P. Mikat, *Die Bedeutung der Begriffe Stasis und Aponoia für das Verständnis des 1. Clemensbriefes* (Cologne, 1969).
41. *Die Quellen der politischen Ethik des 1. Klemensbriefes* (Zurich, 1951).
42. *Enemies of the Roman Order* (Cambridge, Mass., 1966), 48; best examples in Pliny, *Ep.* X 58, 5–6.
43. *Ant.* IV 223.
44. Ibid., V 135. 179 185.
45. Ibid., VI 36. 85; XI 112; XX 229.
46. Ibid., VI 83. 268; XX 229.
47. Ibid., XI 111; XX 234.
48. *Bell.* I 169–170; *Ant.* XIV 91.
49. *Ant.* XX 250–251.
50. *Bell.* II 205. 208; *Ant.* XIX 187.
51. *Bell.* III 401; cf. Suetonius, *Vesp.* 5; Dio Cassius LXVI 1.
52. *Vita* 422–423.
53. *Ibid.*, 428–429.
54. *Ant.* XX 267; Suetonius, *Domit.* 10, 3.
55. Tacitus, *Agric.* 45.
56. I Clem. 5–6.
57. Irenaeus, *Adv. haer.* V 30, 3.
58. MacMullen, *op. cit.*, 252.
59. Dio, *Or.* III 45–47. The quotation must refer to monarchy, not aristocracy.
60. *Leg.* 149; *Conf.* 170.
61. Suetonius, *Gaius* 22, 1.
62. *Domit.* 12, 3.
63. Origen, *C. Cels.* VIII 68. See p. 35.
64. *An seni* 11, 790a.
65. Epictetus III 13, 9–10.
66. *The Ruling Power* (*TAPS* 43, 4, 1953), 942.
67. Ibid., 907 (*Or.* 26, 109).

68. *Apol.* I 3, 2–3.
69. *SHA* M. Antoninus 27, 7.
70. Justin, *Apol.* I 11, 1–12, 1.
71. Ibid., 18, 1.
72. Ibid., 29, 4.
73. Tatian, *Or.* 14, p. 15, 7–10 Schwartz.
74. Theophilus, *Ad Autol.* I 11.
75. Eusebius, *H.E.* IV 26, 7.
76. Herodian I 3, 4; for Nero, M. Aurelius, *Medit.* III 16, 1.
77. Athenagoras, *Leg.* 1, 2.
78. Ibid., 2, 1–2.
79. Ibid., 16, 2.
80. Ibid., 18, 2.
81. Ibid., 37.
82. Irenaeus, *Adv. haer.* III 3, 3; 10, 1; 16, 9; IV 38, 2; V 11, 1; 20, 2.
83. Cf. I John 5:19 (not quoted by Irenaeus).
84. Irenaeus, *Adv. haer.* V 24, 3; cf. Dio Chrysostom, *Or.* I 12–13.
85. Ibid., V 24, 2.
86. Ibid., IV 30, 3.
87. *Dan. comm.* IV 9, 2.
88. Ibid., II 12, 2–7 (Dan. 2:31–43); cf. *De antichr.* 27–28.
89. *Apol.* 25–33.
90. *Adv. Prax.* 3, 2–3.
91. Origen, *C. Cels.* VIII 68.
92. Ibid., VIII 65.
93. Ibid., I 1.
94. Eusebius, *H.E.* VI 42, 3–4.
95. Cyprian, *Ep.* 62, 4; M. Rachet, *Rome et les Berbères* (Brussels, 1970), 238–250.
96. Zosimus I 27–31; A. Alföldi in *Cambridge Ancient History* XII (1939), 146–148.
97. Canonical Epistle in M. J. Routh, *Reliquiae Sacrae* (ed. 2, Oxford, 1846), 253–264.
98. Eusebius, *H.E.* VII 23.
99. Eusebius, *Praep. ev.* XIV 25, 15.
100. Eusebius, *H.E.* VII 11, 18.
101. Eusebius, *Praep. ev.* I 4, 2–4 (trans. E. H. Gifford); cf. R. Farina, *L'impero e l'imperatore cristiano in Eusebio di Caesarea* (Zurich, 1966), 142.
102. Eusebius, *Dem. ev.* VII 2, 22; cf. *Laus Constantini* 3, 6; 16, 2–3;

Theoph. 3; E. Peterson, *Theologische Traktate* (Munich, 1951), 86–93.

103. Eusebius, *Mart. Pal.* 1, 1.

104. Ibid., 3, 5–7; cf. *H.E.* VIII 13, 10–11. 18.

105. Tyrants: *H.E.* VIII 13, 15–14, 18; IX 1, 1–11, 7; *Mart. Pal.* 4, 8; 6, 1. 6; 8, 5; allies of God: IX 9, 1; 11, 9.

106. Artemidorus, *Oneir.* II 34 (pp. 157–158 Pack).

107. *Apol. de fuga* 26 (p. 86 Opitz); *Apol. ad Constant.* 1. 35.

108. Lucifer of Cagliari (PL 13, 767–1008; CSEL 14); Hilary of Poitiers (PL 10, 557–607; CSEL 65, 181–187. 197–205. 227–228); Liberius of Rome (PG 82, 1033; GCS Theodoret, 131–136).

109. W. Nestle in *Klio* 21 (1927), 330–360; W. L. Knox in *JTS* 39 (1938), 243–246; other references in H. Lietzmann, *An die Korinther I–II* (ed. 4; Tübingen, 1949), 62; add Plato, *Rep.* V 462c–d. J. N. Sevenster (*Paul and Seneca* [Leiden, 1961], 170–173) inconclusively stresses differences.

110. Xenophon, *Mem.* II 3, 18f.

111. Livy II 32; cf. Dion. Hal. VI 86; Plutarch, *Coriolanus* 6, 3; etc.

112. Cicero, *De off.* III 22; I 126–127.

113. Epictetus II 10, 4.

114. Seneca, *De ira* II 31, 7.

115. *De clem.* I 5, 1; II 2, 1.

116. Philo, *Spec.* III 131.

117. *Virt.* 103.

118. Josephus, *Bell.* I 507; IV 406.

119. *The Origin of I Corinthians* (New York, 1965), 190–193.

120. I Clem. 37.

121. I Clem. 40–44.

122. Josephus, *Ant.* XIV 235; Acts 18:14–15; 23:29; 25:19.

123. II Cor. 11:24; cf. Acts 5:40.

124. "The Trial of Jesus in the Light of History," *Judaism* 20 (1971), 37–42.

125. Acts 7:58; John 8:59; 10:31 (11:8); cf. II Cor. 11:24.

126. John 8:3–5; E. R. Goodenough, *The Jurisprudence of the Jewish Courts in Egypt* (New Haven, 1929), 253 (examples).

127. Origen, *Rom. comm.* VI 7 (PG 14, 1073A); *C. Cels.* VII 26; *Didasc. apost.*, pp. 238–239 Connolly.

128. Origen, *Ep ad Africanum* 14 (PG 11, 84A).

129. *Sanh.* VII 4 (p. 391 Danby); Philo, *Spec.* III 20.

130. H. Danby, *The Mishnah* (Oxford, 1933), 408 n. 4.
131. I Cor. 5:5; cf. 11:30.
132. I Cor. 6:4. On the whole problem cf. E. Dinkler, "Zur Problem der Ethik bei Paulus," *ZThK* 49 (1952), 167–200. For courts at Qumran cf. M. Belcor, "The Courts of the Church of Corinth," *Paul and Qumran*, ed. J. Murphy-O'Connor (Chicago, 1968), 69–84.
133. I Thess. 5:12; I Cor. 16:15–16.
134. Deut. 19:15; cf. Matt. 18:16.
135. E. Käsemann, *New Testament Questions of Today* (Philadelphia, 1969), 66–81.
136. Ignatius, *Polyc.* 6, 1.
137. *Philad.* 7, 1.
138. Cf. F. Steinwenter in *RAC* I (1950), 915–917; K. M. Girardet, in *Historia* 23 (1974), 98–127.
139. E. Hatch, *The Organization of the Early Christian Churches* (ed. 3; London, 1888), 26–55; W. Telfer, *The Office of a Bishop* (London, 1962), 158–186 ("The Bishop as Trustee").
140. Cf. P. Batiffol, "Le règlement des premiers conciles africains et le règlement du sénat romain," *Bulletin d'ancienne littérature et d'archéologie chrétiennes* 3 (1913), 3–19; id., *Études de liturgie et d'archéologie chrétienne* (Paris, 1919), 84–153.
141. Cf. E. Ferguson in *Church History* 43 (1974), 26–33.
142. Eusebius, *H.E.* VI 29, 3–4.
143. Ammianus Marcellinus XXVII 3, 12–13.

III. TAXATION AND EXEMPTION

1. *The Early Church and the World* (Edinburgh, 1925), 99f.
2. *The Greek City* (Oxford, 1940), 227; he refers to Strabo, 559–560, 567, 577. Later references by F. Millar in *JRS* 61 (1971), 14f.
3. Amounts: Josphus, *Bell.* II 95–97; *Ant.* XVII 318–320; complaints: *Bell.* II 4; *Ant.* XVII 204–205.
4. Josephus, *Ant.* XIV 202f.
5. Appian, *Syr.* VIII 50; cf. F. M. Heichelheim, *ESAR* IV, 235.
6. Josephus, *Bell.* II 118; *Ant.* XVIII 4.
7. Philo, *Spec. leg.* II 113.
8. Josephus, *Bell.* II 433–448; VII 252–406.
9. Suetonius, *Tib.* 32, 2; Tacitus, *Ann.* II 42.

10. Cf. H. Loewe, *Render unto Caesar* (Cambridge, 1940).
11. Cf. Tertullian, *De cor.* 12, 4 and elsewhere.
12. Luke 2:1–5; 23:1–4; Acts 5: 37–38.
13. Matt. 21:31–32; Luke 18:10–13; 19:1–10. Cf. Mark 2:15–16; Matt. 9:10–11; 11:19; Luke 5:30; 7:34; 15:1. See Chapter IV, p. 83.
14. Josephus, *Ant.* XVIII 90; XIX 299 (cf. 326).
15. Ibid., XIX 352.
16. *Bell.* II 273.
17. Ibid., 403–405 (cf. 293).
18. Rom. 13:1–7. According to Prov. 22:8 "the borrower is the slave of the lender," but nothing is said of taxes.
19. Irenaeus, *Adv. haer.* V 24, 1.
20. Hippolytus, *Ref.* V 8, 28.
21. Ibid., citing Matt. 21:31.
22. Philo, *Spec. leg.* I 76–78.
23. K. F.. Nickle, *The Collection* (Naperville, Ill., 1966), 74–84.
24. Philo, *Leg.* 157. 317. 319.
25. Josephus, *C. Ap.* II 77 (cf. *Bell.* II 197).
26. *Bell.* II 409 (cf. 411–417); C. Roth in *HTR* 53 (1960), 93–97.
27. *Bell.* VI 282; cf. II Macc. 3:6–40; IV Macc. 4:2–14.
28. *Ant.* XIV 72. 107 (cf. 110–113).
29. *Bell.* II 50; *Ant.* XVIII 264.
30. *Bell.* II 175; *Ant.* XVIII 60.
31. *Bell.* VI 387–391.
32. *Bell.* VI 317.
33. *Bell.* VI 249–270; VII 433–436.
34. *Bell.* VII 218; cf. Dio LXVI 7, 2. It was still collected in the time of Origen; cf. *Ep. ad Africanum* 14 (PG 11, 81B).
35. *New Testament Studies* 11 (1964–1965), 60–71.
36. Eusebius, *H.E.* III 20, 2.
37. Suetonius, *Domit.* 12, 2.
38. Justin, *Apol.* I 17, 1–2; Tatian, *Or.* 4 (p. 4, 23f. Schwartz); Theophilus, *Ad Autol.* III 14.
39. Tertullian, *Apol.* 42, 8–9.
40. *Acta Scillit.* 6 (p. 86 Musurillo).
41. Justin, *Apol.* I 27, 1–2; cf. Suetonius, *Gaius* 40; H. Herter in *Jahrbuch für Antike und Christentum* 3 (1960), 70–111 (on regulation and taxes, 106–109).
42. Tertullian, *De fuga* 13, 3.

43. W. Cureton, *Spicilegium Syriacum* (London, 1855), 43; cf. *Clem. Hom.* X 22, 3.

44. Theophilus, *Ad Autol.* I 10; Tertullian, *Ad nat.* I 10, 22; *Apol.* 13, 5.

45. T. C. Skeat, *Papyri from Panopolis* (Dublin, 1964), xxvii (P. Panop. 2). For earlier events cf. S. Bolin, *State and Currency in the Roman Empire to 300* A.D. (Stockholm, [1958]).

46. K. T. Erim, J. Reynolds, M. Crawford in *JRS* 61 (1971), 171–177.

47. Lauffer, *Diokletians Preisedikt* (Berlin, 1971).

48. Cf. A. C. Johnson and L. C. West, *Byzantine Egypt: Economic Studies* (Princeton, 1949), 249.

49. Cf. A. C. Johnson, *ESAR* II, 466, cites Jerome: *artaba* = 3⅓ Roman measures.

50. P. Oxy. XXXVI 2798; P. Cair. Isid. 11, 49–50; cf. Lauffer, *op. cit.*, 57–60; also R. MacMullen in *Aegyptus* 41 (1961), 3–5; J. Bingen in *Atti dell' XI Congresso Internazionale di Papirologia* (Milan, 1966) 369–378.

51. Arnobius *Adv. nat.* IV 36.

52. Ibid., I 3. 13. 14. 16; translated by G. E. McCracken, *Arnobius of Sicca* (Westminster, Md., 1949).

53. Lactantius, *De mort. persec.* 7.

54. Ibid., 23. 21.

55. Eusebius, *H.E.* VII 14, 10; X 8, 12; Lactantius, *De mort. persec.* 23, 2; 31, 2.

56. Cf. Zosimus II 38.

57. *Paneg.* IX 3, 5; cf. 16, 1.

58. Julian, *Or.* I, 8B (I, 20 Wright).

59. Eusebius, *Vit. Const.* IV 2–3; cf. Johnson and West, *Byzantine Egypt*, 233.

60. Jones, *Later Roman Empire*, 110.

61. *Paneg.* X 38, 5.

62. C. Poisnel in *École Française de Rome, Mélanges d'archéologie et d'histoire* 3 (1883), 312–327.

63. Julian, *Caes.* 335B (11, 410 Wright).

64. Julian, *Or.* I, 44B (I, 112 Wright).

65. *A Roman Reformer and Inventor* (Oxford, 1952), 110–112.

66. R. I. Frank in *AJP* 93 (1972), 69–86.

67. Salvian, *De gubern. Dei* V 17–45 (pp. 322–346 Garrigue).

68. SIG³ 814 = ILS 8794; Pausanias VII 17, 4.

69. FIRA I² 56 = Wilcken, *Chrest.* 462.
70. FIRA I² 73; Dio LIII 30.
71. Wilcken, *Chrest.* 395.
72. *Dig.* XXVII 1, 6, 2; cf. V. Nutton in *JRS* 61 (1971), 52–63. Cf. also G. W. Bowersock, *Greek Sophists in the Roman Empire* (Oxford, 1969), 30–42; 66.
73. Diodorus I 73, 2–5; on the struggles cf. M. Rostovtzeff, *Social and Economic History of the Hellenistic World* (Oxford, 1941), 884f., 899–903.
74. Josephus, *Ant.* XV 90; *C. Ap.* II 58; Dio LI 5, 5; 17, 6.
75. Strabo XIII 595; cf. *Res gestae divi Augusti* 24, with the notes of H. Volkmann (ed. 2; Berlin, 1964), 42.
76. Dio LI 17, 6.
77. BGU IV 1200.
78. *Social and Economic History of the Roman Empire* (ed. 2; Oxford 1957), 672–673.
79. BGU IV 1198 (5/4 B.C.); 1199 (4 B.C.).
80. BGU IV 1200.
81. OGIS 664.
82. Wilcken, *Chrest.* 84 = BGU I 176.
83. P. Aberdeen 16.
84. Wessely, *Karanis,* 56 and 66 (P. Rainer 107).
85. P. Yale 349 = SB 9328.
86. P. Oxy XXVI 2782.
87. FIRA I² 81 = SB 6944.
88. D. Bonneau, *La crue du Nil* (Paris, 1964).
89. Eusebius, *Vit. Const.* IV 25, 2–3.
90. P. Yale 902 + 906 = SB 9320.
91. BGU I 194 = Wilcken, *Chrest.* 84.
92. P. Lond. II, pp 113–114 = Wilcken, *Chrest.* 102.
93. P. Lund IV 1 = SB 9340.
94. Cf. N. Lewis in *Actes du X Congrès International de Papyrologues* (Warsaw, 1964), 78–79.
95. Tertullian, *Ad. nat.* I 9, 3; *Apol.* 40, 2.
96. W. Otto, *Priester und Tempel in hellenistischen Ägypten* II (Berlin–Leipzig, 1908), 247–251; A. H. M. Jones, *The Greek City* (Oxford, 1940), 228; G. Wissowa, *Religion und Kultus der Römer* (ed. 2; Munich, 1912), 500.
97. OGIS 569; a better text in CIL III 12132.
98. Eusebius, *H.E.* IX 7, 3–14.

99. Ibid., VIII 17, 9–10; Lactantius, *De mort. persec.* 34, 4–5.

100. Ibid., X 5, 4; Lactantius, *De mort. persec.*, 48, 2.

101. Eusebius, *H.E.* X 7; *Cod. Theod.* XVI 2, 2; cf. J. Gaudemet, *La formation du droit séculier et du droit de l'église aux ive et ve siècles* (Paris, 1957), 62 n. 3.

102. For example, Strabo XVII, 794; OGIS 714, 4; P. Oxy. XLI 2978.

103. P. Oxy. XXVII 2476.

104. Mitteis, *Chrest.* 381.

105. IG XIV 956, cited in B. Laum, *Stiftungen* II, no. 213.

106. *JTS* 23 (1972), 132–135.

107. *Cod. Theod.* XVI 2, 3.

108. Ibid., XVI 2, 6.

109. P. Oxy. XXII 2344.

110. P. Oxy. X 1265.

111. *Cod. Theod.* XVI 2, 12.

112. Ibid., XVI 10, 6 and 4.

113. Ibid., XVI 2, 14. Trajan gave the sophist Polemo a travel pass by land and sea; Hadrian extended the privilege to all his descendants (Philostratus, *Vit. soph.* 532–533). Note also that privileges of Aaronic priests are extended to their sons and daughters (Num. 18:11–19.)

114. Ibid., XVI 2, 15; cf. Jones, *The Greek City*, 1373f. n. 65.

115. Epiphanius, *Haer.* 76, 1, 4–6.

116. Ammianus Marcellinus XXII 11, 4–6.

117. *Cod. Theod.* XII 1, 50 = 1, 4.

118. Ammianus Marcellinus XXII 9, 12; XXV 4, 21.

119. Julian, *Ep.* 114 Bidez-Cumont = *Ep.* 41 Wright (August 1, 362).

120. On Alexandria, for example: G. R. Monks in *Speculum* 28 (1953), 349–62; outside the city: E. Wipszycka, *Les ressources et les activités économiques des églises en Egypte du IVe au VIIIe siècles* (Papyrologica Bruxellensia 10, 1972).

121. *Cod. Theod.* XIII 4, 2. In addition Constantine exempted Jewish patriarchs and elders from compulsory public services (Cod. Theod. XVI 8, 2–4), while Theodosius I tried to protect synagogues from over zealous Christians (*ibid.*, XVI 8, 9).

IV. WORK AND OCCUPATIONS

1. Tacitus, *Hist.* V 4.

2. Josephus, *C. Ap.* II 174. 234. 291.

3. *Pirke Aboth* I 10; II 2 (p. 447 Danby).

4. Tertullian, *Apol.* 42, 1.

5. On Jesus cf. Justin, *Dial.* 88, 8; Celsus in Origen, *C. Cels.* VI 34. For Paul's occupation, Origen, *Rom. comm.* X 18 (PG 14, 1279A); Chrysostom in J. Cramer, *Catenae Graecorum Patrum* III (Oxford, 1844), 302, 18; Theodoret (PG 83, 1056C).

6. A. N. Sherwin-White, *Roman Society and Roman Law in the New Testament* (Oxford, 1963), 139–142.

7. Matt. 20:36; Luke 16:3.

8. Acts 20:34–36; H. Conzelmann, *Die Apostelgeschichte* (Tübingen 1963), 119.

9. Epiphanius, *Haer.* XXVI 11, 1–2; cf. Clement, *Exc. ex Theod.* 49, 1; Irenaeus, *Adv. haer.* I 5, 3; Hippolytus, *Ref.* VI 33; 34, 8; Heracleon in Origen, *Ioh. comm.* XIII 50.

10. Matt. 6:25–33; Luke 12:22–31. The kinds of texts involved are those discussed by G. Theissen, "Wanderradikalismus," *Zeitschrift für Theologie und Kirche* 70 (1973), 245–271. On the other hand, the parables of Jesus often portray and approve of men who work hard and gain rewards.

11. A. Fridrichsen, "Zum Stil des paulinischen Peristasenkatalogs 2 Cor. 11 23ff.," *Symbolae Osloenses* 7 (1928), 25–29; "Peristasen katalog und Res Gestae," ibid., 8 (1929), 78–82; "Zum Stil der Peristasenkatalogs," *Kungl. Humanistika Vetenscaps-Samfundet i Uppsala Arsbok 1943*, 31–34. With these discussions one should place Philippians 1:21 and the Greek parallels cited by D. W. Palmer, "'To Die Is Gain,'" *Novum Testamentum* 17 (1975), 203–218, noting with him that Paul rejects the gain for the sake of the community.

12. A. Deissmann, *Light from the Ancient East* (ed. 4; New York, 1927), 314.

13. I Thess. 3:5; I Cor. 15:58.

14. I Cor. 3:8; 9:17–18; II Cor. 11:8 (cf. I Cor. 9:7); Rom. 4:4.

15. I Cor. 3:5, 10; Aristotle, *Met.* I 1, 11–12 (981a 24ff.)

16. I Cor. 4:1–2; cf. J. Reumann in *JBL* 77 (1958), 339–349.

17. Plato, *Rep.* IX 590 C; translated by Y. Simon, *Work,* 145.

18. SVF I 264; Plut. *Mor.* 1034b; Clement, *Str.* V 76, 1; Origen *C. Cels.* I 5.

19. SVF I 611 (via Musonius, fr. 1, p. 34, 22–30 Lutz).

20. Musonius, fr. 3, p. 42, 28–29 (cf. 42, 6); fr. 4, p. 46, 27–28 cf. fr.

11; Dio, *Or.* VII 125; Stobaeus, *Flor.* 85, 21 = Hierocles, pp. 62–63 von Arnim; Epictetus, *Diss.* III 12, 7; 15, 11.

21. M. Aurelius, *Med.* I 5.
22. Musonius, fr. 11, p. 82, 12–15; Phil. 4:11; also the refusal of "rights" in I Cor. 9.
23. Maximus of Tyre, *Or.* XV–XVI Hobein; Heracles, XV 6e–f, p. 190.
24. E. Burck in *Gymnasium* 58 (1951), 161–183 (*labor*, 162–167).
25. Plin. *Paneg.* 24, 2; cf. Dio Chrysostom, *Or.* I 21; III 83.
26. *Roman Social Relations* (New Haven, 1974), 43–44. The comment, "not a word about hard work" (p. 30), is wrong.
27. Col. 3:22–24; I Tim. 6:2; I Clem. 34:1.
28. Ignatius, *Pol.* 1, 3.
29. Barn. 10:4; Did. 12:3–5.
30. Justin, *Apol.* II 10, 8; Athenagoras, *Leg.* 11, 4; cf. Hegesippus in Eusebius, *H.E.* III 20, 2–3.
31. Justin, *Dial.* 3, 3.
32. Justin, *Apol.* I 55, 3; 59, 1.
33. Clement, *Paed.* II 78, 2.
34. *Protr.* 98, 1; *Str.* I 26, 3; VII 28, 4.
35. *Str.* VI 155, 3; cf. Plutarch, *Nicias* 2.
36. Tertullian, *Apol.* 42; see below.
37. *Didasc.*, p. 129 Connolly; citations from Proverbs 6:6–11, Sir. 11:3; 2 Thess. 3:10; ibid., p. 193.
38. *Apost. Const.* II 63.
39. Chrysostom, *II Thess. hom.* 5, 2 (PG 62, 495).
40. Suetonius, *Vesp.* 18.
41. Vatican, Gregorian Profane Museum, Inv. 9998 (*Guide*, 1973, p. 124).
42. Josephus, *Ant.* XX 219–222.
43. Ibid., 220.
44. *The Attitude Towards Labor in Early Christianity and Ancient Culture* (Washington, 1945), 229f.
45. Epiphanius, *Haer.* LXXX 4, 1–5. Theodoret (*H.E.* IV 11, 1) adds that they "give themselves up to sleep and call their dream-fantasies prophecies." This account is hardly complete; cf. J. Gribomont in *TU* 64 (1957), 400–415.
46. Minucius Felix, *Oct.* 31, 6; 8, 4. On *plebs sordida* cf. Z. Yavetz in *Athenaeum* 43 (1965), 295–311.

47. *Gal. comm.* 3 (PL 26, 428A).
48. Seneca, *Ad Helv.* 12, 1–2; cf. R. MacMullen, *Roman Social Relations* (New Haven, 1974), 87.
49. Pliny, *N.H.* IX 117–118.
50. MacMullen, *Roman Social Relations*, 138–141; cf. E. H. Brewster, *Roman Craftsmen and Tradesmen of the Early Empire* (1917; reprinted New York, 1972).
51. Cicero, *De off.* I 150.
52. Seneca, *Ep.* 88, 21–23.
53. Cicero, *De off.* I 151.
54. *ZNW* 30 (1931), 293–300: *Kidd.* IV 14; b. *Kidd.* 82^a; b. *Sanh.* 25^b.
55. *Kiddushin* IV 14, p. 329 Danby.
56. MacMullen (*Roman Social Relations,* 140) cites Cicero, *Ad fam.* X 18, 3; Juvenal VIII 148.
57. Dio Chrysostom, *Or.* X 18.
58. Tertullian, *De praescr.* 30, 1.
59. Origen, *C. Cels.* III 55. Josephus (*Ant.* XVIII 314) especially points out that among Babylonian Jews weaving was not an unsuitable occupation for men. See also Herodotus II 35.
60. *Sanhedrin* III 3, p. 385 Danby.
61. Apollonius in Eusebius, *H.E.* V 18, 11.
62. Cf. Lamer in *RE* XIII (1926), 1910–1912. Trajan was not a gambler, according to Pliny, *Paneg.* 82, 9.
63. Origen, *Ioh. comm.* X 33, p. 207, 16–17 Preuschen.
64. A. von Harnack, *Der pseudocyprianische Tractat De aleatoribus (TU* V 1, 1888), 38–42.
65. Cicero, *Ad Atticum* V 21; VI 1.
66. Cf. R. P. Maloney in *Traditio* 27 (1971), 79–109.
67. Matt. 25:27; Luke 19:23; *Apoc. Petri* 16 (31).
68. R. P. Maloney in *VC* 27 (1973), 241–265. But Chrysostom knows Christians who take usury: *Matt. hom.* 56, 5 (PG 58, 556).
69. Musonius, fr. 11, p. 82, 5 Lutz; Dio, *Or.* VII 103.
70. Cf. H. C. Youtie in *ZPE* 1 (1967), 1–20; J. Donahue in *Catholic Biblical Quarterly* 33 (1971), 39–61.
71. Dio Chrysostom, *Or.* XIV 14; Artemidorus, *Onir.* IV 42, p. 270 Pack; Julian, *Adv. Galil.* 238E.
72. Origen, *C. Cels.* I 62.
73. Philostratus, *Vit. Apollon.* VIII 7, 11 (on pettiness cf. Onasander, *Strat.* I 20).

74. Cicero, *De off.* I 150. W. Miller (Loeb) translated *ludus talarius* as *corps de ballet*, but his footnote was more accurate.

75. Clement, *Paed.* III 26, 2. The same attitude is expressed by Posidonius in Athenaeus VI 273a–275b.

76. Chrysostom, *Matt. hom.* 58, 3 (PG 58, 570 [C]).

77. Socrates, *H.E.* VI 3; Palladius, *Dial.* 5 (PG 47, 18 [B]).

78. Clement, *Paed.* III 27, 1; *Str.* I 26, 3.

79. C. Andresen in *ZKG* 72 (1961), 217–262.

80. Tertullian, *De spect.* 26.

81. Cf. H. Jürgens, *Pompa Diaboli* (Stuttgart, 1972).

82. Cyprian, *Ep.* 2; cf. the synod of Elvira, Canon 62; Arles, 5.

83. *Didascalia*, p. 158 Connolly (pp. 224–226 Funk).

84. Tertullian, *De fuga* 13, 3, had already denounced *beneficiarii* and *curiosi;* cf. G. Lopuszanski in *L'antiquité classique* 20 (1951), 5–46.

85. Cf. H. Herter in *Jahrbuch für Antike und Christentum* 3 (1960), 70–111. Note Dio Chrysostom, *Or.* VII 133ff.

86. Seneca, *Ep.* 88, 3–8. 18.

87. Juvenal III 76–78.

88. Dio, *Or.* VII 114.

89. *Apost. trad.* 9–25; *Const. Apost.* VIII 32.

90. *Cod. Theod.* XIII 4, 2.

91. Theodoret, *Graec. aff. cur.* V (PG 83, 948D).

92. Origen, *C. Cels.* III 55–58.

93. Pliny, *Ep.* X 96, 9.

94. Clement, *Quis dives* 17, 4; *Str.* IV 25, 4.

95. Origen, *C. Cels.* VI 16.

96. Chrysostom, *Matt. hom.* 35, 3 (PG 57, 409B).

97. Eusebius, *Mart. Pal.* 11, 1f (I, 380 Lawlor-Oulton).

98. Chrysostom, *Matt. hom.* 66, 3 (PG 58, 630); see chapter V.

99. Aristotle, *Pol.* IV 10, 4, 1296b.

100. Jones, *Later Roman Empire*, 445.

101. Gregory, *Ep.* VII 26 (PL 77, 881C).

102. Jones, *Later Roman Empire*, 554.

103. E.g., Matt. 8:9; 10:24; 24:45–51; 25:14–30; John 13:16; 15:15.

104. Philo, *Quod omn. prob. lib. sit* 79; cf. Josephus *Ant.* XVIII 21.

105. Col. 3:22–4:1; Eph. 6:5–9; I Tim. 6:1–2; Tit. 2:9–10; I Pet. 2:18–25.

106. Seneca, *Ep.* 94, 1.

107. Did. 4:10–11; Barn. 19:7.

108. Ignatius, *Polyc.* 4, 3.
109. Origen, *Jer. hom.* X 3.
110. Euripides, *Alexandros,* in Stobaeus, *Flor.* 62, 14; Menander, Frag. 796 (F. Poulsen, *Catalogue of Ancient Sculpture in the Ny Carlsberg Glyptotek* [Copenhagen, 1951], 288).
111. Justin, *Apol.* II 12, 4.
112. Eusebius, *H.E.* V 1, 14.
113. Athenagoras, *Leg.* 35, 3.
114. C. J. Cadoux, *The Early Church and the World* (Edinburgh, 1925), 454–455; Origen, *Cels.* V 43.
115. Tertullian, *Ad nat.* I 7, 15; *Apol.* 7, 3.
116. *Apol.* 27, 7.
117. *De cult. fem.* I 5, 1.
118. Diod. Sic. III 12–13; V 38, 1; Strabo XII 3, 40 (562); Pliny, *N.H.* XXXIII 98. 122; cf. H. Kalex, "Uber die Arbeitsbedingungen und den Gesundheitszustand der Arbeiter . . . ," *Sozialökonomische Verhältnisse im alten Orient und im klassischen Altertum,* edited by R. Günther and G. Schrot (Berlin, 1961). 168–179.
119. Jerome, *Ep.* 38, 5; 54, 5; 107, 8 (a cross-reference in 107, 10 to 54, 9–10).
120. Elvira, Can. 5.
121. Gaius, *Inst.* I 53; *Cod. Theod.* IX 12, 1–2.
122. Gangra, Can. 3.
123. *Acta Thomae* 82–83, pp. 198–199 Bonnet (trans. Wilson).
124. Seneca, *Ep.* 47, 5.
125. *Mart. Pionii* 9, 3–4.
126. See Augustine, *Ep.* 108, 18 (PL 33, 416); 185, 15 (799).
127. Symmachus, *Ep.* II 46 (written in 393); on his attitude cf. J. A. McGeachy, Jr., *Quintus Aurelius Symmachus* (Chicago, 1942), 92–94.
128. Gregory of Nyssa, *Res. orat.* III (PG 46, 657C–D)
129. Jerome, *Isa. comm.* XVI 68 (PL 24, 587A–B).
130. Theodore of Mopsuestia, *Phil. comm.,* arg. (II, 262–263 Swete).
131. Theodoret, *I Cor. comm.* (PG 82, 280A).
132. Chrysostom, *Phil. hom.* 3, 2 (PG 62, 718); for the proverb cf. Ignatius, *Rom.* 4, 1.
133. *Const. Apost.* VIII 33, 2–9.
134. Chrysostom, *Matt. hom.* 63, 4 (PG 58, 608).
135. Chrysostom, *I Cor. hom.* 40, 5 (PG 61, 353).
136. Argumentum, ad Philem. (PG 62, 704).

137. *De Anna* 5, 3 (PG 54, 673).
138. *In inscr. altaris* 2 (PG 51, 69); this and the preceding passage cited by L. Daloz, *Le travail selon saint Jean Chrysostome* (Paris, 1959), 105. 36.
139. In general cf. Daloz, *Travail,* 76–88 ("Le devoir du travail"); also Geoghegan, op. cit., 187–193.

V. PRIVATE PROPERTY

1. Origen, *Matt. com.* XV 14.
2. H. J. Cadbury, *The Making of Luke-Acts* (New York, 1927), 60–63. This was one of the few points at which Cadbury agreed with Bruce Barton, *The Man Nobody Knows* (New York, 1926).
3. Acts 5:4; cf. H. Conzelmann, *Die Apostelgeschichte* (Tübingen, 1963), 39.
4. *Manual of Discipline* (1 QS) VI 24f.; Conzelmann, *loc. cit.*
5. References in L. Deubner, *Iamblichi De vita Pythagorica liber* (Leipzig, 1937), 17.
6. Diodorus Siculus X 3,5.
7. Hippolytus, *Ref.* I 2, 16–17; Iamblichus, *De vit. Pyth.* 80–81.
8. Josephus, *Antiq.* XV 371.
9. Damascus Rule, XIV; *Manual of Discipline,* VI.
10. Josephus, *Bell.* II 124.
11. Eusebius, *Hist. eccl.* II 17.
12. Philo, *Vit. cont.* 13–17.
13. *De morte Peregr.* 13.
14. *Apol.* 39, 11.
15. I Cor. 16:1–4; II Cor. 8–9; Rom. 15:25–28. Cf. K. F. Nickle, *The Collection* (Naperville, Ill., 1966).
16. Cf. I Cor. 9:11.
17. Cf. W. Straub, *Die Bildersprache des Apostels Paulus* (Tübingen, 1937).
18. Diogenes Laertius VI 37. 72; cf. Seneca, *De benef.* VII 4, 1.
19. Philo, *Vit. Mos.* I 156–159; cf. *Sobr.* 56–57 (SVF III 603).
20. Lucian, *Hermotimus* 81 ad fin.
21. On this, cf. E. Peterson, "Der Gottesfreund," *ZKG* 42 (1923), 161–193. "Wisdom is rather God's friend than his slave," says Philo (*Sobr.* 55); he then describes Abraham, God's friend, as the archetypal wise man.

22. *Protr.* 122, 3.
23. See my "Chains of Being in Early Christianity" in *Myths and Symbols: Studies in Honor of Mircea Eliade,* edited by J. M. Kitagawa and C. Long (Chicago, 1969), 279–289.
24. Ignatius, *Polyc.* 4:3 (cf. I Cor. 7:23).
25. Philo, *Vit. cont.* 70 (cf. 17).
26. E.g., Justin, *Apol.* I 26, 7.
27. Epictetus, Frag. 15 (Stobaeus, *Ecl.* III 6, 58).
28. Arrian, *Diss.* II 4, 8–11.
29. Life and death: Clement, *Str.* III 5, 2–3. Book: III 6, 1–9, 3.
30. Plato, *Def.* 411e.
31. SVF III 340–348.
32. *Quaest. conviv.* 719b–c.
33. Eyes in common, Plato, *Leg.* 739c. Even Constantine could use such language: "God ... extended the common light to all" (Eusebius, *Vit. Const.* II 71, 4).
34. Compare what Plato says of private ownership in the *Republic* (V 458c–d); also on "mine" and "not mine" (462c); cf. Iamblichus, *Vit. pyth.* 167.
35. According to others, implanted in females too; Musonius Rufus, fr. 14, p. 92, 11 Lutz; Galen, *De usu partium* XIV 2, p. 286, 3–4 Helmreich.
36. Text: H. Chadwick, *The Sentences of Sextus* (Cambridge, 1959). Possessions: Sent. 76, 116, 127; esp. 227, 228. Alms: 47, 52, 246, 247, 330.
37. *Paed.* I 30, 2; *Str.* VI 47, 4.
38. *Paed.* II 119, 3–120, 6.
39. *Paed.* III 36, 1.
40. *Str.* V 30, 1–4.
41. Irenaeus, *Adv. Haer.* IV 30, 1.
42. *Quis dives* 26, 3.
43. *Quis dives* 31, 6.
44. *Matt. comm* XV 15 (pp. 391–392 Klostermann).
45. *Gen. hom.* XVI 5 (p. 142 Baehrens).
46. *Lev. hom.* XV 2 (pp. 487–488 Baehrens); 1 Tim. 6:8.
47. Cf. M. Hengel, *Property and Riches in the Early Church* (Philadelphia, 1974), 62. 80.
48. P. Amherst I 3(a); cf. R. Bogaert, "Changeurs et banquiers chez les pères de l'église," *Ancient Society* 4 (1973), 239–270.

49. "Der heilige Cyprian und die Kreise des römischen Reiches," *Historia* 22 (1973), 479–501.
50. Eusebius, *H.E.* VII 11, 18; 23, 3. Here Dionysius is developing liturgical-imperial eschatology, based on I Cor. 5:7–8.
51. Hippolytus, *Dan. comm.* IV 18–19.
52. Lactantius, *Div. inst.* III 22; cf. Aristotle, *Pol.* II, 1263b.
53. Ibid., V 5–6. Note also that there was no injustice under Greeks or Romans because of inequality (V 14).
54. Ibid., VI 12.
55. Cf. R. I. Frank, "Ammianus on Roman Taxation," *American Journal of Philology* 93 (1972), 69–86. He refers to Salvian, *De gubernatione dei;* but there is exaggeration there.
56. Date about 358, L. W. Barnard in *VC* 28 (1974), 169–175; Pythagorean, R. Reitzenstein in *Sitzungsberichte d. Heidelberger Akad. d. Wiss., Philos. -hist. Kl.,* 1914, Abh. 8.
57. Socrates, *H.E.* VI 3.
58. Ibid., IV 26.
59. E. Salzmann, *Sprichwörter und sprichwörtliche Redensarten bei Libanios* (Tübingen, 1910), 68.
60. Libanius, *Or.* VI–VIII; *Progymn.* IX 5 (-6).
61. Cf. T. A. Kopecek, "The Social Class of the Cappadocian Fathers," *Church History* 42 (1973), 453–466. Ambrose: Paulinus, *Vita S. Ambrosii* 3 (PL 14, 30A); Chrysostom: Palladius, *Dial.* 5 (PG 47, 18 [B]; Augustine: *Conf.* II 3. For Theodoret cf. *Ep* 81 (PG 83, 1261B; cf. *Relig. hist.* 13, PG 82, 1408D–9C); *Ep.* 113 (PG 83, 1317C).
62. Cf. S. Giet, "La doctrine de l'appropriation des biens chez quelques-uns des Pères," *Recherches de science religieuse* 35 (1948), 55–91; Ambrose: B. Maes, *La loi naturelle selon Ambroise de Milan* (Analecta Gregoriana, 162, Rome, 1967), 22–28. 148. 201–202. Basil: Giet, *Les idées et l'action sociales de saint Basile* (Paris, 1941), 96–151. See also E. F. Bruck, *Kirchenväter und sozialen Erbrecht* (Berlin, 1956).
63. *Or.* 14, 26 (PG 35, 889C. 892B).
64. *Or.* 32, 22 (PG 36, 200B–C); cf. I. Seipel, *Die wirtschaftsethischen Lehren der Kirchenväter* (Vienna, 1907), 93–94.
65. I. R. Asmus, "Gregor von Nazianz und sein Verhältnis zum Kynismus," *Theologische Studien und Kritiken* 67 (1894), 314–338; J. Geffcken, *Kynika und Verwandtes* (Heidelberg, 1909), 18–37.

66. Gregory, *Or.* 25 (PG 35, 1197–1225); further references by F. L. Cross in *Oxford Dictionary of the Christian Church* (ed. 2; 1974), 895.

67. F. Martroye, "Le testament de saint Grégoire de Nazianze," *Mém. de la Soc. nat. des Antiquaires de France* 76 (1924), 219–263.

68. John Chrysostom, *I Tim. hom.* 12, 4 (PG 62, 562–564). For the date cf. A. Nägele, "Des Johannes Chrysostomus Homilien zu den Timotheus-Briefen des hl. Paulus und die Zeit ihrer Abfassung," *Theologische Quartalschrift* 116 (1935), 117–142.

69. Examples cited by T. Nikolaou, *Der Neid bei Johannes Chrysostomus* (Bonn, 1969), 84 n. 36; further examples and discussion, O. Plassmann, *Das Almosen bei Johannes Chrysostomus* (Münster 1961), 63.

70. *Adv. Jud.,* 5, 3 (PG 48, 886); also *Matt. hom.* I 4 (SVF I 262).

71. Plato, *Leg.* 739 c.

72. Cicero, *De off.* I 53.

73. *Acta hom.* 11 (PG 60, 94. 96).

74. Socrates, *H.E.* II 13.

75. *Matt. hom.* 66, 3 (PG 58, 630).

76. Ibid., 85, 3 (PG 58, 761–763).

77. Paul Samuelson (*Newsweek,* Sept. 27, 1976, 82) cites incomes of top U.S. 10 percent as fifteen times bottom 10 percent.

78. *Matt. hom.* 85, 4 (PG 58, 763A).

79. *Acta hom.* 11 (PG 60, 97).

80. Augustine, *Conf.* VI 14; P. Brown, *Augustine of Hippo* (Berkeley, 1967), 90. 116.

81. Cynic: Dio Chrysostom, *Or.* VI 60–62; VII 91; X 14–16.

82. Augustine, *De civ. dei* I 10; cf. Giet, *art. cit.,* 77–82; T. Fortin, *Le droit de propriété chez saint Augustin* (Caen, 1906).

83. *Clem. hom.* XV 9, 2–3. But note that teaching about sharing from the *Clementine Recognitions* (X 5, 5–7) passes into the influential pseudo-Isidorian Decretals (*Decretales Pseudo-Isidorianae,* edited by P. Hinschius [Leipzig, 1863], 65, 3–11; also in Migne, PG 1, 506).

84. Aristotle, *Politics* II, 1263a–b.

85. Luke 15:8–10; Theophrastus, *Char.* X 6; Dio Chrysostom, *Or.* XX 5.

86. Galen, *De cogn. cur. animi morbis* 9 (Kuhn V, 49); Herodian I 6, 9; Matt. 13:44–46.

87. Luke 12:16–20; Seneca, *Ep.* 101.

88. James 4:13–17. (James 5:1–6 is simply a diatribe against the rich.)
89. Hermas, *Vis.* III 6, 5; *Mand.* VIII 10; XII 2, 1; *Sim.* I 6. Self-sufficiency (cf. Phil. 4:11) is a Stoic virtue.
90. Hermas, *Sim.* I 11, with an allusion to the Decalogue.
91. I Cor. 16:2; giving, e.g., in II Cor. 9:6–15.
92. *Aeneas Tacticus,* etc. (Loeb Library, 1923), 377 and 383; Onosander I 8. 20.
93. Matt. 6:25–34; Luke 12:22–31.
94. Cicero, *De off.* I 25.
95. Philo, *Leg.* 343.
96. *Fug.* 33.
97. Ibid., 28.
98. Libanius, *Progymn.* IX, Vitup. 5 (VIII, 307 Foerster).
99. Julian, *Or.* I, 15D (I, 38–40 Wright).
100. Chrysostom, *I Cor. hom.* 15, 6 (PG 61, 128).
101. Eusebius, *H.E.* VIII 14, 10.
102. Hippolytus, *Ref.* IX 12, 1.
103. Eusebius, *H.E.* VII 30, 7.
104. Ibid., VII 30, 8; 11, 18.

VI. THE ORGANIZATION OF ALMS

1. Julian, *Ep.* 84a Bidez-Cumont, p. 113 = *Ep.* 22 Wright = Sozomen V 16, 5.
2. *Ep.* 89b, p. 146 = II, 336 Wright.
3. Ibid., p. 130 = II, 302.
4. *Ep.* 84a, p. 114. Cf. *Misopogon* 363A.
5. Deut. 15:10f.; 14:28f.; cf. 10:18 (justice).
6. Prov. 3:27f.; 14:21; 19:17; 31:20; Job 29:12f.
7. Sir. 3:30—4:10; 7:10, 32–36; 12:1–7; 17:22; 29:8–13.
8. Cf. G. F. Moore, *Judaism* II (Cambridge, Mass., 1927), 162–179.
9. A Jewish practice; cf. Moore, *Judaism* II, 167.
10. Matt. 5:41—6:4; 6:19–21; 19:16–22; 26:6–13; 25:31–46.
11. Common: Luke 6:29–38; 12:33–34 (18:18–23 from Mark); special: 3:11; 6:20–25; 10:29–37.
12. Acts 9:36; 10:2, 4; 3:1–10.
13. Acts 6:1–6. Cf. E. Haenchen, *The Acts of the Apostles* (Philadelphia, 1971), 261f.
14. Acts 11:27–30; Gal. 2:10; Acts 24:17.

15. I Cor. 16:1–4; II Cor. 1:16; 8—9; Gal. 2:10; Rom. 15:25–27; cf.
    K. F. Nickle, *The Collection* (Naperville, Ill., 1966); D. Georgi, *Die
    Geschichte der Kollekte des Paulus für Jerusalem* (Hamburg, 1965).

16. Acts 20:33–35; cf. H. Conzelmann, *Die Apostelgeschichte* (Tübin-
    gen, 1963), 119.

17. Gal. 6:9; cf. 5:14 (Rom. 13:8–10).

18. Rom. 12:13; Eph. 4:28.

19. Heb. 13:1–3; 1 Pet. 4:8f.; James 2:14–17 (cf. 4:17); 1 John
    3:17f.; 4:20f.

20. Ignatius, *Smyrn.* 6, 2.

21. Gospel of Thomas, Log. 6 and 14.

22. Clement, *Str.* VII 41, 1.

23. Origen, *De orat.* 5, 1.

24. *Str.*, III 27, 3.

25. Did. 1: 4; cf. J. P. Audet, *La Didaché* (Paris, 1958), 268–280.

26. Did. 1: 5; Irenaeus, *Adv. haer.* I 25, 4.

27. Did. 4: 5–8; 5: 2; cf. 11: 12; 15:4. Similar counsel in Barn.
    19:8–11.

28. Hermas, *Sim.* II 5–7; cf. *Ad Diogn.* 10, 5–6.

29. Hermas, *Mand.* II 4–6.

30. Hermas, *Vis.* III 9, 2–4; for Stoic parallels cf. M. Dibelius *Der
    Hirt des Hermas* (Tübingen, 1923), 475.

31. Hermas, *Sim.* V 3, 7; cf. Dibelius, *Der Hirt des Hermas,* 567.

32. The Roman church, in fact, relieved the poverty of Christians in
    many communities and helped those condemned to work in the
    mines (Dionysius of Corinth in Eusebius, *H.E.* IV 23, 10). For
    systematic relief at Carthage cf. Cyprian, *Ep.* 2, 2; 5, 1; 14, 2; 41,
    1.

33. Justin, *Apol.* I 67, 6; monthly contributions, Tertullian, *Apol.* 39.
    5.

34. Aristides, *Apol.* 15, 7.

35. Lucian, *De mort. Peregr.* 12–13.

36. *De fuga* 13, 1.

37. Cicero, *De off.* I 42ff. (from Panaetius); Seneca, *Dial.* VII de vita
    beata 24, 1–3.

38. H. Chadwick, *Early Christian Thought and the Classical Tradition*
    (New York, 1966), 61 with n. 152, p. 147.

39. Origen. *Matt. comm. ser.* 61.

40. Moore, *Judaism* II, 166–167. It is not peculiarly Jewish, how-
    ever; R. Taubenschlag (*Opera minora* II [Warsaw, 1959], 259–

260) notes that "the standard of maintenance among free people varied according to their legal or social position."

41. *Das Almosen bei Johannes Chrysostomus* (Münster/Westf., 1961).
42. Chrysostom, *Matt. hom.* 45, 2 (PG 58, 474).
43. Chrysostom, *I Cor. hom.* 21, 6 (PG 61, 179).
44. Chrysostom, *Matt. hom.* 66, 4 (PG 58, 630); cf. E. J. Bruck, *Kirchenväter und soziales Erbrecht* (Berlin, 1956), 25.
45. Bruck, *Kirchenväter*, 26–27.
46. Tertullian, *Apol.* 39, 16.
47. *Didasc. apostol.*, p. 88 Connolly.
48. Ibid., p. 90.
49. PG 58, 629–630.
50. Justin, *Apol.* I 67, 6.
51. Tertullian, *Apol.* 39, 5.
52. ILS 7212.
53. Tertullian, *Apol.* 39, 6.
54. Hug in *RE* III A (1929), 2538–2540; G. Wissowa, *Religion und Kultus der Römer* (ed. 2; Munich, 1912), 428–430; cf. A. D. Nock, *Conversion* (Oxford, 1933), 82 and 286.
55. Tertullian, *Apol.* 42, 8.
56. C. Blinkenberg, *Lindos: Fouilles de l'Acropole 1902–1914*, II Inscriptions, ii (Berlin–Copenhagen, 1941), no. 419.
57. Cf. F. Sokolowski in *HTR* 47 (1954), 153–164. On tithes, Koch in *RE* IV (1901), 2423–2424; Liebenam, ibid., 2306–2014; Cicero, *De nat. deor.* III 88 with the note of A. S. Pease; on first-fruits: Stengel in *RE* I (1894), 2666–2668.
58. M. P. Nilsson in *Oxford Classical Dictionary* (ed. 2; 1970), 1079.
59. Cf. G. Wissowa, *Religion und Kultus der Römer* (ed. 2; Munich, 1912), 277–278; A. S. Pease on Cicero, *De nat. deor.* III 88 (p. 1207).
60. ILS 3216.
61. Athenaeus VI 226e.
62. *Or.* 45, 28 Keil (p. 360, 21–25).
63. *De opere et eleemos.* 13.
64. Josephus, *C. Ap.* I 188.
65. Josephus, *Ant.* IV 68–75. 205. 240–243.
66. H. Danby, *The Mishnah* (London, 1933), 1–98.
67. Luke 18:12; Matt. 23:23.
68. Josephus, *Ant.* XX 179–181.
69. Josephus, *Vit.* 29. 63. 73. 80.

70. Josephus, *Ant.* XVIII 22.
71. Mark 12:41–44; Luke 21:1–4.
72. *Adv. haer.* IV 18, 2.
73. *Str.* II 51, 1; 86, 3.
74. OGIS 319.
75. OGIS 179.
76. S. L. Wallace, *Taxation in Egypt* (Princeton, 1938), 176.
77. *Adv. haer.* IV 17, 5.
78. Did. 13:3–7; cf. J. P. Audet, *La Didaché* (Paris, 1958), 457–458.
79. *Apost. Trad.* 28.
80. *Num. hom.* XI 2.
81. *Didasc. apost.*, p. 87 Connolly.
82. *Apost. Const.* VII 29; VIII 30.
83. Did. 11:6. 12; 12:3; 13:1–2.
84. Cf. H. Danby, *The Mishnah,* 93–98 (first-fruits); E. Schürer, *A History of the Jewish People in the Time of Jesus Christ* II, 1 (Edinburgh, 1885), 237–238.
85. Matt. 10:10; Luke 10:7.
86. A. H. M. Jones, *The Roman Economy,* edited by P. A. Brunt (Oxford, 1974), 348–349; Cyprian, *Ep.* 34, 4; 39, 5.
87. II Cor. 8:14; cf. 9:8–12.
88. Apollonius in Eusebius, *H.E.* V 18, 2.
89. Ibid., 4. 7.
90. Anonymous in Eusebius, *H.E.* V 28, 10.
91. *Ref.* IX 12, 13.
92. Irenaeus, *Adv. haer.* I 4, 3 (p. 36 Harvey); 13, 3 (pp. 118–119).
93. *Church Society and Ethics,* edited by D. Baker (Oxford, 1975), 24ff.
94. Cf. A. R. Hands, *Charities and Social Aid in Greece and Rome* (Ithaca, N.Y., 1968), 103–106.
95. Appian, *Bell.* civ. II 120.
96. Philo, *Leg.* 158; "The common benevolence" also in P. Oxy. XL 2918, 16; 2919, 9–10.
97. Hands, *Charities and Social Aid,* 103.
98. ILS 1539.
99. ILS 977.
100. P. Oxy. XL 2941.
101. D van Berchem, *Les distributions de blé et d'argent à la plèbe romaine sous l'empire* (Geneva, 1939), 98–100.
102. Eusebius, *H.E.* VI 43, 11.

103. Ibid., VII 21, 9.
104. J. Rea, *The Oxyrhynchus Papyri* XL (London, 1972).
105. Zosimus I 61, 3.
106. Jones, *Later Roman Empire*, 696–698.
107. Theophanes, *Chron.*, p. 29 de Boor.
108. Cf. H. I. Bell, *Jews and Christians in Egypt* (London, 1924), 69.
109. Athanasius, *Apol. c. Ar.* 9, 3–4; 87, 1; compare the case of Sopater (Eunapius, *Vit. Philos.*, pp. 462–463 Boissonade; Zosimus II 40, 3).
110. Athanasius, *Apol. c. Ar.* 18, 2.
111. Eusebius, *Vit. Const.* IV 28.
112. Theodoret, *H.E.* I 11, 2.
113. Ibid., III 7, 1.
114. Ibid., IV 4, 1–2.
115. *Cod. Theod.* XVI 2, 6; for the context see Chapter III, n. 108.

VII. TEMPLES, CHURCHES, AND ENDOWMENTS

1. Acts 1:13; 12:12; 18:7; 19:9; 20:8; 28:30.
2. F. V. Filson in *JBL* 58 (1939), 105–112.
3. Cf. A. M. Schneider in *Festschr. zum 200 jährigen Bestehen der Akad. der Wiss. in Göttingen* II, Philo-hist. Kl. 1951, 166–198; also J. M. Peterson in *VC* 23 (1969), 264–272.
4. The basic text is given by J. U. Powell, *Collectanea Alexandria* (Oxford, 1925), 68–71; translation and comments by A. D. Nock, *Conversion* (Oxford, 1933), 50–54; cf. H. Engelmann, *Die Delische Serapisaretalogie* (Beiträge zur klassischen Philologie 15, 1964).
5. OGIS 594, 595 = IGRR I 420, 421. Part of the second inscription is translated in N. Lewis and M. Reinhold, *Roman Civilization* II (New York, 1955), 196–197. Cf. Nock, *Conversion*, 66.
6. Evidence for Rome and Ostia: M. J. Vermaseren, *Corpus Inscriptionum et Monumentorum Religionis Mithriacae* I (The Hague, 1956); on Rome, Vermaseren, *De Mithrasdienst in Rome* (Nijmegen, 1951); id., *Mithras, The Secret God* (London, 1963), 37; on Ostia, S. Laeuchli, ed., *Mithraism in Ostia* (Evanston, Ill., 1967), 91–93.
7. F. Cumont, *Textes et Monuments figurés relatifs aux mystères de Mithra* II (Brussels, 1898), 536: index s. v. "temples et mobilier sacre"; id., *The Mysteries of Mithra* (Chicago, 1903), 169–170.
8. Cf. W. Rordorf in *ZNW* 55 (1964), 110–128.

9. R. Krautheimer, *Early Christian and Byzantine Architecture* (Harmondsworth, Eng., 1975), 42; 484 n. 12.

10. B. Laum, *Stiftungen in der griechischen und römischen Antike,* 2 vols. (Leipzig-Berlin, 1914); A. R. Hands, *Charities and Social Aid in Greece and Rome* (Ithaca, N.Y., 1968). Additional evidence: E. Ziebarth in *RE* Suppl. VII (1940), 1236–1240; A. Mannzmann, *Griechische Stiftungsurkunden* (Münster/Westf., 1962), esp. n. 2, pp. 17–18; for the empire, G. Le Bras in *Studi in onore di Salvatore Riccobono* III (Palermo, 1936), 23–67.

11. Laum, *Stiftungen,* II, nos. 175–176 (Greek); cf. nos. 50b and 114 (Latin).

12. A. C. Johnson, *ESAR* II, pp. 661–662; text in *Archiv für Papyrologie* 2 (1902/3), 565, no. 121*. Shops as endowment: cf. Laum, *Stiftungen,* I 135.

13. Mart. Justini 3, 3 *(Myrtinou* or *Martinou tou Timiotinou).*

14. Clement, *Str.* VII 28–29; Minucius Felix, *Oct.* 32, 1. For these and other references cf. J. G. Davies, *The Secular Use of Churches* (New York, 1968), 1–9.

15. Eusebius, *H.E.* VII 13; IX 10, 11; X 5, 17.

16. Ibid., VIII 1, 5.

17. Ibid., X 4.

18. Ibid., X 4, 42.

19. *Vit. Const.* I 42, 2 (cf. *H.E.* X 2, 1).

20. Maxentius: Augustine, *Brevic. Coll. c. Donat.* 34; Galerius: Eusebius, *H.E.* VIII 17, 9; Lactantius, *De mort. persec.* 34, 5; Maximin: Eusebius, *H.E.* IX 10, 11; Constantine and Licinius: Eusebius, *H.E.* X 5, 9–11; Lactantius, *De mort. persec.* 48, 9; proconsul: Eusebius, *H.E.* X 5, 15–17; fields and gardens, Eusebius, *Vit. Const.* II 39 (p. 58, 10–14 Heikel).

21. Laum, *Stiftungen,* I, 134–140.

22. P. Oxy. XXXIII 2673.

23. Ed. T. Mommsen, *Monumenta Germaniae Historica. Gesta Pontificum Romanorum* (Berlin, 1898); L. Duchesne, *Liber Pontificalis,* 2 vols. (Paris, 1886–1892; supplement by C. Vogel, 1957); translated by L. R. Loomis, *The Book of the Popes* (Liber Pontificalis) I (New York, 1916).

24. Hailed: Lactantius, *De mort. persec.* 26, 3; Aurelius Victor, *Caes.* 40, 5; died: Lactantius 44, 6; *Paneg.* IX 17, 1; Zosimus II 16, 3; disbanded: Aurelius Victor 40, 25; Zosimus II 17, 1.

25. E. Josi in *Rivista di archeologia cristiana* 11 (1934), 349.

26. Cf. E. Nash, *Pictorial Dictionary of Ancient Rome* (ed. 2; New York, 1968), 214–218; cf. S. S. Alexander in *Rivista di archeologia cristiana* 47 (1971), 284.

27. Òptatus, I 23 (CSEL 26, 26).

28. *Liber Pont.* 34 (pp. 54–56 Mommsen); on the silver *fastigium* cf. M. T. Smith in *Rivista di archeologia cristiana* 46 (1970), 149–175.

29. J. M. C. Toynbee and J. W. Perkins, *The Shrine of St. Peter and the Vatican Excavations* (New York, 1956), 6; 196–197.

30. *Liber Pont.* 34 (pp. 57–60 Mommsen).

31. On the "funeral halls" cf. Krautheimer, *Architecture*, 51–54; *Corpus Basilicarum Christianarum Romae* IV (Vatican City, 1970), 147.

32. For a subsidizing bishop, note Eugenius of Laodicea Combusta (MAMA I 1 170).

33. Epiphanius, *Haer.* XXX 4, 1; 11, 10.

34. Eusebius, *Vit. Const.* III 54, 2.

35. Iohannes Malalas, *Chron.* 13 (p. 324 Dindorf): Sun, Moon, Aphrodite.

36. Eusebius, *Vit. Const.* III 55–57.

37. Jerome, *Chron.*, p. 233 Helm; Theophanes, *Chron.*, p. 28 De Boor.

38. Cf. *Anon. Vales.* 6, 34.

39. Julian, *Or.* VII, 228b; Libanius, *Or.* XXX 6 (cited by A. Alföldi, *The Conversion of Constantine and Pagan Rome* [Oxford, 1948], 136).

40. E. A. Thompson, *A Roman Reformer and Inventor* (Oxford, 1952), 94 and 110.

41. Eusebius, *Vit. Const.* III 56; cf. E. J. and L. Edelstein, *Asclepius* (Baltimore, 1945), I, 419–420 (T. 818).

42. *Or.* XXX 39 (T. 817).

43. IG IV² 438.

44. Lucian, *De dea Syria* 9; Clement, *Protr.* 13, 5.

45. *Vit. Const.* III 55, 3.

46. Julian, *Ep.* 79 Bidez-Cumont = *Ep.* 19 Wright.

47. Ammianus Marcellinus XXII 5, 2; cf. J. Bidez and F. Cumont, *Iuliani Imperatoris Epistulae* (Paris, 1922), 47–49.

48. Sozomen V 5, 2.

49. Libanius, *Or.* XVIII 126.

50. Zonaras XIII 12; cf. Edelstein, *Asclepius*, I, 420–21.

51. Julian, *Ep.* 115 Bidez-Cumont = *Ep.* 40 Wright. In 388 the situation was different. After Christians at Callinicum on the Euphrates burned down both a Valentinian chapel and a Jewish

synagogue, Theodosius ordered the local bishop to rebuild the synagogue. Under pressure from Ambrose he rescinded the order. Cf. Jones, *Later Roman Empire,* 166–167.

52. Theodoret, *H.E.* IV 4.
53. *Cod. Theod.* V 13, 3.
54. Ibid., IX 16, 9 and 7.
55. Ammianus Marcellinus XXIX 1–2; Libanius, *Or.* XXX 7.
56. Jerome, *Ep.* 107, 2.
57. ILS 4938.
58. Ambrose, *Ep.* 17, 10 (PL 16, 1004B).
59. A. Cameron in *JRS* 58 (1968), 96–102.
60. Cf. R. O. Edbrooke, Jr. in *AJP* 97 (1976), 40–61 (58).
61. Jerome, *Ep.* 52, 6 (PL 22, 532).
62. Livy I 20, 3.
63. F. Blume, et al., *Die Schriften der römischen Feldmesser* I (Berlin, 1848), 235, 4–8.
64. Cf. A. D. Nock, in *HTR* 23 (1930), 251–274.
65. Cf. G. Wissowa, *Religion und Kultus der Römer* (ed. 2; Munich, 1912), 97 n. 1.
66. Symmachus, *Ep.* I 68.
67. *Epp.* IX 108–109; 147–148.
68. Dio LXVII 3, 3.
69. Ambrose, *Epp.* 17–18; 57, 3 (PL 16, 1225C); *Cod. Theod.* I 6, 9; Prosper of Aquitaine, *De promiss. Dei* III 38 (PL 51, 834B).
70. Libanius, *Or.* XXX *(pro templis; Opera,* edited by R. Foerster, III (Leipzig, 1906), 87–118; French translation and notes by R. Van Loy, *Byzantion* 8 (1933), 7–39; 389–404; date, P. Petit, *Byzantion* 21 (1951), 285–310.
71. *Cod. Theod.* XVI 10, 10–11. Is it a coincidence that at Apamea early in 391 donors to a synagogue building do not hesitate to state their names—and even to call it a temple? Cf. B. Lifschitz, *Donateurs et fondateurs dans les synagogues juives* (Paris, 1967), 38 and 40.
72. Ambrose, *Ep.* 57, 5 (PL 16, 1226B); cf. *Cod. Theod.* XVI 10, 10,
73. Ambrose, *Ep.* 57 as a whole.
74. Zosimus IV 59; cf. *Cod. Theod.* XVI 10, 19.
75. Zosimus V 38.
76. Jones, *Later Roman Empire,* 1167 n. 11; references from *Cod. Theod.* (X 3, 4 of 383; X 10, 24 of 405; X 10, 32 of 425) and *Cod. Justin.* (VII 37, 2 of 387; others).

Bibliography

I. THE CHRISTIAN POPULATION OF THE ROMAN EMPIRE

Berchem, D. van. *Les distributions de blé et d'argent à la plèbe romaine sous l'empire.* Geneva, 1939.

Boak, A. E. R. "The Population of Roman and Byzantine Karanis." *Historia* 4 (1955): 157–162.

Broshi, M. "La population de l'ancienne Jerusalem." *Revue Biblique* 82 (1975): 5–14.

Crook, J. *Consilium Principis.* Cambridge, 1955.

Downey, G. "The Size of the Population of Antioch." *Transactions of the American Philological Association* 89 (1958): 84–91.

Dreizehnter, A. "Die Bevölkerungszahl in Attika am Ende des 4. Jahrhunderts v. u. Z." *Klio* 54 (1972): 147–151.

Duncan-Jones, R. P. "City Population in Roman Africa." *JRS* 53 (1963): 85–90; revised in *The Economy of the Roman Empire.* Cambridge, 1974, pp. 259–287.

Fichman, I. F. "Die Bevölkerungszahl von Oxyrhynchus in byzantinischer Zeit." *Archiv für Papyrusforschung* 21 (1971): 111–120.

Gerkan, A. von. "Die Einwohnerszahl Roms in der Kaiserzeit." *Mitteilungen des Deutschen Archaeologischen Instituts, Roemische Abteilung* 55 (1942): 149–195.

————. "Weiteres zur Einwohnerszahl Roms in der Kaiserzeit." Ibid. 58 (1943): 213–243.

Greenwood, M. "A statistical mare's nest?" *Journal of the Royal Statistical Society* 103 (1940): 246–248 (on *Digest* XXXV 2, 68).

Hertling, L. von. "Die Zahl der Christen zu Beginn'des vierten Jahrhunderts." *ZKTh* 58 (1934): 243–253.

Hopkins, K. "The Probable Age Structure of the Roman Population." *Population Studies* 20 (1966–1967): 245–264.

Jacoby, D. "La population de Constantinople à l'époque byzantine: un problème de démographie urbaine." *Byzantion* 31 (1961): 81–110.

Kötting, B. "Christentum (Ausbreitung)." *RAC* II (1954): 1138–1159 (ancient statistics, 1139).

La Piana, G. "Foreign Groups in Rome during the First Centuries of the Empire." *HTR* 20 (1927): 183–403 (not quantitative).

Lehmann, A., "Christentum III. Ausbreitungsgeschichte." *Die Religion in Geschichte und Gegenwart* I (ed. 3, 1957): 1705–1712 (esp. 1707).

Packer, J. E. "Housing and Population in Imperial Ostia and Rome." *JRS* 57 (1967): 80–89; cf. *The Insulae of Imperial Ostia*, Memoirs of the American Academy in Rome, 31 (1971).

Russell, J. C. *Late Ancient and Medieval Population. TAPS*, N.S. 48, 3 (1958).

Russell, J. C. "Recent Advances in Medieval Demography." *Speculum* 40 (1965): 84–101.

Welles, C. B. "The Population of Roman Dura." *Studies in Roman Economic and Social History*, edited by P. R. Coleman-Norton (Princeton, 1951), pp. 251–274 (not quantitative).

II. CHRISTIAN DEVOTION TO THE MONARCHY

Alföldi, A. "The Crisis of the Empire (A.D. 249–270)." *Cambridge Ancient History* 12 (1939): 165–231.

Alföldy, G. "Der heilige Cyprian und die Krise des römischen Reiches." *Historia* 22 (1973): 479–501.

Barker, E. *From Alexander to Constantine: Passages and Documents Illustrating the History of Social and Political Ideas 336 B.C.–A.D. 337.* Oxford, 1956.

Batiffol, P. "Le règlement des premiers conciles africains et le règlement du sénat romain." *Bulletin d'ancienne littérature et d'archéologie chrétiennes* 3 (1913): 3–19.

Baynes, N. H. *Byzantine Studies and Other Essays.* London, 1955 (1960).

Cadoux, C. J. *The Early Church and the World.* Edinburgh, 1925.

Case, S. J. *The Social Triumph of the Ancient Church.* New York, 1933.

Crook, J. *Consilium Principis.* Cambridge, Eng., 1955.

Delcor, M. "The courts of the Church of Corinth and the courts of Qumran." *Paul and Qumran,* edited by J. Murphy-O'Connor (Chicago, 1968), pp. 69–84.

Delling, G. "Philons Enkomion auf Augustus." *Klio* 54 (1972): 171–192.

Dinkler, E. "Zur Problem der Ethik bei Paulus." *ZThK* 49 (1952): 167–200.

Dölger, F. J. "Zur antiken und frühchristlichen Auffassung der Herrschergewalt von Gottes Gnaden." *Antike und Christentum* 3 (1932): 117–127.

Dvornik, F. *Early Christian and Byzantine Political Philosophy.* 2 vols. Washington, 1966.

———. "The Emperor Julian's 'Reactionary' Ideas on Kingship." *Classical and Medieval Studies,* edited by K. Weitzmann (Princeton, 1955), pp. 71–81.

Eger, H. "Kaiser und Kirche in der Geschichtstheologie Eusebs von Cäsarea." *ZNW* 38 (1939): 97–115.

Eggenberger, C. *Die Quellen der politischen Ethik des l. Klemensbriefes.* Zurich, 1951.

Farina, R. *L'impero e l'imperatore cristiano in Eusebio di Cesarea.* Zurich, 1966.

Ferguson, E. "Origen and the Election of Bishops." *Church History* 43 (1974): 26–33.

Gaudemet, J. *La formation du droit seculier et du droit de l'église aux ive et ve siècles.* Paris, 1957.

Girardet, K. M. "Appellatio." *Historia* 23 (1974): 98–127.

Goodenough, E. R. *The Jurisprudence of the Jewish Courts in Egypt.* New Haven, 1929.

———. "The Political Philosophy of Hellenistic Kingship." *Yale Classical Studies* 1 (1928): 55–102.

Grant, F. C. "The Idea of the Kingdom of God in the New Testament." *The Sacral Kingship.* Supplements to Numen, 4 (Leiden, 1959): 437–446.

Grant, R. M. "The Coming of the Kingdom of God," *JBL* 67 (1948): 297–303.

———. "The Trial of Jesus in the Light of History." *Judaism* 20 (1971): 37–42.

Hatch, E. *The Organization of the Early Christian Churches.* 3d. ed., London, 1888.

Hurd, J. C., Jr. *The Origin of I Corinthians.* New York, 1965.

Isichei, E. A. *Political Thinking and Social Experience: Some Christian Interpretations of the Roman Empire from Tertullian to Salvian.* Christchurch, N.Z., 1964.

Knox, W. L. "Parallels to the N.T. Use of *Sōma.*" *JTS* 39 (1938): 243–246.

Larsen, J. A. O. *Representative Government in Greek and Roman History.* Berkeley–Los Angeles, 1955.

Lietzmann, H. *An die Korinther I–II.* 4th ed., Tübingen, 1949.

MacMullen, R. *Enemies of the Roman Order.* Cambridge, Mass., 1966.

Meneghelli, R. *Fede cristiana e potere politico in Clemente Romano.* Bologna, 1970.

Mikat, P. *Die Bedeutung der Begriffe Stasis und Aponoia für das Verständnis des I. Clemensbriefes.* Cologne, 1969.

Millar, F. "Paul of Samosata, Zenobia and Aurelian: The Church, Local Culture and Political Allegiance in Third-Century Syria." *JRS* 61 (1971): 1–17.

Nestle, W. "Die Fabel des Menenius Agrippa." *Klio* 21 (1927): 330–360.

Oliver, J. H. *The Ruling Power. TAPS* 43, 4. Philadelphia, 1943.

Peterson, E. "Der Monotheismus als politisches Problem." *Theologische Traktate* (Munich, 1951), pp. 45–147.

Rachet, M. *Rome et les Berbères.* Brussels, 1970.

Scott, K. "Humor at the Expense of the Ruler Cult." *Classical Philology* 27 (1932): 317–328.

Sevenster, J. N. *Paul and Seneca.* Leiden, 1961.

Starr, C. G. "The Perfect Democracy of the Roman Empire." *American Historical Review* 58 (1952): 1–16.

Syme, R. *The Roman Revolution.* Oxford, 1939.

Telfer, W. *The Office of a Bishop.* London, 1962.

Wheeler, M. "Aristotle's Analysis of the Nature of Political Struggle." *AJP* 72 (1951): 145–161.

Wolfson, H. A. *Philo.* 2 vols. Cambridge, Mass. 1947.

Ziegler, A. W. "Entwicklungstendenzen der frühchristlichen Staatslehre." *Kyriakon: Festschrift J. Quasten* (Münster, 1970), pp. 40–58.

III. TAXATION AND EXEMPTION

Bingen, J. "L'Édit du Maximum et les papyrus." *Atti dell' XI Congresso Internazionale di Papirologia* (Milan, 1966), pp. 369–378.

Bolin, S. *State and Currency in the Roman Empire.* Stockholm, 1958.

Bonneau, D. *La crue du Nil divinité égyptienne.* Paris, 1964.

Bowersock, G. W. *Greek Sophists in the Roman Empire.* Oxford, 1969.

Broughton, T. R. S. "New Evidence on Temple-Estates in Asia Minor." *Studies . . . in Honor of Allan Chester Johnson,* edited by P. R. Coleman-Norton (Princeton, 1951), pp. 236–250.

Chadwick, H. "The Origin of the Title 'Oecumenical Council.'" *JTS* 23 (1972): 132–135.

Déléage, A. *La capitation du Bas-empire.* Macon, 1945.

Erim, K. T., et al. "Diocletian's Currency Reform; A New Inscription." *JRS* 61 (1971): 171–177.

Evans, J. A. S. "The Temple of Soknebtunis." *Yale Classical Studies* 17 (1961): 149–283.

Ferrari dalle Spade, G. "Immunità ecclesiastiche nel diritto romano imperiale." *Atti dell' Instituto Veneto di Scienze, Lettere ed Arti* 99, 2 (1939/40): 107–248.

Frank, R. I. "Ammianus on Roman Taxation." *AJP* 93 (1972): 69–86.

Gaudemet, J. *La formation du droit séculier et du droit de l'église aux ive et ve siècles.* Paris, 1957.

Gilliam, E. H. "The Archives of the Temple of Soknobraisis at Bacchias." *Yale Classical Studies* 10 (1947): 179–281.

Grant, F. C. *The Economic Background of the Gospels.* Oxford, 1926.

———. "The Economic Background of the New Testament." W. D. Davies and D. Daube, eds., *The Background of the New Testament and its Eschatology* (Cambridge, Eng., 1956), pp. 96–114.

Guild of St. Ives. "Churches and Taxation Revisited." *St. Luke's Journal* 17 (1974): 44–71.

Hahn, I. "Theodoretus Cyrus und die Frühbyzantinische Besteuerung." *Acta Antiqua* 10 (1962): 123–130.

Hombert, M., and Préaux, C. *Recherches sur le recensement dans l'Egypte romaine.* Papyrologica Lugduno-Batava, 5. Leiden, 1952.

Johnson, A. C., and West, L. C. *Byzantine Egypt: Economic Studies.* Princeton, 1949.

Johnson, A. C. Roman Egypt = T. Frank, ed., *ESAR* II (Baltimore, 1936).

Jones, A. H. M. *The Cities of the Eastern Roman Provinces.* Oxford, 1937.

———. *The Greek City.* Oxford, 1940.

———. *The Later Roman Empire.* 2 vols. Norman, Okla., 1964.

———. *The Roman Economy,* edited by P. A. Brunt. Oxford, 1974.

Kubitschek, W. "Centesima." *RE* 3 (1899): 1928–1929.

Kübler, B. "Munus." *RE* 16 (1933): 644–651.

Lauffer, S. *Diokletians Preisedikt.* Berlin, 1971.

Leist. "Auction." *RE* 2 (1896): 2269–2272.

Lewis, N. "Exemption from Liturgy in Roman Egypt." *Actes de Xe Congres International de Papyrologues* (Warsaw, 1964), pp. 69–79; *Atti dell' XI Congresso Internazionale di Papyrologia* (Milan, 1966), pp. 508–541.

Loewe, H. *Render unto Caesar.* Cambridge, 1940.

MacMullen, R. "Diocletian's Edict and the 'castrensis modius.'" *Aegyptus* 41 (1961): 3–5.

Millar, F. G. B. "Immunitas." *Oxford Classical Dictionary.* 2d ed. (1970), p. 542.

Montefiore, H. "Jesus and the Temple Tax." *New Testament Studies* 11 (1964–1965): 60–71.

Morrison, C. D. *The Powers That Be.* Studies in Biblical Theology, 29. London, 1960.

Nutton, V. "Two Notes on Immunitas." *JRS* 61 (1971): 52–63.

Otto, W. *Priester und Tempel in hellenistischen Agypten.* 2 vols. Berlin–Leipzig, 1905, 1908.

Parássoglou, G. M. "A Prefectural Edict Regulating Temple Activities." *ZPE* 13 (1974): 21–37.

Poisnel, C. "Recherches sur l'abolition de la vicesima hereditatium." *Mélanges d'Archéologie et d'Histoire. École Française de Rome* 3 (1883): 312–327.

Rostovtzeff, M. I. *Social and Economic History of the Hellenistic World.* 3 vols. Oxford, 1941.

———. *Social and Economic History of the Roman Empire.* 2d ed. Oxford, 1957.

Roth, C. "The Debate on the Loyal Sacrifices." *HTR* 53 (1960): 93–97.

Volkmann, H. "Immunitas." *Der Kleine Pauly* II (1967): 1376–1377.

Wallace, S. L. *Taxation in Egypt from Augustus to Diocletian.* Princeton, 1938.

Wesener, G. "Vicesima hereditatium." *RE* 8 A (1958): 2471–2477.

———. "Vicesima manumissionum." *RE* 8 A (1958): 2477–2479.

Wessely, C. *Karanis.* Denkschriften der Kaiserliche Akademie der Wissenschaften, Wien, Philosophisch-Historische Klasse 47 (1902), no. 4.

Wissowa, G. *Religion und Kultus der Römer.* 2d ed. Munich, 1912.

Zawadski, T. "Quelques remarques sur l'étendue de l'accroissement des domaines des grands temples en Asie Mineure." *Eos* 46 (1952–1953), part 1, 83–96.

Ziegler, K. "Immunitas," *RE* 9 (1914): 1134–1136.

Zucker, F. "Priester und Tempel in Ägypten in den Zeiten nach der decianischen Christenverfolgung." *Akten des VIII. Internationalen Kongresses für Papyrologie* (Vienna, 1956), pp. 167–174.

IV. WORK AND OCCUPATIONS

Albrecht, M. von. "Arbeit." *Der Kleine Pauly* 1 (1964): 490–494.

Andresen, C. "Altchristliche Kritik am Tanz." *ZKG* 72 (1961): 217–262.

Bienert, W. *Die Arbeit nach der Lehre der Bibel. Eine Grundlegung evangelischer Sozialethik.* Stuttgart, 1954.

Bogaert, R. *Banques et banquiers dans les cités grecques.* Leiden, 1968.

———. "Changeurs et banquiers chez les pères de l'Église." *Ancient Society* 4 (1973): 239–270.

———. "Geld (Geldwirtschaft)." *RAC* 9 (1975): 797–907.

Brabant, O. "Classes et professions 'maudites' chez saint Augustin, d'après les *Enarrationes in Psalmos.*" *Revue des Études Augustiniennes* 17 (1971).

Brewster, E. H. *Roman Craftsmen and Tradesmen of the Early Empire.* 1917; reprinted New York, 1972.

Burck, E. "Drei Grundwerte der Römischen Lebensordnung." *Gymnasium* 58 (1951): 161–183.

Daloz, L. *Le Travail selon saint Jean Chrysostome.* Paris, 1959.

Davis, W. S. *The Influence of Wealth in Imperial Rome.* New York, 1910; reprinted 1933.

Della Corte, M. *Case ed abitanti di Pompeii.* 3d ed. Naples, 1965.

Donahue, J. "Tax Collectors and Sinners." *Catholic Biblical Quarterly* 33 (1971): 39–61.

Finley, M. I., ed. *Slavery in Classical Antiquity*. Cambridge, Eng., 1960; reprinted 1964.

Gagé, J. *Les classes sociales dans l'empire romain*. Paris, 1964.

Garnsey, P. *Social Status and Legal Privilege in the Roman Empire*. Oxford, 1970.

Geoghegan, A. T. *The Attitude towards Labor in Early Christianity and Ancient Culture*. Washington, 1945.

Glotz, G. *Ancient Greece at Work*. New York, 1926.

Greeven, H. *Das Hauptproblem der Sozialethik in der neueren Stoa und im Urchristentum*. Gütersloh, 1935.

Gülzow, H. *Christentum und Sklaverei in den ersten drei Jahrhunderten*. Bonn, 1969.

Harnack, A. "Der pseudocyprianische Tractat De aleatoribus." *TU* V 1. Leipzig, 1888.

———. *"Kopos." (kopian, hoi kopiountes)* im frühchristlich Sprachgebrauch." *ZNW* 27 (1928): 1–10.

Hauck, F. "Arbeit." *RAC* 1 (1950): 585–590.

———. *"Kopos." Theologisches Wörterbuch zum Neuen Testament* III (1938), 827–29.

Herter, H. "Die Soziologie der antiken Prostitution." *Jahrbuch für Antike und Christentum* 3 (1960): 70–111.

Jeremias, J. "Zöllner und Sünder." *ZNW* 30 (1931): 293–300.

Joly, R. *Hermas: Le Pasteur*. Paris, 1958.

Judge, E. A. *The Social Pattern of Christian Groups in the First Century*. London, 1960.

Kalex, H. "Ueber die Arbeitsbedingungen und den Gesundheitszustand der Arbeiter." *Sozialökonomische Verhältnisse im alten Orient und im klassischen Altertum*, edited by R. Günther and G. Schrot. Berlin, 1961, pp. 168–179.

Kleinfeller. "Lenocinium." *RE* 12 (1925): 1942.

Lamer. "Lusoria tabula." *RE* 13 (1926): 1900–2030 (esp. 1909–1912).

Laukamm, S. "Das Sittenbild der Artemidor von Ephesus." *Angelos* 3 (1930): 32–71.

Lopuszanski, G. "La police romaine et les chrétiens." *L'Antiquité classique* 20 (1951): 5–46.

MacMullen, R. *Roman Social Relations*. New Haven, 1974.

Maloney, R. P. "Usury in Greek, Roman and Rabbinic Thought." *Traditio* 27 (1971): 79–109.

————. "The Teaching of the Fathers on Usury." *VC* 27 (1973): 241–265.

Plankl. W. "Wirtschaftliche Hintergrunde der Christenverfolgungen in Bithynien." *Gymnasium* 60 (1953): 54–56.

Reekmans, T. "Juvenal's View on Social Classes." *Ancient Society* 2 (1971): 117–161.

Reumann, J. "'Stewards of God'—Pre-Christian Religious Application of *Oikonomos* in Greek." *JBL* 77 (1958): 339–349.

Ste Croix, G. E. M. de. "Early Christian Attitudes to Property and Slavery." *Church Society and Politics*, edited by D. Baker. Oxford, 1975, pp. 1–38.

Schwer, W. "Beruf." *RAC* 2 (1954): 141–156.

Sherwin-White, A. N. *Roman Society and Roman Law in the New Testament*. Oxford, 1963.

Simon, Y. *Work, Society and Culture*. New York, 1971.

Straub, W. *Die Bildersprache des Apostels Paulus*. Tübingen, 1937.

Westermann, W. *The Slave Systems of Greek and Roman Antiquity*. Memoirs of the American Philosophical Society, 40. Philadelphia, 1955.

Yavetz, Z. "Plebs sordida." *Athenaeum* 43 (1965): 295–311.

Youtie, H. C. "Publicans and Sinners." *ZPE* 1 (1967): 1–20.

V. PRIVATE PROPERTY

Barbieri, G. "Problemi della ricchezza nei primi scrittori cristiani." *Economia e Storia* 2 (1954): 126–141.

Behm, J. "Kommunismus im Urchristentum." *Neue Kirchliche Zeitschrift* 31 (1920): 275–297.

Derrett, J. E. M. "Ananias, Sapphira, and the Right of Property." *Downside Review* 89 (1971): 225–232.

Dudley, D. R. *A History of Cynicism*. London, 1937.

Farmer, W. R. "The Economic Basis of the Qumran Community." *Theologische Zeitschrift* 11 (1955): 295–308.

Farner, K. *Theologie des Kommunismus?* Vol. 1 Frankfurt/Main, 1969.

Fortin, T. *Le Droit du propriété chez saint Augustin*. Caen, 1906.

Giet, S. "La doctrine de l'appropriation des biens chez quelques-uns des Pères. Peut-on parler de communisme?" *Recherches de science religieuse* 35 (1948).

Hauck, F. *Die Stellung des Urchristentums zu Arbeit und Geld*. Gütersloh, 1921.

Hauschild, W. D. "Christentum und Eigentum. Zum Problem eines altkirchlichen 'Sozialismus,'" *Zeitschrift für Evangelische Ethik* 16 (1972): 34–49.

Healy, P. J. "The Fathers on Wealth and Property."*Catholic University Bulletin* 17 (1911): 434–458.

Hengel, M. *Property and Riches in the Early Church.* Philadelphia, 1974.

Liboron, H. *Die Karpokratianische Gnosis.* Leipzig, 1938.

Lovejoy, A. O., and Boas, G. *A Documentary History of Primitivism and Related Ideas.* Vol. 1. Baltimore, 1935.

Maes, B. *La loi naturelle selon Ambroise de Milan.* Analecta Gregoriana, 162. Rome, 1967.

Nikolau, T. *Der Neid bei Johannes Chrysostomus unter Berücksichtigung der griechischen Philosophie.* Bonn, 1969.

Pöhlmann, R. von. *Geschichte der sozialen Frage und des Sozialismus in der antiken Welt.* 3d ed. by F. Oertel. Munich, 1925.

Ste Croix, G. E. M. de. "Early Christian Attitudes to Property and Slavery." *Church Society and Politics,* edited by D. Baker (Oxford, 1975), pp. 1–38.

Schilling, O. *Reichtum und Eigentum in der altchristlichen Literatur.* Freiburg/Br., 1908.

———. "Der Kollektivismus der Kirchenväter." *Theologische Quartalschrift* 114 (1933): 481–492.

Schubert, H. von. *Der Kommunismus der Wiedertäufer in Münster und seine Quellen.* Sitzungsberichte der Heidelberger Akademie der Wissenschaften, 1919, Abh. 11.

Schwalm, M.-B. "Communisme." *Dictionnaire de Théologie Catholique* 3 (1908): 574–596.

Seipel, I. *Die wirtschaftsethischen Lehren der Kirchenväter.* Vienna, 1907.

Weiss, E. "Kollektiveigentum." *RE* 11 (1922): 1078–1098.

VI. THE ORGANIZATION OF ALMS

Bell, H. I. "Philanthropia in the Papyri of the Roman Period." *Hommages à J. Bidez et à F. Cumont* (Brussels, 1949).

Bolkestein, H. *Wohltätigkeit und Armenpflege in vorchristlich Altertum.* Utrecht, 1939.

Bruck, E. F. *Kirchenväter und sozialen Erbrecht.* Berlin, 1956.

———. "St. Paul, the Fathers of the Church and the 'Cheerful Giver' in Roman Law." *Traditio* 2 (1944): 97–121.

Chastel, E. *Études historiques sur l'influence de la charité.* Paris, 1953.

Clark, W. P. *Benefactions and Endowments in Greek Antiquity.* Ph.D. dissertation, University of Chicago, 1928.

Constantelos, D. J. *Byzantine Philanthropy and Social Welfare.* New Brunswick, N.J., 1968.

Downey, G. "Philanthropia in Religion and Statecraft in the Fourth Century after Christ." *Historia* 4 (1944): 199–208.

Duff, P. W. "The Charitable Foundations of Byzantium." *Cambridge Legal Essays* (1926): 84–99.

Gapp, K. S. "The Universal Famine under Claudius." *Harvard Theological Review* 28 (1935): 258–265.

Hands, A. R. *Charities and Social Aid in Greece and Rome.* Ithaca, N.Y., 1968.

Jones, A. H. M. *The Later Roman Empire.* Norman, Okla., 1964.

Koukoulis, P. "L'assistance aux indigents dans l'empire byzantin." *Memorial L. Petit* (Bucharest, 1948), pp. 254–271.

Leclercq, H. "Liberalités des fidèles." *Dictionnaire d'archeéologie chrétienne et de liturgie* 9 (1930): 489–497.

McGuire, M. R. P. "Epigraphical Evidence for Social Charity in the Roman West," *AJP* 57 (1946): 129–149.

Mott, S. C. "The Power of Giving and Receiving: Reciprocity in Hellenistic Benevolence." *Current Issues in Biblical and Patristic Interpretation,* edited by G. F. Hawthorne (Grand Rapids, 1975), pp. 60–72.

Nickle, K. F. *The Collection.* Naperville, Ill., 1966.

Plassmann, O. *Das Almosen bei Johannes Chrysostomus.* Münster/Westf., 1961.

Quispel, G. "Love Thy Brother." *Ancient Society* 2 (1970): 83–93.

Rogers, R. S. "The Roman Emperors as Heirs and Legatees." *Transactions of the American Philological Association* 68 (1947): 149–158.

Schwer, W. "Armenpflege." *Reallexikon für Antike und Christentum* 1 (1950): 698–698.

Vischer, L. *Tithing in the Early Church.* Philadelphia, 1966 (also, *ZKG* 70 [1959]: 201–217).

VII. TEMPLES, CHURCHES, AND ENDOWMENTS

Alexander, S. S. "Studies in Constantinian Church Architecture," *Rivista di archeologia cristiana* 47 (1971), 281–330.

Armstrong, G. T. "Imperial Church Buildings in the Fourth Century," *Biblical Archaeologist* 30 (1967), 90–102.

Bloch, H. "A New Document of the Last Pagan Revival in the West," *HTR* 38 (1945), 199–244.

Cameron, A. "Gratian's Repudiation of the Pontifical Robe," *JRS* 58 (1968), 96–102.

Campenhausen, H. von. *Ambrosius von Mailand als Kirchenpolitiker.* Berlin, 1929.

Cumont, F. *The Mysteries of Mithra.* Chicago, 1903.

———. *Textes et Monuments figurés relatifs aux mystères de Mithra.* 2 vols. Brussels, 1896.

Davies, J. G. *The Secular Use of Churches.* New York, 1968.

Dill, S. *Roman Society in the Last Century of the Western Empire.* 2d ed. London, 1910.

Dudden, F. Homes. *The Life and Times of St. Ambrose.* Oxford, 1935.

Edbrooke, R. O., Jr. "The Visit of Constantius II to Rome in 357." *AJP* 97 (1976): 40–61.

Edelstein, E. J. and L. *Asclepius.* 2 vols. Baltimore, 1945.

Erim, K. T., et al. "Diocletian's Currency Reform; a New Inscription." *JRS* 61 (1971): 171–177.

Filson, F. V. "The Significance of the Early House Churches." *JBL* 58 (1939): 105–112.

Geffcken, J. *Der Ausgang des griechisch-römischen Heidentums.* Heidelberg, 1920.

Hengel, M. "Die Synagogeninschrift von Stobi." *ZNW* 57 (1966): 145–183; reprinted J. Gutmann, ed., *The Synagogue: Studies in Origins, Archaeology and Architecture* (New York, 1975), pp. 110–148.

Jones, A. H. M. *The Greek City.* Oxford, 1940.

———. *The Later Roman Empire.* Norman, Okla., 1964.

Klein, R. *Symmachus.* Darmstadt, 1971.

Krautheimer, R. *Corpus Basilicarum Christianarum Romae.* 4 vols. to date. Vatican City, 1937–1970.

———. *Early Christian and Byzantine Architecture.* Harmondsworth, Eng., 1975.

Latte, K. *Römische Religionsgeschichte.* Munich, 1960.

Laum, B. *Stiftungen in der griechischen und römischen Antike.* 2 vols. Berlin, 1914.

LeBras, G. "Les fondations privées du Haut Empire." *Studi in onore di Salvatore Riccobono* 3 (Palermo, 1936): 23–67.

Leclercq, H. "Propriété ecclésiastique." *Dictionnaire d'archéologie chrétienne et de liturgie* 14 (1940): 1906–1924.

Lifschitz, B. *Donateurs et fondateurs dans les synagogues juives.* Cahiers de la Revue Biblique, 7. Paris, 1967.

Loy, R. Van. "Le 'pro templis' de Libanius." *Byzantion* 8 (1933): 7–39; 389–404.

Manzmann, A. *Griechische Stiftungsurkunden.* Münster/Westf., 1962.

Matthews, J. F. "Symmachus and the Oriental Cults." *JRS* 63 (1973): 175–195.

McGeachy, J. A. *Q. Aurelius Symmachus and the Senatorial Aristocracy of the West.* Chicago, 1942 (over-critical review by N. H. Baynes in *JRS* 36 [1946]: 173–177).

Nilsson, M. P. "Pagan Divine Service in Late Antiquity." *HTR* 38 (1945): 63–69.

Nock, A. D. "A Diis Electa." *HTR* 23 (1930): 251–274; reprinted *Essays on Religion and the Ancient World,* edited by Z. Stewart (Oxford, 1972), 1: 252–270.

———. *Conversion.* Oxford, 1933.

Paschoud, F. "Reflexions sur l'idéal religieux de Symmaque." *Historia* 14 (1965): 215–235.

Petersen, J. M. "House-Churches in Rome." *VC* 23 (1969): 264–272.

Petit, P. "Sur la date du 'pro templis' de Libanius." *Byzantion* 21 (1951): 285–310.

Pharr, C. *The Theodosian Code.* Princeton, 1952.

Piganiol. A. *L'empereur Constantin.* Paris, 1932.

Robinson, D. N. "An Analysis of the Pagan Revival of the Late Fourth Century with Especial Reference to Symmachus." *Transactions of the American Philological Association* 46 (1915): 87–101.

Rordorf, W. "Was wissen wir über die christlichen Gottesdiensträume der vorkonstantinischen Zeit?" *ZNW* 55 (1964): 110–128.

Schneider, A.-M. "Die ältesten Denkmäler der römischen Kirche." *Festschrift zum 200 jährigen Bestehen der Akademie der Wissenschaften in Göttingen* 2, Philologisch-historische Klasse, 1951, pp. 166–198.

Seeck, O. "Symmachus 18." *RE* 4 A (1931): 1146–1158.

Thompson, E. A. *A Roman Reformer and Inventor.* Oxford, 1952.

Toynbee, J. M. C., and Perkins, J. W. *The Shrine of St. Peter and the Vatican Excavations.* New York, 1956.

Vermaseren, M. J. *Corpus Inscriptionum et Monumentorum Religionis Mithriacae.* Vol. 1. The Hague, 1956.

Voelkl, L. *Die Kirchenstiftungen des Kaisers Konstantin im Lichte des römis-
    chen Sakralrechts.* Cologne, 1964.
Wissowa, G. *Religion und Kultus der Römer.* 2d ed. Munich, 1912
Ziebarth, E. "Stiftungen." *RE* Suppl. 7 (1940): 1236–1240.

Indexes

I. Subjects and persons
II. Biblical references including the Apocrypha
III. Ancient authors and books
    A. Jewish and Christian
    B. Pagan
IV. Modern authors

Note that Part II contains references to footnotes as cited in the text of the book, since the biblical passages ordinarily illustrate a point being made. In Part III, however, the references are to the pages where the authors are actually named, because the names are often absent from the discussions in the text.

I. SUBJECTS AND PERSONS

II. BIBLICAL REFERENCES INCLUDING THE APOCRYPHA

III. ANCIENT AUTHORS AND BOOKS

A. Jewish and Christian

IV. MODERN AUTHORS